D0626997

A Great Connection

SHANNON

JAPAN

A
GREAT
CONNECTION

J. H. Krehbiel, Sr. / Molex

CONTENTS

THE FIRST FIFTY YEARS

The boys and I are, I think, good examples of hard–working people, and I think that's the best way in the world to convince people of what you expect. Because if you're a good example, they'll follow you. There's nothing original about that. It's true the world over. I'd follow a guy who's a good worker. I wouldn't follow a guy who's a lazy lout.

—JOHN KREHBIEL, SR.—

IN 1988, when Molex celebrates its Fiftieth Anniversary, John H. Krehbiel, Sr., the chairman of the board, will be eighty-two years old. If John's late brother-in-law, Bill Veeck, were still around they would be emblazoning the skies with the fireworks display they had been promising themselves for years. Well, they were really going to buy a fireworks factory and let the whole thing go up at once. But why quibble?

In those fifty years, John Krehbiel—with the help of his two sons—has taken a company that began life as the manufacturer of a noxious plastic and built it into a global supplier of electrical connectors, terminals, and switches. It employs more than five thousand people in thirty manufacturing plants situated in thirteen different countries. In its Golden Anniversary year it expects to do a half-billion dollars worth of business. Five or six years later, if all goes well, they will be entering the golden portals of the Billion Dollar Club.

Molex is not the biggest company in its field. It is in there against some of the giant corporations in the country. In size and sales, Molex ranks third in the fiercely competitive interconnection industry. What makes the company such a jewel, and so intriguing to stock analysts, is that in growth and profitability it has historically ranked either first or second. If you had gotten in on the ground floor in 1966 when Molex stock first became available, every dollar you invested would now be worth more than $500. Stick around, and we'll tell you about somebody who did. As for John himself, he was forced to become a multimillionaire, and according to *Forbes Magazine* John's stock holdings in Molex have made him one of the 400 wealthiest men in the nation.

What intrigues analysts even further is that in strict defiance of the rules of growth and management as laid down by the gnomes of Wall Street and the gurus of the Harvard Business School, the company is being run by a pair of owner-managers. John Krehbiel, Jr., is the president of the domestic division, and his brother Fred is president of the booming international division.

What's the secret of Molex's success?

"The old man had a vision," Junior says, "to get us into products where some innovation was required. That, of course, is the kind of guy he is. He'd start out by working to meet the needs of a customer, and he'd scrounge enough dough from the customer he was designing it for to help pay for the tooling. Then he would get the customer to let him sell it throughout the industry.

"Here's a guy who understands how to design the product. He understands how to price it so that it makes a profit, he understands how to manufacture it, and he's worked in shops so he knows how to do the stamping and the molding. And he knows how to sell it. Here's a guy who can do it all." He also knows how to administer a growing business, how to pass his vision and his values on to his employees, as he had already done to his sons.

John Krehbiel believes that it is the responsibility of the company not only to establish an environment that will allow people to do the best work they are capable of, but to get out of their way and let them do it. "I think it's terribly stultifying if you have people with ability who also have imagination, and they are restricted by boundaries," he says. "And this is what they all really like about Molex. They say you can examine your own ideas, investigate and find out whether you're right or wrong. And that's what it's all about, isn't it?"

People are the difference, Fred Krehbiel says. "There isn't one big home run that has made Molex. If anything, its just a group of very diverse people who were given an opportunity and who have run with it. We have good equipment, but it's not that much better. We have developed some very fine products which have helped us tremendously. But by and large, our products are not that much better. I think it's just that Molex created an atmosphere which gets the maximum out of people who are involved with the company. They are able to achieve more, I think, than they thought they could, or maybe could have achieved somewhere else."

What does Senior say? "You know, people have asked what's different about Molex compared to other companies. I really can't say. I believe one of our strengths is that we're pretty good generalists. We're not great engineers, we're not great financial people, we're not great salespeople, we're not great processors. I think we do all these things fairly well, none of them outstandingly. We pay attention to the small details. I think that's an advantage in that you'll see companies that have a brilliant engineer running them, and he's so wrapped up in the engineering that he'll forget the salesmanship, the marketing, or something else. Same thing if they're being run by a money man. Invariably, those companies will go down the drain."

What Molex has done is to provide its customers with not only connectors and terminals but also the equipment the customer needs in his factory to install the Molex products. "The razor and the razor blade," John Sr. calls it. Rent him the razor, sell him the blades, and you profit at both ends.

"The only way you can keep growing is by reinvesting in machinery and equipment," Senior says. "My father taught me that, and I have impressed it, in turn, on my sons."

If you're getting up there in age yourself, we've got even better news for you. When the stock went public in 1972, John Krehbiel was sixty-six years old. The great success of the company, and most certainly his own introduction to great wealth, came well after he had passed the age in which a benevolent government tells you to go sit on a rock, admire the sunset, and collect Social Security. "It's the biggest waste of people and brains I can imagine," John says.

During the last years of his wife's life, they had a house in Lompoc, California, alongside the Vandenberg Air Base. "Beautiful place. Nice golf course. They are all colonels and generals and admirals there. Probably pretty smart fellows when their minds were being pressed to work. But you should hear these guys now. They talk about how someone is behind on his golf dues at the club or somebody's dog is running across his lawn and wetting on his bushes."

Is that what retirement is? he asks. "For myself, I feel I've done a hell of a lot of things since I was sixty-five years old. And I hope I'm doing a lot of things now."

It's not easy to retire at Molex. You have to fight your way past the chairman of the board. You say you've grown tired of the daily grind? OK, you are invited to make out your own schedule. You're sick of getting up in the morning? OK, what time do you want to come in?

If you're an engineer, you can work on a consulting basis for whatever period of time will allow you to make however much money you want to make. The Krehbiels take the position that the oldtimers are doing them a favor by staying. "We have more projects than we have people to handle them," John Krehbiel, Jr., says. "They are invaluable."

Once, during the 1974 recession, a list was drawn up of people who might have to be laid off. When the list was submitted to John Jr., his eyes went immediately to the name of a guy whom he knew to be over sixty-five. "This goes into the wastebasket," Junior said. "It would take me a week to scrape the old man off the ceiling." Actually, the man had volunteered to go on the list because he was thinking of retiring at the end of the year anyway, and he didn't want to see some young guy with a family laid off. "OK," Junior said. "But he stays until he says he's ready to leave."

The Krehbiels absolutely fascinate the people who work for them, and there is an ongoing discussion as to how much control Senior maintains over company policy. Ivor Redmonde has an excellent overview. Molex is the fifth connector company Ivor has worked for during his thirty-six years in the business, and he has always known the heads of the companies intimately. In all five companies, he notes, the man who started the company was an airplane pilot. Since the odds against that happening are about 30 million to one, one is tempted to conjecture on the kind of personality that finds a compatibility between the intricacies of the interconnector business and the mysteries of the skies. But that isn't what Ivor is getting at here. Ivor is interested in drawing an analogy on the degrees of control. In the days when planes were held together by baling wire, the pilot had to be in charge of every part of the plane; had to react to every situation. Compare that, says Ivor, with the highly instrumented airplane of today. "Molex is a very finely tuned, excellent aircraft. Fred Krehbiel, John's son, is one of the main features of the aircraft, and John, Jr., his other son, is another main feature of the aircraft. They drive the aircraft, but John Sr. put the aircraft together and he'd be right there, in my opinion, if something was out of line. Today John is still a very active chairman of the board. And he's the head of the Advanced Development Committee."

Ask the people at Molex to sum up the boss with a quick adjective or phrase and you will invariably hear these words:

> integrity
> down to earth
> common sense
> work ethic
> perseverance
> vitality

John Krehbiel is, pure and simple, the most comfortable man in the world to be around. If John were talking to the head man from IBM one minute and the guy sweeping the floor the next, he'd be calling them both by their first name and treating them exactly the same. "When I first came to the company," one oldtime manager says, "it used to take him 15–20 minutes to get from the door to his office because he'd sit down at people's desks, talk to them—what are you doing?—and that's kind of nice. If he'd see someone in the corridor it would be, Hi, Jim, or Hi, Bob."

Kerry Krafthefer has climbed the ranks to become a corporate officer. "Senior is one of our best salesmen," Kerry says. "So if we had a technical presentation to a customer he would go in with us. Back in the late seventies, we went to GE in Lynchburg, Virginia, to put on a presentation, and we invited several of the engineer and purchasing people out to dinner. Senior was sitting next to an engineer, and he got along with him very well. The guy would fill up an ashtray, Senior would get him another one. A couple of times during dinner he got up to fill the guy's glass or something. As the evening wore on this guy said, 'John, what do you do at Molex?' And John said, 'I'm the chairman,' and the guy just about fell out of the chair. He couldn't believe the chairman would be that regular a guy. He is just so unassuming. You could talk to him for an entire evening and have no idea of the scope of his accomplishments."

He is the easiest person in the world to know, says Mary Frances Veeck, his sister-in-law, because he is so curious about everything. "He really listens to what you have to say. He wants to know if he can learn from you."

Common sense is what engineering is really all about. You want to get from here to there. What's the best way of doing it? Finding the better way, to John, has always been finding the simpler way.

Kerry Krafthefer gives a perfect example of the way Senior's mind works:

We are dealing with something as familiar to us all as the light switch on a refrigerator. You open the door and the light goes on, right? Here was the problem: Underwriters Laboratories, the consortium of insurance companies that establishes industry-wide codes and standards, had determined that when housewives washed the door jamb of their refrigerator, the water tended to collect inside the switch and eventually short it out. So U.L. made a ruling that refrigerator switches had to be redesigned to withstand washing.

Molex didn't make those switches. "But," Kerry explains, "whenever a specification, a ruling, or a standard is changed, that represents a potential opportunity for us." When U.L. ruled that the switch had to withstand washing, it had to define what washing was—the size of the sponge, the amount of water—and set up a test wherein the switch had to function a specified number of times after being doused with a specified amount of water.

How would you go about keeping water away from a switch? Most manufacturers, Molex included, attacked the problem by sealing off the switch. What, after all, could be more logical? Or, as far as the manufacturers were concerned, more expensive? You and I might not think an extra 10 cents on the construction of as high priced an appliance as a refrigerator would bother anybody. But if you were a manufacturer, turning out ten thousand refrigerators a day, the cost of doing business had just gone up $1,000 a day—or a minimum of $260,000 a year. (In the connector business, a fraction of a penny can make the difference between getting a contract and not getting it. Perfect illustration: Molex sells a certain little connector to Zenith for a penny apiece. Every television set Zenith makes has three hundred of those connectors. That's $3 worth of connectors per set. Zenith turns out 2 million sets a year. That's $6 million dollars, at a penny a shot.)

Senior said, "Instead of trying to keep the water out, let's design a switch that is very open, so the water will run right through." And so, says Kerry, "we designed a switch that had a couple of little slits along the sides and at the bottom of the housing, made it a rocker switch instead of a plunger to provide a kind of protective covering at the point of entry, and while we were at it, recommended that the switch be built down at the bottom of the door, instead of halfway up. Passed the test, got the order." For most of the refrigerators that were made in the country.

Integrity could be said to be a function of the down-to-earthedness. Or maybe its the other way around. "John has less guile than anyone I know," says Bob Pribish and Pribish is also John's golfing partner, racquetball opponent and friend. "You always know exactly where you stand with him." What comes across, instantaneously, is a combination of total competence, easy confidence, and quiet strength. He is a man who is comfortable to be with because he is so clearly comfortable with himself.

When Molex decided to have outside directors, the first person whom Senior interviewed was Lew Platt. Platt had joined Hewlett-Packard at a time when it was in pretty much the same position as Molex was in 1980. In other words, he had the background to recognize both the opportunities and the pitfalls confronting a company that was poised to grow as explosively as Hewlett-Packard had. When Lew came home after the interview he told his wife, "I really hope they decide to put this

Outside Board together and to ask me to be on it. Because I've just met the most extraordinary old gentleman and I would like to get to know him better."

Understand, Lew Platt is the executive vice president of Hewlett-Packard. His picture has graced the cover of major business magazines. While the experience of serving on the board of a company like Molex was obviously going to be a good move for him at that stage in his career, he is obviously nobody's pushover. "My wife, of course, has since met John," Platt says, "and thinks he's absolutely the most charming person she's ever known. I think he has that impact on a lot of people. You can't get enough of him. He doesn't wear on you at all. You want to be around him more and more."

He'll get no argument on that from Fred Krehbiel's wife, Kay. "I don't know what the dickens this man does to you. It's perhaps that there's nothing pretentious. He's so wholesome. You ask him to do something, you can rest assured it will be done. He gave the children a trampoline a few years ago, and just yesterday I called to ask him if he could recall where he had bought it because we needed new springs. And I know that I'll get a note or a call within the next two days telling me. He bought a trampoline for Posey and John's kids years ago. He went up north to Lake Forest where they live to buy it, because if anything needed to be fixed, he wanted it to be convenient for them. Just as he made sure to get ours down here to make it easier for us."

Through the early years, he grew the company by ploughing the profits back into it. Theoretically, his salary ran from $20,000–$25,000 during those years. In practice, he took what he took. There was one stretch where he went without any salary for eight straight months, and there were other times when he actually loaned the company money in order to meet that week's payroll.

And finally: John has had a passion for golf ever since he was a caddy in grammar school. And yet for the eight years that Johnny and Fred were going, successively, to college he gave up his membership in the Naperville Golf Club in order to pay for their tuition. Ed Healy was a rep for Molex for many years and also one of John's closest friends and golfing partners. "I've learned a lot about living from John," Healy says. "I'm not just saying that. I've told him the same thing. Like giving up golf for those eight years, knowing as I do how he loves the game. He was willing to make a sacrifice, and I think that's all part of living too. You've got to make a sacrifice along the line if you're going to accomplish anything."

If common sense is what engineering is all about, then the work ethic is what John Krehbiel and Molex are all about.

A few years back, a couple of guys went parading through the administration building carrying a poster that read, "Molex is a great place to work for if you want to work like hell. If you don't want to work, its awful." The signmakers had summed up the prevailing atmosphere so succinctly that similar signs were soon cropping up in offices all over the building.

John Krehbiel summed it up even better while he was still grieving over the death of his beloved wife, Peg, early in 1986. "There is only so much fishing, there is only so much golf. But work lasts forever. Work is the one thing you can never get enough of."

There is a corps of engineers who came on the job in the late sixties and early seventies, to comprise the management cadre for the first period of explosive growth. The profiles are remarkably similar. They were young, they were all grossly underqualified for the tasks that were assigned to them, and the more they were willing to do the more they were given to do. There is one other attribute they have in common. Talk to the old hands, from the guys on the floor to the top managerial level, and sooner or later they will be saying, "It's exciting. It's fun. I've worked here for umpteen years, and I still can't wait to get back in the morning." It takes a certain nuttiness amounting to something like a personality defect, they will also agree, to want to work that hard.

Tom Schneider was twenty-six years old, and only two years out of college when he was hired to work on a special project relating to the company's first move into automation. He is now vice president in charge of Application Tooling and Manufacturing Services. His first impression of Molex was coming in at 5:00 in the morning to catch up on his work and finding the three Krehbiels already there. "When Fred is home—and more often than not he's at one of the international facilities—it's very seldom that he doesn't have the first parking space." What that means is that Junior had to settle for second.

There are more than one thousand employees at the Lisle headquarters, and it has always been first come, first served. There are no reserved spots for the executives. Arrive a little late, and you can be sure that you'll be parking your car down in the lower parking area, otherwise known as the South 40.

The driving force behind the U.S. company is these latter years has been John Jr., and when Junior is on a rampage he has been known to call a meeting for 5:00 in the morning and to keep everybody there until 9:00 at night.

It was at such a meeting that Bob Pribish spoke the line that turned him into a Molex immortal. Pribish had come traipsing into the conference room at 5:15 A.M., carrying a box of doughnuts, and Junior was giving him the hard eye. "Hey," Pribish said, letting his own eyes run down the long table. "It's a bitch finding a parking spot this time of day."

"The Krehbiels demand a lot from the people who work for them," Schneider says, "especially those who work with them directly. You work hard, don't get home at night, your family is often secondary. It's a career—either you want to do it or you don't want to do it." Schneider was so eager to do it that only later could he appreciate how unprepared he was to tackle some of the assignments he brought off. "The responsibilities are great, and the rewards are commensurate. You know the company is growing and you take satisfaction in that. And it's always so exciting. It's been eighteen years now, and I still can't wait to get back in the morning."

John Stipanuk came in 1974, which puts him on the outer edge of the second cadre. He came in as an engineer and designer, worked up through various levels of management in technical areas into general management. He is also a member of Senior's Advanced Development team.

"There's a striving for excellence here," he says. "The work ethic is part of it. And it's not just words. From top management on down it's lived. Everybody works very hard even though we've been enormously successful.

"You never seem to sit back and say, Well, we finally did it. It's always out there in front of you. Exactly how is that conveyed? Certainly one way is the example given by the top executives. John Jr. works probably harder than anybody in the company. He could sit back and say, Well, we've made our profit, we've grown our business, we have more money than I could ever possibly use. And the same with Senior. But it's always what's next, there's always this drive going. And then the rewards that follow. In many cases you don't even have time—hah!—to realize the rewards, you're moving on to the next project. So it's winning and working harder to continue to win in the business, and you never look back and say, We won. It's How am I going to win the next one?" Those who have the kind of personality that needs to make a pit stop in order to savor success, those who have a need, in Stipanuk's words, to say, Well, I did it, and then live off it for a time, don't last very long. "There have been a lot of people who have dropped in, hung around for a while and dropped out."

There are also those who never came. Bill Gruhn, one of the top managers, turned down his wife's request to recommend a relative. "He's not the Molex type," Bill told her, after sleeping on it. "He doesn't want to work that hard." That doesn't make him a bad guy, Bill is more than willing to concede. It might even make him a better guy. Bill declined, in the end, even to set up an appointment for an interview. "Look," he told his wife, "he can do that himself if he wants to. I just don't want to get involved in something that has no chance of working out for either him or the company."

It works the other way too. Ted Tomkiewicz, vice president of Engineering, thought he was doing something nice when he offered to put in a word for a friend who had been caught in a mass layoff at a rival company. "I've heard about you guys," his friend told him. "You guys are a sweatshop over there. I wouldn't work that hard for anybody. Not for any amount of money."

There is a sign on Senior's desk that reads: Nothing Takes the Place of Perseverance.

You never give up. And you never give in. Whether it's pursuing the solution to an engineering problem, or penetrating a target company. It took twelve years to get into Xerox, but when they did get in, they got in big with a breakthrough product that is one of the important items in Molex's future. "Tenacity," John Psaltis, the treasurer, explains. "We put together a plan to penetrate an account, and we focus on it, and we work on it, and if we don't succeed we develop another plan and work on that. Eventually the entire cast of characters may change but we continue to go after that account until we win."

Call it perseverance. Call it tenacity. Call it single-mindedness. It is the one quality from which all other qualities flow. Single-mindedness will get the job done for you, and get it done every time.

Lou Hecht is the corporate secretary and general counsel. That means he's Senior's lawyer, a job you wouldn't wish on a dog. Senior's most unfavorite people are those blighted and benighted souls who practice the professions of law and politics. Or, as Senior customarily refers to them, "those goddam lawyers" and "those goddam lawyers in Congress." Lou Hecht stands about 5'6" when he's bragging. "I am symbolically the bearer of the cross of the legal profession," he says. "I used to be 6'6"."

To make the case against lawyers airtight, they are also the people who have been put upon the earth to tell you what you can't do. Lou Hecht knows better. "Senior has taught me that the most overrated commodity in business life, if not life itself, is talent. Talent by itself doesn't get you anywhere. It may get your foot in the door. It doesn't make you successful. I don't mean this in a derogatory sense, but if you work with John you realize that he's successful because he's single-minded, he's driven. He gets it done. He doesn't articulate this, he does it by example."

John reacts toward a negative opinion in precisely the same way he would react to a failed engineering approach, or to a failure in life itself. To wit: Have you tried any other way?

"He has taught me not to accept things," Hecht explains, "especially things that aren't good. He will not accept something that he does not want to hear. He will test it, retest it, test it again. He will question you even when you're sure. And more often than not there is a way around it."

Having discovered many years ago that it is not pleasant to tell Senior that something he wants to do cannot be done, Hecht sees no reason to go rushing in with the bad news. He puts it off for a day, he sleeps on it. "He has taught me that if you think about something hard enough, there's usually a way. It may not be easy, but I never want to go to him with only one answer, when that answer is no. I am going to provide him with options." Perhaps Option A will be: It can be done your way, but you're going to have to spend a million dollars. Option B: This other way is not exactly what you want but it'll only cost you $100,000. Option C: Given those alternatives, there is always the option of not doing it at all.

There are plaques hanging on Lou Hecht's wall. "I'm the only person in this company who has them up and I have them up for a purpose. Because I know that John Sr. doesn't think much of lawyers and doesn't think much of education per se, unless it's toward engineering. I want to succeed for him, and I want him to recognize that there are some people who are educated, who are lawyers, who can still fit in at Molex and be his type of person."

Senior has that effect on people. He has the ability, as Lou Hecht demonstrates, to make people want to please him. Lou also believes—and he is far from alone in this—that the one blind spot in Senior's perception of the people around him is that he does not accept their respect and admiration. "He's a private person. He doesn't like the adulation at all."

Ted Tomkiewicz puts it this way: "There are two things you cannot do with any Krehbiel. You cannot beat them to work and you cannot open a door for them." God knows Teddy has tried. "I've grabbed Senior by the arm to show him through a door and he'll just push me out of the way. Goddammit, I think I ought to open the door for him."

Teddy believes he has it figured out. "I believe they have respect for and a realization that the people are the overall strength of this company, and that is so embedded in them that they say, OK, if he works here he goes first, I don't. I'm only here because he's here also. And I think the reverse: I'm only here because he's here."

Perseverance is not so much a quality of mind as a test of character. And, when it entails an eighty-one-year-old-man engaging in sports, the state of his health. John is a flight A competitor in the Molex golf league. Carries his own bags. And he is a fierce competitor. A few years ago, when they were playing on a cold, windy, rainy, all-around rotten day, Ken Kufner was in the foursome ahead of him. "We finished the front nine and didn't want to play anymore. For one thing, we were freezing our butts and, for another, it was impossible to play well. John came in, he had his rain slicker and his rain hat on. He looked in a pretty good mood. Had some food, and took right off. I found out later he had shot a 39 on the front nine, which was incredibly good in those conditions, and he played the back nine, and won the low gross championship. He was really happy. It reminded me of *Caddy Shack*, where the priest played in lightning and thunder."

One hesitates to call an eighty-one-year-old man an athlete, but not for long. Senior still plays raquetball every week. Has the court reserved for seven o'clock in the morning. He doesn't get around well enough any more to play singles, he says. And that is his only concession to age. He plays a tough, stay-out-of-my-way game. Crowd him and you'll get an elbow in the ribs. And, of course, he hates to lose. When he loses, he'll throw his racquet down and let out a stream of "damns" and "hells." For many years, the three other players in the match-ups were John Klein and Larry Kosseck, both in their mid-thirties, and Bob Pribish. All former athletes. A few years back, John got whacked so hard above the eye by Kosseck's racquet that the blood spurted and the eye swelled up like a golf ball.

After the others had helped him off the court, they prepared to get him to a doctor. "Put a bandage on it," Senior said. John Klein was his partner. "So we went up and got a butterfly bandage and we slapped it on, and he insisted that he was going to go back in and play. He and I continued to a finish, and we won." The next day Junior came up to Klein's office, "What did you do to my father yesterday?" he asked.

Turned out that Junior had taken him to the hospital later in the day and they'd had to put in eight stitches. "Four or five days later," Klein says, "I saw Peg. And she started to touch that spot over her eye and laugh."

Senior was seventy-seven years old at the time.

Jim Geiser is the purchasing director. "This Larry Kosseck was a hell of an athlete, and one time he came off the court with an eye blackened by John. He couldn't see, and Senior hired a limousine to take him home. The next day Junior walked into Kosseck's office and said, "Larry, you have to stop playing with those kids, 'cause they're going to kill you."

In 1985, the Board of Directors held its summer meeting in Shannon, Ireland, which happens to be the site of Molex's first overseas factory. All the members of the board, except John, had taken the precaution of arriving a day early to obviate the effects of jet lag. Senior took an all-night flight to London and then flew up to Shannon. He arrived at the hotel shortly before the meeting was scheduled to start, went up to his room to shower and change, and he was ready. "The rest of us had all had a good night's sleep," Lew Platt says. "Yet by midafternoon we were all very tired and yawning, the way you are when you're in Europe on that first afternoon. Senior is still going strong. Comes early evening, some of us are saying maybe we'll go to bed instead of having dinner. Senior says, 'Come on down.' There he is, the most energetic of anybody in the room." The others have seen him do the same thing many times.

Last year, John and Bob Pribish went to Bob Toski's golf school in Florida for a week to try to improve their game. Pribish felt they should be able to knock two or three strokes off their score. "What are you talking about?" Senior said. "Five strokes is more like it."

You would think that an eighty-one-year-old man would have an arthritic swing. Quite the contrary. The short putting game has gone, but the swing is as smooth as ever.

Toski told Pribish that he had a good mechanical swing but that he wasn't a natural golfer. To Senior he said, "You're a natural. Of all the people here, you're the one with the most natural swing. You know why I like your swing so much? Because you swing the way I do."

Maybe he gets it from chopping wood. That's something else he still does.

More likely, it shows that you just can't beat those genes. John's father, Frederick A Krehbiel, the inventor of Molex plastic, came to the office every day until he was eighty-six. He told John as he was leaving one day that he wouldn't be back, and died two years later.

FINDING THE PATH

I've seen a lot of brilliant men who came along with highly imaginative concepts but lacked the practical experience to make them work. If I had my way, every American engineer would spend his first two years after college working out in the shop.

—JOHN H. KREHBIEL, SR.—

WHEN John Krehbiel was thirteen years old, he and his parents got into their Pathfinder automobile and drove down to Salem, Indiana, to take a look at the farm his father had recently purchased.

The distance from Hinsdale, Illinois, was three-hundred miles, a long day's journey over the predominantly narrow dirt roads of that time. When they were ready to return, the car broke down. Mr. Krehbiel, who was a mechanical engineer, knew what was wrong right away. "You see," he told his son, "the engine is running fine, but you put it in gear and nothing happens." Better jack up a wheel and take a look. Aha. One of the back wheels is turning and the other isn't. There was something wrong in either the differential or the axel. "So Dad jacked it up and took the differential apart and, sure enough, the gears were driving all right but one axel was not turning. And, of course, those are made so that one wheel can go around a curve faster than the other wheel. That's the reason you have a differential."

Immediately, Mr. Krehbiel diagnosed the trouble with the unhappy words: "What we have here is a busted axel." Off comes the wheel, and sure enough, the axel is parted in the middle. "So what do you do? You look for a place where you can get a new axel."

This is 1919 we're talking about. In those days they did not have an automobile mechanic around every corner, let alone a neighborhood supply store. The axel, as they discovered soon enough, would have to be shipped down from Chicago. If they were lucky, it probably wouldn't take more than a week.

What they did have in Salem, Indiana—and in every other little town in the USA—was a blacksmith shop. "The blacksmith shop was closed, it was either a Saturday or a Sunday. My dad got the blacksmith to open up. A blacksmith shop had all different kinds of steel shapes—squares, rounds, and slabs—and Dad told the guy he'd pay him for whatever steel he used. Took off his jacket, rolled up his sleeves, and forged himself a new axel. Put it in the fire, hammered it and shaped it, and before the day was over he had made a rear axel, installed it in the car, and got the car going. And the thing was that the car ran all the way home. Got us back to Hinsdale that night."

19

To know how things work and to be able to fix them when they break down. That's what will do the job for you. You betcha. That's what will get you home and sleeping in your own bed every time.

The Old Man was some piece of work himself, huh?

What does the story of the Pathfinder tell you? Well, it tells you that the Krehbiels were pretty well off. The Pathfinder was an open car. A summer car. A second car.

It tells you that John idolized his father. ("You bet I was impressed. You probably couldn't find one in a million who could do that today.")

And it tell you by his loving description of differentials and axels that John Krehbiel is so fascinated by the way things work that he takes particular pleasure in lingering over the details.

Frederick Augustus Krehbiel came by his knowledge of differentials and axels honestly. His own father, John Jacob Krehbiel, had been a wagonmaker back in Newton, Kansas, where Frederick was born. Not only was blacksmithing an essential part of the wagonmaking process, but J.J. had actually owned a blacksmith shop in his younger days.

Krehbiel (Kray-bule) is a Swiss name. Somewhere along the line the name had been shortened from Krehenbuehl (which means "crow's nest") in the hope of making it more palatable to the American ear. ("I had the J. H. Krehbiel Company when I was a young man," John says, chuckling. "And every time I'd call someone he'd ask me how it was spelled. I'd spell it out slowly and he'd say, 'Yeah, John, what can I do for you?' ")

The Krehbiels were Swiss Mennonites. John's mother, Lucille Pemberthy, was the daughter of a mining engineer, from Colorado. Her grandfather was the inventor of the Pemberthy injector, a device that enabled engineers to inject water into boilers where the steam pressure was higher than the incoming water pressure.

Mennonites are pacifists. The entire Krehbiel family had left Switzerland and crossed into Germany after it was decreed that every male citizen be issued a rifle and enrolled in the National Guard. In Germany, they found out what real militarism was and, in the 1820s, emigrated to America. "My dad's family settled in Newton, Kansas, started a wagonbuilding facility, and became wheat farmers." His grandfather, John J. Krehbiel, was one of the three founders of Bethel College. He gave the land for the college campus and was the first chairman of its board.

Mennonites are a tiny sect, the smallest identifiable religious sect in America today. They are a principled people, and the Krehbiels ceased to be Mennonites on a matter of principle. One of the payments that J. J. Krehbiel had pledged to Bethel came due during the time of the land panic of 1896, and when his request for a period of grace was turned down by the church elders, he was forced to sell off a great deal of valuable farmland at severely depressed prices. The Mennonites got their money, and the Krehbiels became Episcopalians. They continued to support Bethel College, however, and so does John. As soon as he could afford to he began to contribute to Bethel as something of a family obligation.

Frederick didn't finish high school. There was the farm and there was the wagon factory. "They built farm wagons and buggies, and they also repaired steam tractors. And Dad was working as an apprentice in the shop and learning all these trades, and finally he asked his dad, 'Who designed those steam tractors?' And his father said, 'An engineer.' After his father had told him what an engineer was, my dad told him that was what he wanted to be, an engineer. The first thing he did was to go to Kansas University, in Lawrence, to get his high school diploma. Took his freshman year of college there and went up to Chicago to Armour Institute which had an excellent professor in steam plant power. When he'd learned everything he could about that, he asked the professor who was the best man in the country in designing generating equipment, and he said it was a fellow at Cornell. So Dad went to Cornell to study with him." By the end of the year he had the credits to graduate as either a mechanical engineer or an electrical engineer, but they wouldn't give him two degrees in the same year and he wasn't going to go back a second year just to pick up a diploma. Instead he joined a company in Chicago called Arnold Engineering. He worked with Sargeant-Lundy, which designed all the Commonwealth Edison plants, and eventually took off with a couple of other Lundy engineers to start his own business, Krehbiel Engineering. "I can remember as a young kid being there on Saturdays. They had the whole top floor of the Manadnoc Building. I think it was one of the first skyscrapers in the world, as well as in Chicago." That, of course, was before the Depression hit.

Fred Krehbiel was a strict disciplinarian with a well-developed Swiss-German work ethic. On the other hand he had been raised in an environment where accomplishment was more important than formal schooling, and so it didn't bother him at all that Johnny, who was always a high-spirited kid, spent as much time swimming in the quarries as attending classes. "Dad wasn't so concerned with attendance as with accountability. How was I doing at the end of the year?" And during Johnny's first two years of high school, he was bringing home very good report cards. Why wouldn't he? He was making them out himself. "I thought I was so clever. You don't realize that every kid in the world has thought of doing the same thing."

Every kid in the world didn't have a father who was on the School Board. And when the time came, as sooner or later it was bound to, when the reports from Johnny's teachers did not exactly accord with the report cards he had been signing, Fred Krehbiel went into the master files and took a look for himself. Then he took Johnny out to the woodshed and gave him the whaling of a lifetime.

He also gave him an ultimatum. There would be no college tuition unless he graduated with his class. "So I had to get busy the last two years and work like hell to squeeze through. But the one thing he was smart enough to insist on was that I was to work for at least a year before college. He didn't say that I was too immature, which I was, he just said that I'd be better off on my own. And that was probably the smartest thing he ever told me."

When the year was up, his father gave him $2,000, the full tuition for a four-year college education, and informed him that it was his money to use in any way he wished.

What John really wanted to do, as his father undoubtedly suspected, was to learn the tricks of every trade. While he was in high school, he had built a small steam engine down in his father's basement workshop, and when he saw that the thing actually worked, he built an electric generator so that it would have something to drive. He had also spent his last summer vacation in high school working in a Chicago machine shop, Lammert & Mann, making heavy machinery and commercial oil burners. "We had a steel-cutting lathe in the basement, and we had good wood-working tools and a good tool bench, too. My brother, Ed, and I both had a pretty good idea what kind of work you did on what kind of machines. I just wanted more experience, so I'd know how to run milling machines, drill presses, shapers, and the rest."

In the seven years before he went into business for himself, he worked at a machine shop, an iron foundry, a brass and aluminum foundry, and a ready-mix cement company. And if initially it was not so much the knowledge as the application of the knowledge that interested him, he learned what he had to learn in night schools as he went along. While he was working at Lammert & Mann, he took advanced courses in machine shop. But only, interestingly enough, after he had taken a course to make up his deficiency in math. During his time at the brass foundry he took courses at the Robie Institute (which eventually combined with Armour to form the Illinois Institute of Technology) in metalurgy and metallography. And when he went into business with his next-door neighbor manufacturing a highly explosive material, he went to the University of Chicago for courses in both organic and inorganic chemistry. But that was as much to learn the vocabulary the chemists were pitching at him as anything else. "My father had told me never to let anybody snow me with language. 'Any time you don't understand what somebody is supposed to be telling you,' he said, 'it isn't your fault, its theirs.' My two sons aren't scientific kids, either, and I've told them the same thing: 'Don't ever let somebody with a Ph.D snow you.' "

He had still been working in the machine shop, however, when his father gave him the money, and the decision about college had to be made. He still wasn't interested. He had seen machining castings that were being shipped in from a foundry, and he wanted to find out how they were made. For the next three-and-a-half years, he worked in foundries on the west side of Chicago, first a cast iron foundry and then a brass and aluminum foundry.

And for a boy who had been brought up in the affluent community of Hinsdale, there were lessons to be learned. At Fearon Foundry, his coworkers were mostly Polish and blacks. "I learned to respect native intelligence," he comments now. The intelligence of the hands. The values of good common sense.

Even today, Senior can look back and remember every detail of the casting process.

"The trade of core-making consists of making the sand cores by using molds called core boxes, and baking them in ovens for the insides of castings. From that I went to floor molding, which is molding big objects on the floor of the foundry, as well as bench molding, which is the same except that it's done on benches at waist height for the smaller parts."

Physically, the toughest job was tending the furnaces to melt the metal in order to create alloys for the castings. "Pouring the hot metal was the hardest, even in winter. The windows were all knocked out of the frames, and the birds would fly around this high-ceilinged factory room that took the fumes off the steaming molds as the metal was being poured." That was in the summer. In the winter you'd have snow coming in and swirling around the factory.

"Summer or winter, you'd strip to the waist. You'd have a leather apron over the main part of your body to keep the hot metal from splashing on you, but your arms and much of the rest of your body was bare, and for that there was no protection."

It was the foundry work itself—a technology that has all but disappeared—that fascinated him:

The reason the molds would steam when you poured the metal was because you make them out of damp sand so that the thing holds its shape. You put a pattern in of whatever you are going to mold. First you put some sand in the bottom of the frame, which is called a drag. A cope and a drag. The drag was the bottom half. You then put this piece in and you packed the sand around it, see if there was enough sphere. You'd put the sand about halfway in the thing, you'd put the cope on top of the frame and you'd sprinkle in the sand, and then you'd start pounding it with a mallet. The back end of a shovel handle was one of the best things you could use, although they also had a big round wooden mallet that did the packing in the sand.

The sand had to be damp enough to hold itself together—as a matter of fact, you had molasses in it—and then you patterned out, put the parts back together. And you took out an awl-like instrument and cut out a hole for the metal to pour in. Then the metal went along this parting line where you parted those two molds and flowed in this particular pattern. When it cooled down enough you'd separate them out, and take metal out of the thing. Clean the sand off of it, cut the screw off; the screw was the thing that took sand down to this sphere. Now that you had a sphere, you could machine it or whatever you were going to do.

Once he had learned what there was to know about steel casting, he moved on to the Faunt Brothers Brass and Aluminum Foundry. "Here I learned a great deal more about casting metals, as well as the formulas and formulations of different brass and bronze alloys."

The move out of the factory and into sales and eventually into his own business began when his father bought an interest in a company that designed and built the first of the big concrete mixers. Here was a business with a future, Fred Krehbiel told his son. "You ought to get into it."

Having learned everything there was to learn about making cement in about a day and a half, he became a salesman out of sheer boredom and discovered that he was such a natural that he was able to pick up clients as he went along. His big item was Haydite tile, a lightweight concrete block made out of burned clay aggregate. Being so light, Haydite was not only considerably cheaper to make, but so much easier for the masons to work with that their productivity went way up. You have a product that's both cheaper and better, how can you miss? "We sold these products to architects and engineers in Chicago and the western suburbs for apartments, hospitals, public buildings, and residences. Couldn't get enough of the stuff."

Having discovered that he could sell, he also discovered that he could be sold. One of the principles of the firm told him to hock the family jewels and invest in the commodities market. "He said, 'I tell you guys in the office if you don't have a cent, you'd better beg, borrow, or steal whatever you can and put it in wheat.' Wheat was about to go through the ceiling. I thought this guy was the greatest thing since sliced bread and he was my boss and if he said to beg, borrow, or steal, I was ready to go out and hold up some guy in the street."

Remember the context. This is 1928, the stock market is booming, and Chicago was—as it has always been—the center of the commodities market. "I put all I had, the $2,000 my father had given me, into the wheat market, and in less than two weeks it was gone."

Best lesson he ever learned. Cheap at the price. "I learned a lesson that has stayed with me for sixty years. Never risk your money on something you don't know or understand." And never take somebody else's word for it.

John's philosophy is that there is nothing wrong with making a mistake so long as you learn from it. That, in fact, you want your people to make mistakes so that they will be able to learn from them. Look how lucky he was, he can say, that he blew his whole wad at a time when he was young enough not to have much of a wad to blow.

As for John himself, moving the screen back to the twenties, he followed the commodities disaster by signing on with the Ready Mix Concrete Company of Chicago. A tremendous product. The mixer was part of the truck. The manufacturing process was built into the delivery system. Yet with all that going for it, the company was practically bankrupt, because both of the owners were poor businessmen and even worse salesmen. "I took the job on the basis that I would get a very low salary and my commission would be applied toward stock. The agreement was that when I had achieved enough sales I would own 25 percent of the company." It took him eighteen months to build up the credits for the agreed upon purchase. In the process, he had also built up the company to where he was no longer needed. The owners kept putting him off by telling him they were having trouble getting the stockholders together, an excuse which might have been considerably more convincing if John hadn't been well aware that they were the only two stockholders.

Just as he was on the point of giving up, his contacts at Commonwealth Edison advised him they were looking for someone to make a fireproofing compound for their cable. That didn't sound so bad. If he couldn't have 25 percent of somebody else's company, he could have 100 percent of his own. At age twenty-six, he started his own business, J. H. Krehbiel Co. He had a contract with Edison to manufacture 100,000 bags of the fireproofing material in 100-lb. bags, and he borrowed the money to build a plant especially designed to fulfill these requirements.

The fireclay needed in the mix came from a clay pit in Anna, Illinois, about four hundred miles south of Chicago. He signed a contract to lease the pit. He bought some used equipment—a 200-HP gasoline engine, a crusher to break up the clay, and a conveyor. Set it up, got it running, made a deal with a foreman to hire a crew and move right into production.

And then everything started to go wrong. On the day the first carload was supposed to arrive from Anna, he called the foreman and was told that they hadn't been able to get the engine going. "Have you choked it?" John asked him. Did he know how to choke it? Had he done this, that and the other thing? When the long-distance instructions proved to be unavailing, there was nothing to do except to go down there himself. "I drove all night, arrived before the foreman or crew, turned the engine over a couple of times, choked it, and then turned it on—exactly as I had instructed them—and it started up on the next cranking."

Raised holy hell with the crew about having to drive four hundred miles down, and four hundred miles back, to turn on an engine. Stood by while they started it up several times. Stayed there until they actually had the clay going through the crusher and down the conveyor and into the rail car. And then he had to rush back to Chicago to contend with some other pressing problems of the operation.

The next day, it was the foreman who called him. "They had knocked off the night before with the car only half-loaded, and when they'd tried to start the machinery up again they couldn't get the engine going."

Again the frantic and unavailing telephone instructions. Again the four hundred mile drive to Anna. This time they had overchoked and flooded the engine. "They never did finish loading that first car. And what really had me worried was that they didn't seem to care."

So he got a truck and a mechanic to pick up the machinery and bring it back to Chicago so that he could sell it. And contracted the job out. (He found out later that the foreman had hired a bunch of hillbillies who were on welfare, and were obviously quite willing to stay on.) The worst was yet to come. "Being a young guy in business, I did not notice that the contract had no completion date on it." Edison had never talked in terms of using anything less than 100,000 bags a year. When they signed the contract they had fully intended just that. Unfortunately for everybody, the Depression clamped down on the country in 1932. And Edison clamped down on young John Krehbiel.

"Instead of using 100,000 bags in one year, it took Edison three years to use that amount of material. But it was another good lesson. It not only taught me something about contracts but, in a very direct way, it got me into the material business. In order to meet the notes covering the construction cost of the plant, I had to expand the fireproofing compound business into the manufacture of electrical insulating materials which were used in high voltage cables."

Wherever high voltage lines went into a building, they had to be pushed through an opening. These junctions were called potheads, and they had to be lined with a high quality insulation material in order to keep the cables from shorting out when they were whipped against the building material in a high wind. The J. H. Krehbiel Co. manufactured the material for both the overhead lines and the underground cables and sold them to Commonwealth Edison, Public Service of Northern Indiana, Public Service of Northern Illinois, and several other utilities including the Cleveland and Philadelphia Electric companies.

With J. H. Krehbiel Co. beginning to prosper, John got into another business. The manufacture of nitrocellulose. Nitrocellulose is a form of gunpowder. Gunpowder is the stuff that blows up. It didn't happen to him once. It happened twice.

The neighbor who got him involved was Bill Regnery. In a manner of speaking, they lived across the street from each other. In reality, they lived on successive corners of Ayres Street. The Krehbiels lived on Lincoln Street, the Regnerys on Washington Street. The Regnerys owned the block between the two houses. William Regnery, Sr., was the owner of Western Shade Cloth Company. An excellent businessman, a shrewd investor and, fortunately for Hinsdale, a very civic-minded man, because in the worst years of the Depression, Mr. Regnery remained spectacularly solvent.

The families were very close. Fred Krehbiel and William Regnery liked to walk to the railroad station together so they could practice their German on each other. Bill Regnery, the oldest son, and John were members of a group of five cardplayers who would get together at either John's or Bill's house a couple of times a week.

"What do you know about nitrocellulose?" Bill asked him one night, in the middle of a poker game. That was easy. "Absolutely nothing."

"The reason I'm asking you," Bill Regnery said, "is because we buy it in carload lots." And paid for it almost the same way. There were only three companies from whom the stuff could be bought. Dupont, Hercules Powder, and American Powder; otherwise known as "The Powder Trust." In theory, the government had broken up *The Powder Trust* in a well-publicized anti-trust suit a few years earlier. In practice, Bill Regnery could tell him, the three giant companies were still colluding to keep the price up.

Bill was about five years out of Amherst at the time. And he was not only the heir apparent to the Western Shade Cloth Company, he was independently wealthy. Well, kind of independent. William Regnery had four sons and a daughter, and he had given each of them a trust fund of something like a million dollars as soon as he felt they were equipped to handle it.

Bill's proposition was that he would put up all the money and run the business while John would run the factory and do the selling. They named their company Illinois Manufacturing Chemists. John went out and did a lot of research. Talked to experts, heard the word "hazardous" more often than he'd have liked to, hired a consultant, picked out a factory site, and bought some equipment—all before Bill Regnery got around to letting his father in on their plans.

And, of course, the old man hit the ceiling. Bill was his oldest son, and he had been grooming him to take the business over. "But the old man was smart. He wasn't going to say, no, you can't, because he knew he had started it on his own. So he said, 'Well, Bill, the family can't afford this because we need you in the business. But, he also said, "I'll tell you what we will do. We'll finance John Krehbiel in the business and you can oversee the financial end of Illinois Manufacturing Chemists.' And the Western Shade Cloth Company would still have the benefits of a competitor to the Powder Trust."

To nail it down, Mr. Regnery promptly put up $200,000 of his own money and then proceeded to keep his son so busy at the Western Shade plant that Bill Regnery very quickly became an invisible partner.

But Bill Regnery's basic thinking had been correct. The day the plant opened, the quotation for nitrocellulose dropped about 25 percent to the Western Shade Cloth Company. "And even at that price, Mr. Regnery showed me how we could make a good profit." In fact, it was clearly to his benefit at that point to make sure that they did.

Western Shade Company made book cloth by running cotton cloth through a solution of this nitrocellulose dissolved in solvents and, with added coloring, made a lacquer out of the solution. After it hardened, it would be run through embossing rolls to give it a grain, such as you see on imitation leather books, upholstery, and the like.

"In addition, we sold a great deal of material to companies like Sherwin Williams for use in lacquer and the various paint companies around Chicago that are manufacturers of lacquers and varnishes. The most difficult customer to please was a small company that made a very clear lacquer for silverware to prevent it from tarnishing. They were very critical buyers but we finally landed their business as well."

When you build yourself a plant to make nitrocellulose you do not build it to last through the ages. Nor do you build it anywhere near where a school bus might run. John built his plant in Calumet City, down by the railroad tracks. It was constructed mostly of tin and designed so that the sides would blow out with a minimum of encouragement.

A very dangerous business. As long as the cotton was wet, there were no serious problems. Dry was something else again. Over a period of time, dust particles would accumulate along the windowsills and every once in a while—*whisssh*—you'd see a streak of fire go dancing by.

John would take each new employee and try to scare the hell out of him. "Have you ever seen gun cotton?" John asks. "It's like cotton linten. Like the stuff you get out of your navel. If you put the stuff down and you light a match, it's gone in a poof. Like a magician's trick. It goes so damn fast you can't see it go, and there's no ash left behind. We've got four tubs out there on the floor with 6,000 pounds of the stuff in each of them. After I had given my demonstration, these guys would go in there shaking. A week later, you'd see the same guys smoking in the tub house."

They had been in operation for about a year when the place went up. John and Peg were staying at Peg's mother's house in Hinsdale, and so when the phone rang early one morning John took the phone into the bathroom so as not to disturb anybody. Bill Veeck saw the light from across the court and called to find out what was going on.

"We've got a fire at the factory," John said.

"I'm going with you," said Bill.

By the time they got there, the factory had burned to the ground. Like everything else about the operation, the two-story factory had been designed to allow for the volatility of the product. The three heavy tubs sat on the first floor, and there were three matching centrifuges on the second. The basic problem was that you couldn't ship the stuff dry, because it was like an explosive. And you didn't want to ship it in water and force the customer to drain it all off himself. So you boiled the cotton lintens in tubs containing 6,000–7,000 gallons of water, stirring constantly all the while, and after it had soaked for about a week, you drained the water through a very fine screen. Then you put fresh water in and start pumping the material up to the centrifuges.

"The centrifuge," John explains, "was nothing but a fast moving big bucket with a screen inside. The centrifugal force threw the water out and kept the cotton lintens inside. You'd get that down to the point where you had maybe 30 percent water in it and the balance was the cotton, and that's all the water you could get by centrifugal force. Then, behind it, you pumped alcohol—pure alcohol—and this would go into the cotton as it was being swirled around in the centrifuge, and it would grab onto the excess water and get rid of it." And then you would collect the alcohol, redistill it, and start the process all over again.

When the customer unpacked the nitrocotton that was saturated with alcohol he was able to use the alcohol as a solvent for the material he was going to introduce into the mixture to produce his own particular lacquer. Great system.

The alcohol also provided a safety factor, of a sort. So long as the stuff was wet, you couldn't have an explosion. Right? The worst you could have was a bad fire. When it came to shipping it, that was something else. The stuff was packed in airtight, waterproof drums. If there were a fire, the alcohol inside the drums would start expanding and . . . well, if you didn't want to call that an explosion, it would do until the real thing came along.

"We were situated right across from the main line of the New York Central tracks, and when Bill and I got there the fire chief told us these drums were being launched over the tracks like they'd been shot out of a cannon. Zoom . . . zoom . . . zoom. If the 20th Century Limited had been going through there, it would have been carnage. Those steel drums weighed about 55 pounds apiece."

Mr. Regnery was more than willing to start over. "He wasn't the kind of guy to be discouraged by failure. And, of course, he didn't want the price of nitrocellulose to go back up again, either."

Illinois Manufacturing Chemists prospered for another five years before the factory blew up again. By then, nobody really cared. The United States was at war, and a whole new set of economic factors had come into being. John Krehbiel was married, he had a couple of kids and also a couple of other companies to worry about. In addition to his own J. H. Krehbiel Co. he was a partner with his father and brother in a company called Molex, and his father was urging him to come into the company in a more active capacity.

THE HOUSE IN DOWNERS GROVE

It's funny, I was thinking about John and Peg the other day when I saw the picture Crocodile Dundee. *That was the quality John had. Lots of vitality. Lots of fun. He'd walk in and things would begin to happen. He was the youngest guy in the group, but people were just drawn to him.*

—JOE BLACKMAN—

"WHEN Margaret Ann Veeck married John Krehbiel," oldtime Hinsdale residents can still say, "all of Hinsdale wept."

Peg Veeck was the darling of Hinsdale. Her father was William L. Veeck, best known as the president of the Chicago Cubs. He was also president of the Hinsdale Golf Club and, with his wife Grace, a social leader of what was one of the more affluent communities in the country. After the census of 1916, it was said that there were five thousand people living in Hinsdale, and seven hundred of them were millionaires.

Wealthy or not, there was the right side of the tracks and the wrong side of the tracks. The south side was the right side, the north side was the wrong side, and as far as the kids were concerned the twain rarely met until they came together at Hinsdale High.

An explanation is in order. The dividing line hadn't been firmly established at the time Frederick Krehbiel built his home on Ayres Street, and if it had he probably wouldn't have noticed or cared. But it was said of his wife, Lucille, that "she spent her whole life regretting that it hadn't been built on the south side."

Joe Blackman was the son of a member of the town council. South side all the way. And although Joe grew up to become both a lawyer and a banker (two of John's most unfavorite professions), they have been friends throughout their adult years. "I didn't know John before high school," Joe says. "I knew *about* him. Every kid in town knew about John and his motorcycle accident. He was one of those north side rowdies. That's exactly what we called them, north side rowdies."

But it wasn't a north side-south side thing, really. As Henry Regnery, who was a classmate of Peggy's can attest. "There was a woman who lived across the street from us on Ayres Street who later moved to the other part of town. She was a great friend of Peggy Veeck's, and she was saying just the other day how shocked they all were that Peggy had married John. She thought it was quite terrible. This nice girl married to John Krehbiel. She visits us often, and she still talks about it, talked about it no more than two, three weeks ago at our house. How shocked everybody was. You see, Peg was sort of the belle of Hinsdale. And with all that tremendous energy and drive of his, Johnny had been in a lot of scrapes."

He was also a ladies man. His nickname, for as long as anybody could remember, was Huggus. The name was pinned on him when he was about eight years old by the brother of a little girl he was smooching it up with on her front porch. And if the name had stuck through all those years, it was not because he had gone to any heroic lengths to get rid of it.

"John was a banger," says Red Thayer, his best friend for more than seventy years.

"Red was a hellion," John chuckles, returning the favor.

The banger and the hellion came together when they found themselves in the same Boy Scout squad, and although Red was twelve, and John was only ten, each recognized a kindred spirit.

John enjoyed scouting so much that he actually ended up as an Eagle Scout. To this day, the Boy Scouts have no stronger advocate. "I got a lot out of it," he will say. "What it does is try to make a kid a broader person, not just make a hell of a good guy at tying ropes or swimming or something. It takes something like twenty-five or thirty merit badges in order to be an Eagle Scout, and each badge requires the development of a particular skill." John earned his lifesaving merit badge, as it were, on the field of battle. Or, at least, the high seas. So OK, make it a lake.

The Scouts had opened a new camp at Lake Delavan, Wisconsin, and useful kid that he always was, John was there to help build the tent platforms and the piers. While he was about it he rescued a boy who was in the process of both choking and drowning after swallowing a massive ball of gum. "John swam for the Hinsdale Club in the center of town," Red says. "He was a competitive swimmer and could have made a name for himself, I always thought. He was a good athlete."

He and Red also caddied and played golf together at the country club, and through Red's friendship with the groundkeeper's son, they were hired on the crew of kids who were paid something like 30 cents an hour, during the summer, to rid the greens of crabgrass and dandelions.

The famous motorcycle caper took place right alongside one of those greens. John remembers it as happening during a lunch break. But there obviously was some kind of ceremony going on because half the kids in town seemed to be gathered along that particular stretch of the golf course.

At any rate, John's dad had allowed him to purchase a used motorcycle on time. Not that John was part of a motorcycle gang or anything like that. There weren't enough motorcycles around in 1921 to make up a decent gang. To Fred Krehbiel's way to thinking, what better way for a fifteen-year-old kid to learn about engines and the value of a dollar at the same time.

Gang or not, a certain statement is being made when you opt for a motorcycle over a car. Not unlike the difference between joining the marines instead of going into the army. John was pretty well demonstrating that difference by zooming his motorcycle up and down the dirt road (now Ogden Avenue) alongside the golf course, performing every fancy trick in his repertoire for the edification of the gathered girls and boys. ("I don't know what they call it these days, the technical term back then was showing off.") At any rate, he zoomed full tilt into a chuck hole and went straight up over the handlebars. Johnny was a rather small kid, he only weighed about 120 pounds, and what everybody still remembers is the truly remarkable height he was able to achieve before he descended back to earth, head first. He landed on his head, and was in a coma for forty-eight hours.

Exit the motorcycle. "Dad decided it wasn't worth having the kid learn about engines if it was going to get the kid killed."

What did not exit, however, was his thirst for speed, thrills and fast cars.

As a kind of sideline, Lammert & Mann machine shop had contracted to rebuild racing-car engines for a stable belonging to a leading driver of the area, Cliff Woodbury. It was natural enough that John would want to discover everything possible about the high-powered engines of the day, and natural too that he would begin to pester Woodbury for a chance to drive one of his cars in a race.

"I'm sure he thought about it and decided, Some kid in the shop back there. I'll try to be nice to him so I can get my engines done faster."

They were the old-fashioned racing cars of 1924, thick wheels, little square windshield in front to protect the driver. "It was a quarter-mile dirt track called Sante Fe Park. Being an amateur I was placed in the back row, the gun went off, and I never saw another car because of the dust."

Nor did he want to. He was afraid that if he did see another car, it would be because he was climbing up its back. "The only way I knew the race was over was that the dust had started to settle in front of me."

He was not really cut out, Johnny concluded, to be a race car driver. He had already congratulated himself on getting out of the race alive.

But the kid wasn't through yet. If there were not that many motorcycles around Hinsdale, there were far more automobiles than you might imagine. It was the custom in Hinsdale, among the country club set at least, to present their sons and daughters with an automobile on their sixteenth birthday. A Chrysler roadster was the thing to have. Peg Veeck had to make do with a custom-built Packard roadster. Red Thayer had a Dodge roadster. But the truly awesome car, as all serious students of the Roaring Twenties know, was the Stutz Bearcat. The Stutz was really a modified race car, an open car with an engine so powerful that if you were able to get more than four miles to the gallon you were doing well. Whatever statement you made zooming along on a motorcycle, you made an even more flamboyant statement when you gathered the girls in your Stutz. It is the Stutz Bearcat, along with the hip flask, the raccoon coat, and the flapper, that was to become the symbol of Flaming Youth.

There were perhaps two Stutz Bearcats in town. One of them was owned by a guy named Billy Kimball (of the Kimball Piano family), who was the very personification of Flaming Youth in Hinsdale. Billy Kimball's Stutz was up for sale, and Johnny Krehbiel lusted after it. His father told him he couldn't afford it. Not just the original cost, but the upkeep.

So Johnny bought it anyway, and kept it in the garage behind Red Thayer's house. (There was a precedent. He had kept his motorcycle in Red's garage for some time after his parents believed it had been sold.)

Came the day he and Red drove the Stutz over to pick up something in the garage. And he did the one thing that he didn't want to do. He hit the curbing as he was swinging into the driveway, and the car stalled. In order to start any car in those days, you had to get out and crank it. Johnny was doing exactly that when—as fate ordains these things—his folks came driving by on their way to the movies.

"Is there anything we can do to help you?" his father asked.

"No, Dad," said Johnny.

"What car is it?" asked his father.

"It's a Stutz," answered Johnny.

"That's THAT Stutz," gasped Lucille Krehbiel in a voice that sounded remarkably like the voice of doom.

And that was the end of the Stutz, and the beginning of a running joke. For sixty years now, Johnny and Red have been able to break themselves up by chorusing whenever remotely applicable, "That's THAT Stutz."

In the pursuit of fun and games, there was one other form of revelry that defined the Roaring Twenties. It was the Age of Jazz, and Chicago was its hotbed. Johnny had scarcely set foot in Hinsdale High before he organized his own band. Johnny was the drummer and he doubled on a one-string bass fiddle. "He got an old oil drum," Red Thayer says, "attached a wooden handle to it, made a string out of something or other and it went boom . . . boom . . . boom. John could always make something out of nothing."

The first time Joe Blackman ever saw him, as far as Joe can remember, Johnny and his band were playing at what would become the regular Friday night dance in the church building in downtown Hinsdale. "Admission was a buck a couple. Johnny was the guy who started that."

The trumpet player (who doubled on sax) was Mundy Peale. A great name for a jazz artist, huh? This Mundy Peale grew up to become the president of Republic Aviation.

As for John himself, he remained such a jazz buff that Bill Veeck, another aficianado, presented him with an honest-to-goodness bass fiddle during the celebration of the Cleveland Indians' victory in the 1948 World Series.

Red Thayer didn't play an instrument. "I just hummed along. The thing we did together more than anything else in those days was to play golf." The other two regulars in their foursome were E. E. (Laddy) Meyers, who was an Olympic pole vaulter, and Karl Ostrum, who was the best golfer in the area. They would drive fifty miles to Fox Lake on Sunday morning and play twenty-seven holes. Maybe thirty-six holes, maybe forty-five holes. And meet again a few times a week to join with Bill Regnery in the card games.

Red Thayer: "John had fixed up a little room in the basement of his house. We'd go over there and play poker, bridge, red dog. John and I made some brew in the basement and most of it blew up during the night. From what John told me, it sounded like a machine gun had gone off. I came over to help him clean up the mess. His mother, of course, was furious. She had given him strict orders to get rid of all those bottles. So we cleaned the place up, and looked at each other, and said, well, if she insists . . . and drank whatever was left. We had an awful lot of fun."

And then there was the fire. The five musketeers had gathered at John's house to play cards one night when his folks were on vacation. Along about midnight, they decided to go to a roadhouse and somebody apparently dropped a lighted cigarette in the wastebasket as they were leaving. Disaster was averted when Red Thayer's brother came by with his girlfriend, just in time to see the curtain go up in flames. "Don't worry," John told his friends. "I'll have the place looking as good as new before my folks come back." He knew the insurance guy, so he was able to hustle up a quick settlement. He bought matching curtains, and he did a remarkable job of matching the wallpaper. Unfortunately, his folks came back a couple of days early and walked into a house filled with scaffolding and ladders and paperhangers and painters.

His father called him at work. "Your mother is upset," he said. "You'd better stay away for a couple of days." That wasn't so unusual. Lucille Krehbiel was a woman who, as the saying went, "enjoyed ill health." (She took to her bed somewhere along the road to middle age, and then arose at the age of almost seventy to take up painting, and began to turn out really fine, professional still lifes.)

Her confidante was Mrs. Regnery. As Henry Regnery recalls very well. "She used to call up my mother and tell her about these things. Johnny had done this and that, and she had got mad and put him out." Three or four days later, he was back and everything was fine. "My Johnny is just the best boy in the whole world," she would tell Mrs. Regnery. "Do you know what he just did for me?"

In the end, it was Johnny and Red who decided they were getting too old to live at home. John was twenty-seven years old and the owner of his own business. Red was living with his four brothers in a converted barn at the back of the house. "John was the sparkplug of the thing," Red says. "He went out scouting for the land, he negotiated the deal, and he bought it." Actually, Johnny had had his eye on five acres of wooded land, complete with a stream, along the southern edge of Hinsdale. Just perfect for hunting and fishing.

The plans for the house had already been drawn up. Hinsdale had an architect, named Harrold Zook, who had achieved such renown that to live in "a Zook house" was a mark of distinction. (It still is. A Zook log cabin in Lake Toneba was recently bought for $400,000.) Although Zook was probably in his late fifties, he and John had become quite friendly. And since nobody was building houses during the deep Depression, Zook drew him a set of plans for a home in the woods.

Depression or no, the cost of the land was out of sight. John was looking for five acres of land he could buy for $1,000. The parcel of land he hungered for was quoted at $2,000 per acre.

"So we went out north of Hinsdale where the land was supposed to be cheaper and quickly ran into Frank O. Butler." Another older man. Frank Butler was a very successful paper merchant and builder. (His son, Paul Butler, would become Butler Aviation.)

From the beginning, Butler was intrigued at the notion of a couple of young guys set on building a house with their own hands, and when he also learned that they were going to be building themselves a Zook house, he invited them to come to his house and show him the plans. "We spread the plans across the floor of his living room, and he said, 'I wish to hell I'd done this when I was a kid. I think you fellows are great.' " Having said that, he told them that as much as he wanted to help them, he didn't want to sell any land in that area because he was trying to accumulate as large a parcel of land as possible. "What I will do," he said, "I'll lease you five acres for ninety-nine years."

It would be several years before John discovered that Butler was buying up all the land in the area to build the village of Oakbrook. "We would have been right in the middle of Oakbrook, as it turned out. But we had grandiose ideas. Here's a businessman, probably sixty years old, and he's being so gracious and telling us how much he wants to help us, and we tell him, Nah, if we can't buy it, the hell with it."

So John went southwest toward Downers Grove and ran into a farmer named Chilvers who owned everything in sight. "A very shrewd guy. Completely illiterate. Owned all the land, owned apartment houses in town." And was always ready to deal. Farmer Chilvers was perfectly willing to take John Krehbiel's $1,000 if John Krehbiel was willing to take five acres of heavily wooded, absolutely raw land in the middle of nowhere. The middle of nowhere turned out to be a full thousand feet off the gravel road. So far back that they needed an easement to bring in a line for electricity.

"The first thing we had to do," John says, "was lay down a narrow gravel road back to our property."

"The next thing we did," Red says, "was build a sort of garage to give us a place to camp out on weekends, so we'd have more time to work."

They purchased a used Ford pickup truck for hauling sand and gravel.

There was no water out there, so they hired a couple of strong farm kids to help them dig a well.

Red Thayer: "We both had experience in building shacks and, really, buildings that were much larger. And, as everyone knows, John is very good at learning and finding out how to do things."

Armed with nothing except picks and shovels, they began to dig a hole for the foundation on Decoration Day of 1933. By working on weekends and whenever else they had time, they were able to move into their house on Decoration Day of 1934. And during that year, the house going up in Downers Grove became famous. During the early days, Harrold Zook himself showed up to help them dig the hole and build the foundation. And—however much John tried to discourage him—to sketch in an improvement here and there on his original plans. "This guy could draw a couple of lines," John says, "and the cost would go up $20,000. I'd have to tell him, Harrold, I can't afford it."

There was only one thing in the house they didn't build themselves. As the centerpiece of what was essentially a showcase two-story living room, Zook had designed a huge A-shaped fireplace which extended from the floor up through the ceiling. Zook was adamant in insisting that the fireplace had to be made of stone. He also advised them on the best place to get it. The town of Lemont, seven miles to the south, had been built as a quarry town. Although the quarries had been played out for commercial production, Zook had every confidence that they could find some beautiful stuff there.

"One of the Chilvers farm boys we had hired took us to a woman who owned one of these abandoned quarries. To show how interesting it became, this woman told us that the big stones that came out of there were the ones used for State Street in Chicago in the days before concrete." They paid her 25 cents a ton, but they had to dig the great stone boulders out of the quarry wall themselves.

So John learned still another trade: "You put some poles in there and some dynamite, and shake it up, and shovel off the dirt. Then, using a pitch fork as a crow bar, you raise it up and that will bust a big hunk loose."

Zook had also warned them, however, not to try to build the fireplace themselves. Building a fireplace, it seems, is a tricky business under the best of circumstances. To begin with, you have to make sure that the fireplace is deep enough for the height of the chimney, and in this high cathedral-like living room Zook had designed, the fireplace was so huge that you would eventually be able literally to walk into it. And, of course, it worked both ways. "The stones were 4 feet wide and 4 feet thick, and where it extended through the roof to become the chimney, you also had to make sure that the chimney opening was wide enough to accommodate that depth."

If he tried to lay out a formula for them, Zook told them, he'd only be kidding them. "The only rule was the rule of thumb, and if the draft wasn't pulling exactly right we'd have the smoke coming back at us. For an amateur to do it, he said, was out of the question. There were few enough masons who were able to get it right, even for much smaller fireplaces."

Fortunately, John also happened to know the best mason in Hinsdale. "He was a marble setter really, and he was out of work like everybody else. So he came out there and in three-and-a-half days he laid up this fireplace, from the base of the floor right up on through the roof. This man was something to see. He had these two farm kids going crazy. They couldn't get the mortar and stones to him fast enough. And in more than fifty years, there has never been a wisp of smoke escape into the house."

The mason did more than that. He became so fascinated with the project that when he had finished with the fireplace, he helped them put in the timbers for the ceiling. "These were pretty good-sized timbers, and they were exposed on the inside. He helped us lay the timber out so that it was properly morticed and fitted. And then he helped us put it in place."

All the carpentry work, plumbing, painting, and electrical wiring they did themselves. Also the concrete and stone masonry. Because, in addition to using the Lemont stone for the fireplace, they were able to use it for the outside wall of the house. "That was another reason why the old Lemont quarry was particularly attractive to Zook. He had told us to look for stone where the rusty water from the corrosion that had taken place over the years had run down over it and stained it with a distinctive design." As always, the architect knew what he was talking about. The stone on both the chimney inside and the flagstone outside is stained in a way that lends it a pattern and character all its own.

Now, we have said that they built it themselves, and for the most part that is true. But let's not overlook the unskilled labor. In addition to the farm boys, their friends would come by during the weekend to help out. As the place began to take shape, they set out barbecues for their helpers, and by the time they were finished, the barbecues had turned into full-blown parties.

Joe Blackman's most vivid memory is going out there one rainy Saturday, shortly after the rafters had been put in place. "They had hired this little guy, Shorty, to do some work. This guy was like a little monkey, a real 5 x 5 and really strong. This Shorty got a little beer in him, and got rambunctious, and the next thing you knew he was swinging on the rafters. We thought he was going to kill himself."

Jane Dyas Ostrum, who was Peg's close friend all her life, remembers the first party she came to out in the woods. "The ladies room was a chair out by the garage, with the seat cut out. There was no staircase. To get to the bedroom on the second floor, you had to climb a ladder."

From somewhere, they had picked up a Filipino servant, named Ivory, who was usually drunk. Neither John nor Red could remember where he came from, or how they had hired him. He had apparently come by one night, stuck around, settled into the little servant's room by the kitchen, and made himself useful enough so that they didn't mind him drinking their booze.

In that regard, they had no trouble at all. "We got hold of a bootlegger in Wisconsin who used to make regular trips down to our part of the country once a month. He rode this regular circuit, and he put us on his route. He used to bring us a cute wooden barrel, with five gallons of booze in it. It was White Lightning. He made it in the bathtub, put it in the barrel, and delivered it. He'd say, 'You have to let it age.' We'd have a couple of barrels up in the attic and we'd let it age until we got thirsty and then we'd start drinking the stuff. Two weeks was a lot of aging."

Prohibition was so openly violated that there was a place along Ogden Avenue, right around Kensey Avenue, where Al Capone had his delivery point. When Johnny was working at the brass foundry he would drive past there every night. "You'd drive by and you'd find these big square, 5-gallon cans stacked along the curb. Four high, four or five deep, and twenty long. I'll never forget, once I picked up a 5-gallon can on the way home. While I was there some guy came in and he was violently mad. He said, 'Look at my car out there. Goddam it, when I pulled in I had wheels on it.' Some guy had jacked it up and pulled all four wheels off.

"This guy who was running the local alcohol distributing place got on the phone and said, 'You son of a bitch, this is one of the guys we do business with. You get his wheels back here right away.' Five minutes later the wheels were back on the car. The group that was stealing them was part of the same syndicate. That's how open the thing was. I suppose those 5-gallon cans were out there all night." Who, after all, was going to steal from Capone?

Given the times, given the stories about Flaming Youth, and given the weekend parties, you can imagine what the farmers around Downers Grove thought was going on. "We were under suspicion from the beginning," John admits. Downers Grove was a very small town. But it was an old town, a very conservative German and Italian town. Farmers built their homes as close to the road as possible. The road, after all, was their lifeline. And here were two young guys buying a piece of land that was back a thousand feet from the road. "And they think, why would a guy want to do that? The talk all along had been that we were going to run a whorehouse and gambling joint. They had everything pegged for that." The parties merely served to confirm their worst suspicions.

It had taken exactly one year for John and Red to build the house, and it took five months for Red to get married and leave. Red Thayer met a young lady named Marjorie Bowes, and just like that they became engaged. The first time Marjorie came out she brought her best friend along to meet Red's roommate. Her best friend's name was Margaret Ann Veeck. Marjorie and Margaret Ann had just finished touring Europe together. In October 1934, Red married Marjorie. Two months later, John married Peg.

When Red got married he sold out his share of the house to John.

John Krehbiel got married and brought his bride out to the "wilderness" and they lived there for fifty-one years.

The home, as originally constructed, had a small kitchen and a servant's room downstairs, in addition to the massive living room, and a bedroom and bath upstairs. The toilet, which was the last thing they had installed was such a wonder in that area, that Farmer Chilver's eight-year-old daughter took to dropping by two or three times a day to ask Mr. Red and Mr. John if she could use it. There wasn't anything wrong with the little girl's kidneys, she just liked to flush the toilet and watch in wonder as the water went swirling down the hole.

After Johnny was born, John built two more bedrooms and another bath upstairs. While he was about it, he added a second living room and a "mud room" downstairs. He later constructed a screened porch, and in 1975, as Peg's heart became so weak that she had trouble negotiating the stairs, he had a bedroom glass porch and bath added onto the first floor.

Five years later, he built a summerhouse for Peg down by the pond, as a birthday present. And that is how the House in Downers Grove stands today, fifty-three years after John brought home his bride.

She had always been called Margaret Ann growing up. And she had always been the darling of Hinsdale. When the children of the town were twelve or so, they were sent to dancing school to be instructed in the social amenities. The boys would sit in their best suits on one side, and the girls, white-gloved and beribboned, on the other. Henry Regnery, who was the same age as Peg, remembers those classes fondly. On a given signal, the boys would walk across the room and ask the girls of their choice for a dance. "Everybody would head for Margaret Ann. She'd sit there, modest and demure, with her eyes downcast. Everybody loved her. Even the other girls weren't jealous of her."

It was not really so surprising that she and John had never met. For one thing, Peg was five years younger. They would not have been in high school at the same time even if she had been attending public school. As it was, she had attended Hinsdale High for only one semester and had then been sent to the Ogontz School in Philadelphia to be instructed in the social amenities. She learned to curtsy to the queen. She did the Grand Tour of Europe. Given the proper audience, Peg could tell some hilarious stories about her chaperone, a world-class flapper with the wonderful name of Dutchen Stansbury, who was always trying to break loose and do a bit of hip-swinging on her own.

By the time they did meet, Peg was twenty-three years old. She'd had two serious romances. Everybody had always assumed that she would marry Fred Regnery, her childhood sweetheart. Fred was the flamboyant member of the Regnery clan, given to the grand gesture. Sal Dreher is now in her nineties. In the great old days her husband, George, was William Veeck's best friend, and Sal still loves to tell the story about the day the Drehers and the Veecks were in Atlantic City with the Wrigleys for what must have been the 1929 World Series against the Philadelphia Athletics. "Fred Regnery walked in while we were all having breakfast at the Courmaine Hotel, got down on his knee to Peggy, and said, 'I'll give you anything in the world if you marry me.' Poor Peg was so mortified, she was blushing. Then she was going to marry Dave Brittain, and John just came in and swept her off her feet."

John thought she was the loveliest thing he had ever seen. And John was a man who never hesitated to go after what he wanted. What John represented to her, we can surmise, was strength and comfort, at a time in her life when Peggy was badly in need of those qualities. Because when Peg met John, she was still recovering from the death of her father.

William L. Veeck was born in Booneville, Indiana, in 1877. He was the son of a cabinet maker. William Veeck's ambition was to be a newspaperman, and he was a voracious reader, a passion he passed on to his two children. (You don't have to believe this if you don't want to, but both Peg and Bill Veeck read a minimum of three books a week throughout their entire lives.)

Veeck married his childhood sweetheart, Grace DeForest. Grace was the daughter of the area's only doctor and one of its largest landholders. Dr. DeForest was far from pleased with the thought of his daughter roaming the country with an itinerant reporter. But Grace knew what she wanted. ("Gracie was born knowing what she wanted," her oldest friends say. "And what Gracie wanted, Gracie got.") She was going to marry

William L. Veeck, she told her father, and William L. Veeck was going to be a great success. Gracie knew what she was talking about. William Veeck became a reporter for the *Louisville Courier*, and then went up to Chicago to work for William Randolph Hearst's *American* in the glory days of Chicago journalism that have been immortalized in Hecht and MacArthur's *The Front Page*.

There was something about William Veeck. He was a natural leader. He was a doer. When he was handed the newspaper's sports byline, he became so critical of the way the Chicago Cubs were being operated that William Wrigley, who owned the team, invited him to become their president and try to do better.

And he did. He won pennants in 1929, and 1932, and set a Chicago attendance record along the way that lasted for forty years. But he was more than that. The newspaperman who had so impressed William Wrigley rapidly became such a power in the inner circles of baseball that in his second year on the job he became one of the small group of base-ball men who pushed through the election of Judge Kenesaw Mountain Landis as commissioner of baseball in the fallout from the Black Sox scandal.

He very well may have been the man who first put Landis's name forward, because Landis, who was a federal judge, was another personal friend.

Jane Ostrum: "Mr. Veeck always called Peg 'sister-girl,' and he used to take us to the ball games and arrange for us to sit up in the press box and get autographed baseballs and all the good food for nothing. We'd also go down to his office. I remember one day he said, 'My, sister-girl, you have the loveliest friends.' He was just darling."

He was a powerful figure, and Peg adored him, and she always felt that she was being shipped off to Ogontz and to Europe because her mother wanted to keep him all to herself. And then, suddenly, William Veeck was stricken with leukemia, and within a matter of weeks he was dead.

Jane Ostrum, who was there to support her friend during the death watch, can still relate to the trauma of those final days. "One reporter said to Billy in the hospital, 'You let me have the scoop on when your old man kicks the bucket—those were the words—and you'll have the best cover-age the Cubs ever had.' And Billy just said, 'You will never write another word about the Cubs.' I thought he was going to knock him down."

And then the funeral almost turned into a circus. "They had the Andy Frain ushers from the ballpark all down Park Avenue and into the house, and we went past this open coffin and out into the yard, and all the Cubs were there, and all kinds of horrible sightseers trying to sneak in through the bushes. It was terrible."

When Peg went out to the house in Downers Grove with her friend, Marjorie Bowes, to meet Marjorie's fiancé, it was probably the first time she had gone out socially since her father's death.

Johnny Krehbiel looked at her with his lively blue eyes and called her "Snooks," a pet name that would last through life and, as Sal Dreher says, swept her off her feet.

They were coming home from dining and dancing at the Congress Hotel where Eddie Duchin was performing and, as had become their custom, they stopped off at a White Castle for a sandwich. White Castles were little hamburger and coffee joints that were not frequented by the rich and famous. John proposed to her over a sandwich.

Because it was less than a year after her father's death, nobody wanted a big wedding. Least of all Peg's mother. That was fine with John. He made a deal with his bride. "I told her that I wouldn't have any drinks before the ceremony, if she didn't have any more than fifty guests. But for every guest over fifty, I was going to have one drink." Peg got the list down to fifty. "There were no extra guests and no extra drinks."

The wedding was held in her mother's house. Marjorie Bowes was the maid of honor. And, as a final indication of how John felt about his father, he asked him to be his best man.

When the ceremony was over, Frederick Krehbiel put out his hand and in a gallant and bantering tone said, "Son, my heartiest congratulations." George Dreher, acting as a kind of spokesman for the bride's father, said, "Young man, you'd better treat this little girl right, or you'll answer to me."

When you're ninety years old, like Sal Dreher, you can speak your mind. "Grace liked the Krehbiels but she felt her daughter had married a rowdy. She couldn't bear to send her out to the cold woods alone. She sent her own maid, Jenny, out there." In fact, Jenny had reached the age where it was sometimes difficult to tell who was taking care of whom.

The first thing Peg did was get rid of Ivory, the Filipino houseboy. And just in time. Ivory, who had been able to read the signs very well, had become ill after gobbling an entire fruit cake that had been delivered to the house as a gift. John took Ivory to town, came back for his suitcase, and found that he had loaded it down with most of the silverware that had been given to them as wedding gifts.

Looking back over fifty years, John says, "It didn't occur to me, really, what a contrast coming out here was for her. She had led a very protected life. She had lived in a pretty glorious environment, and I'm sure that a lot of the adulation of the whole Veeck family had surrounded her. And when she came here, there was nobody else around at all. The road was private. There was a farmer about half-mile west and there were a couple of old gals that had a farm back there. But there was nothing else between our house and the hard road, which was Main Street then (Lemont Road now), almost a mile away."

And there was no telephone. The telephone line ran down Main Street, and the power company wasn't going to string a line three-fourths of a mile for one customer. "When we wanted to telephone we had to go down to the radio station, which was WNR, on the other side of the street. We got to know those people very well, and they let us in to make a phone call at some godawful times."

"There was nothing out there," Jane Ostrum says. "Nothing. Peggy and John had to go to bed with boots and mittens at night in case they had to cross the field to get help. And this delicate girl, who'd had every luxury in the world, couldn't have been happier."

There were plenty of times they weren't able to get to the radio station. That's where the fireplace proved to be a blessing. The power would go off every time there was a storm, and John always had a plentiful supply of cordwood ready, cut and stacked, to throw into the fireplace for both heating and cooking purposes.

In that regard: In order to have oversized fireplace tools to go with the oversized fireplace, he had gone down to the local blacksmith shop and, with a little help from the blacksmith, forged them himself. Remind you of anything?

Half the time they seemed to be shoveling themselves out. And even after they had shoveled a path to the road—a herculean task in itself— Plainfield Road was such a minor artery that the snow plow would probably not have got to it.

On the other hand, and especially in retrospect, it sounds as if it was kind of fun. The best times, after all, are the struggling times. The you-and-me-against-the-world times. You listen to John as he recalls those times and you see the two of them kneeling down on the floor of the huge living room, with the fireplace crackling behind them, building a snow fence together. Like this:

"Once it was 20 below zero, and we were shoveling out this damn snow. The wind would sweep through the area of the woods where there weren't any trees, and that would start a drift and cover the path again. What we did—I had bought a bundle of laz and some wire—we'd start with a couple of wires here and a couple of wires there, and lay the laz down in between the wire. Then we'd roll it up and lay it down where the drifting was, and we had a snow fence and it did an excellent job."

Or going back in periodically to warm their insides with a good jolt of whisky. You can almost hear them groaning and laughing, first as they shook the snow off and then as they got themselves ready to go back out and grab their shovels. Listen:

"One of those storms was so tough that we were snowed in and practically out of food. The company where we purchased those tank car lots of alcohol that we used to remove the water in the nitrocellulose process was naturally enough also in the commercial liquor business, and they had given me a case of their labels as a Christmas present. Vodka, rum and whisky. We were out shoveling and we'd go back to the house and take a swig and go back out and back in, and that's what kept us going until we were able to shovel ourselves out."

The worst of the blizzards came when Peg was about seven months pregnant. They were running out of food and huddled by the fireplace, when all of a sudden—a little *Twilight Zone* music here, professor—they heard a rapping on the door. "We thought what the hell is going on? There's nobody within miles of us. But there at the door were Bill Veeck and his first wife, Ellie. They had called the radio station and been told there was no way to get hold of us." They had set out by car with a supply of food, got caught in a jam of stalled cars at the wide "S" curve in Downers Grove, found another couple there with a sled, and had managed to push through the rest of the way. "After that, Mother Veeck decided it would be a good idea for us to come back to civilization until the baby was born. And, of course, she was right."

And that was why John and Peg were at her mother's house when the call came about the fire at the nitrocellulose plant.

The snow frolics came to an end for Peg with the birth of Johnny on Valentine's Day, 1937. Or, more accurately, she had found it necessary to curtail that kind of activity in the early days of her pregnancy after an examination had revealed a slight irregularity in her heart beat. It was eventually determined that her heart had been scarred as a result of a childhood attack of rheumatic fever.

The delivery proved to be so difficult that the doctor told her there was no way she could have another baby. "She was absolutely determined that she was not going to bring up a child by himself," John says. "So she went to bed for practically the full nine months with Fred, which was the way they did it back then."

There's a story about that too. Back in the first days of the construction work, John and Red had saved themselves a lot of work by digging the well under the foundation hole. In other words, they were already 6 or 7 feet under ground level before digging another 15 to 20 feet to hit water. After Johnny was born, John boarded the well over, intending eventually to put a furnace over that spot. But he still had a pump down in the well, and he had built a kind of manhole over the opening, barely wide enough for him to squeeze through. "Johnny was down there with me one day when he was young, and Peg was pregnant with Fred. Peg was sitting out in the sun and when I came up I said, 'Where's Johnny,' and she said, 'I thought he was with you.' "

Immediately, John tore down the stairs, heard some splashing and jumped into the well, scraping both of his sides against the manhole. "Of course, it was pitch black, but I found him and shoved him up, and of course Peg was beside herself. She had come down and she grabbed hold of him when I handed him up. She always said that probably induced Fred to come quicker than normal because she was just scared to death. As was I. There was probably 6 feet of water in there. I suppose Johnny saw this manhole, looked down and tipped over, and instinctively started swimming and kept himself up."

Not long after Johnny was born, they awoke to find that they had a neighbor. Chuck Ide, a twenty-four-year-old mink rancher, had bought twelve and a-half acres from Chilvers and pitched a tent about 100 yards away. Three years later, he brought home a bride, Julie, and until they were able to throw up a little house, they lived in the barn with the food-grinding equipment.

The Krehbiels and Ides did not always get along. Especially when the Ide's mink would get loose and wreak havoc on the Krehbiel's chicken coops. Minks are mean, sharp-toothed little animals. All you have to know about the odor they emit when they are unhappy is that they are members of the skunk family. And if the wind happens to be blowing your way during their mating season, you might as well book passage to Europe. Even on a simple day-to-day basis . . . well, Julie Ide says it herself: "The smell when it gets real hot, especially if you don't clean the manure out all the time, can be awful. Sometimes we didn't and John would come storming over. But we owned our land, too."

There were also arguments about land ownership and access. But whatever strains may have arisen between the parents passed quickly enough and were never reflected in their relationship with either set of kids.

"We were poor together," Julie says. "John had a chicken house and they used to sell eggs. I'd come into the kitchen, and Peg would be stamping them, *Krehbiel's Eggs*. We were so poor ourselves that we were living in a barn. Even later, Peg and I would go to town and we could buy ice cream cones for our children but not for ourselves."

But there is a nice part of the story too. They were poor together, and they became rich together. And we all know which is better.

The one thing John Krehbiel and Chuck Ide had in common was that they worked seven days a week and plowed all the profits back into their business. Somewhere in the midfifties, Chuck Ide and John Krehbiel bumped into each other coming off the elevator at the old Sherman Hotel in Chicago. John was there to arrange for a profit-sharing plan for his employees. Chuck was there to give out the annual awards for the Great Lake Mink Association, of which he was a director. Actually, it was Chuck Ide who hit it first. Mink pelts are sold at auction, and in 1951 and 1952, Ide's Autumn Haze pelts bought a higher price than any other pelt sold anywhere in the world. And the Ides were finally able to build themselves a lovely house on the same spot where Chuck had pitched his tent. Chuck also added more than one hundred acres to his holdings. In recent years he has sold off enough of that acreage to developers so that he is able to hold his head up when the millionaires get together.

"We weren't social friends," Julie Ide says. "We were neighbors. Peg was older than me, and her children were older, and she helped me raise my kids. And I loved her children. Her two boys are the politest children you will ever meet. And it's the woman who raises the children, don't ever forget that. We were together for forty-four years. She wasn't a well woman, but I never once heard her complaining about anything. Never complained about her house, her finances, anything. Not once. Now, that's remarkable."

Posey Krehbiel: "Peg was fifty when I came on the scene, and she was not in such good health then. In fact, she was very sick when I met her, and then she had her first open heart operation and thankfully got much better. She went back for a new valve in 1971, and had seven or eight very good years."

In 1979, the valve went out of whack and she almost died on the operating table. The first time they repaired the damaged valve, the second time they replaced it. They had to go back in the very same day to repair the repair, and stop the bleeding. And then a couple of years before her death her heart began to fibrilate, and she had a very small pacemaker, about the size of a quarter, implanted in her chest under the skin.

Kay Krehbiel: "Peg was just a very gentle person. If you look at her pictures when she was younger, there was a softness and gentleness about her face. I would say to Peg, nobody is going to believe that you're disabled, you look too good. On good days, Peg would come over here and she'd look absolutely dazzling."

The early upbringing, the years at Ogontz, had left their indelible imprint. For years she almost never went out in public without wearing a hat, white gloves, and high heels. She was a tall (5'8"), handsome woman, well proportioned and long of limb. You could put a sack on her, as Kay would tell her, and she would look good.

After the second operation, John bought a home in Lompoc, California, to get her out of the harsh Chicago winter. An absolute necessity. Lompoc is on a little knob of land west of Santa Barbara. The climate is incredibly warm and stable. John and Martha Flaherty, old friends from Downers Grove, were already living there. The Healys came soon after. Red Thayer lived only about one hundred miles to the south in Sierra Madre.

It was difficult for her. John was always a man on the move. So restless that, even when among friends in Lompoc, he was ready to leave at the end of a week. Two weeks and he was really stretching it. So he'd commute back and forth.

Still, even in the early years, when he was out on the road selling, he took his family role seriously enough always to come home over weekends.

He was completely devoted to Peg. As nobody knows better than John Flaherty. "John and I traveled a lot together, and stayed together in more hotels than I care to remember. And every single night he'd call Peg. Now I'm devoted to Martha, but I have never called her and never would. I used to say that if the plane crashes she'll hear about it on the ten o'clock news."

Peg lived on very little for almost thirty years. Theoretically, John was drawing $25,000 in salary. In practice, he'd cut his own salary to keep key employees in place. He'd mortgage the house to meet expenses. Or even lend money to the company himself in order to meet the payroll.

Posey: My God, people usually take everything out of a business. Gramps never took a cent. I would have thought that Peg, looking at Kay and me living in clover, and knowing it was her sacrifices that got us there would be resentful. Nothing at all like that. Never."

Peg never babied herself. She rode the lawnmower around the grounds. She'd drive around in her old Thunderbird. A few years before she died, John had built the summerhouse for her down by their pond, and she loved to go down there for a drink.

Kay Krehbiel: "We'd go out there on a Sunday afternoon and they'd be watching a ball game. Up until literally the last day. You'd go out there and they were drinking a Bloody Mary and holding hands."

In the September before she died, they went to Ireland and up to England and Scotland to play golf. She still looked good, but she didn't always have the energy. She was frequently out of breath.

John always took a positive attitude. When they'd come back from a trip she'd say she was sure it would be their last one. And he'd say, "That's what *you* think." He kept making plans. "We can always cancel them," he'd tell her. But they never did.

But in the last couple of years, it became increasingly difficult for her. The last time she went to Lompoc, she had to get on the plane in a wheel chair, and she hated that.

Along toward the end, she had to spend one day a week in bed.

Twice there were emergency trips to the hospital by ambulance; once in Lompoc, and again in Downers Grove.

She always said her greatest fear was that something would happen to her and John wouldn't be there.

On January 10, 1986, while they were watching the evening news, she gave a quiet sigh and passed away.

MOLEX

You have to be in the right place at the right time. You also have to be the right person in the right place at the right time. I think the company is only as good as the people. Molex is based on people. But products made Molex. If Molex made shoestrings we never would have had that success. You have to give Senior credit. From the terminal blocks, we went to crimp termination. To electronics. We go where the sales are. That has to be part of the success too.

—BRUNO BAUMANIS—

IF Molex didn't achieve its great success until after John Krehbiel was sixty-five, what could be more fitting? Fred Krehbiel didn't invent the plastic from which the company derives its name until after he was sixty-five. The plastic he developed had qualities unlike any other plastic of the time. As well they should have. Fred Krehbiel had concocted it out of waste products.

A great story in its own right.

Back at the turn of the century, Frederick Krehbiel had built the power systems for several of the larger midwestern cities, including Kansas City and Cincinnati. Not to mention a multitude of commercial enterprises. On the strength of his background as both a mechanical engineer and an electrical engineer, he had been hired to build the tipples over various kinds of mining fields. A tipple is the superstructure constructed over a working mine. Much like an oil rig over an oil well.

They have to build a superstructure up from the mine level, and this has a hoist in it. And they hoist the coal, stone or asbestos or whatever up and bring it to a higher level, and it dumps the raw material onto a combination of shaker screens. First they have a crusher, which crushes the material to the size they want and sends it down to the shaker screens. The shaker screens are full of holes and slots. The finer material starts falling out first and goes down into a railroad car, and the smaller pieces drop through into the next railroad and then the coarser pieces, and so on down the line.

"Going back, Dad had designed a lot of these things, and built the machinery that was associated with the hoisting of the materials and the movement of the shaker screens and the loading into cars. He had done a lot of it in Indiana and southern Illinois. And then along came World War I. And what happened was we had almost no toluol in this country. Trinitro-toluol is TNT, and we didn't have the TNT we needed because we had been buying it from Germany. Well, toluol is a by-product of coal. The government brought all the mine owners together and told them to come up with a refinishing plant to generate toluol."

So they got ahold of Dad, and Dad designed a plant which was down in Terra Haute, Indiana. And they refined the coal, just like

57

you'd refine anything else. You put the stuff in a still and start heating it, and you start driving off these vapors. The first one that comes off is naptha, the next is benzine, then toluol, and after the final refractions have been driven off, what's left in the still is coal tar pitch, which looks like coal when it cools off. Except that it's so hard that to get it out of the still you have to use air hammers.

"And this stuff was creating great big piles out there. They didn't know what to do with it. They couldn't burn it. It was what was left after they'd burned everthing off." Frederick Krehbiel would look out at those great black piles and think about the possible uses for a substance that could be made pliable under heat but wouldn't burn. And then he would take out his notebook and begin to scribble.

Some years later, his firm was hired to build the tipples over some asbestos mines in Canada. And something very similar happened there. "They had tremendous piles, stories high, of nothing except the tailings from the asbestos. They had uses for all the other sizes that came down off the shaker screen, but nothing for those first fine little strands."

What could be better during a time of Depression, Mr. Krehbiel asked himself, than to develop a product out of the materials that nobody wanted? If he could take these two waste materials, he mused, and mix them together into some kind of plastic, he would have his basic raw material for nothing more than the cost of hauling it away.

The coal tar pitch would make a perfect binder, the asbestos would serve as the filler, and for the reinforcing agent he could take the limestone which abounded in that part of the country and melt it down to extract yet another inert substance, rock-wool fiber.

As a pragmatic man, Fred Krehbiel had no intention of wasting his time and effort to produce a product that had no commercial value. And that took him right back to Commonwealth Edison and those underground cables.

They have duct lines under the manholes that go from manhole to manhole, and the cables are wrapped around the thing under each of the manholes so that if one blows out it won't take the whole system with it. All these cables are in pipes depending on who's doing it. Edison just digs down in the ground and pours a pipe, or five or six pipes, depending on how big the duct line is. Puts the pipes in, pours it with concrete around it to separate them. And then they draw the cable through them, and bring them together to connect up with the cable that's carrying the power.

In order to pull the cable throught the cement pipe, they covered it with grease. John knew all about that process, because it was his company, J. H. Krehbiel, that made the grease. "It was a very expensive way to do it, and Dad said, 'Gee, if we can extrude these kinds of pipes out of this plastic we could have a big piece of business.' Because all the public utilities, telephone companies, and telegraph companies had those underground cables."

The old man designed an extruding machine and brought his sons in to help him crank the stuff out. After a period of trial and error, they managed to extrude any length of pipe.

When it came to molding for the T or L fittings that were needed for the connection points, however, they found that the limestone filler made the plastic so stiff and brittle that the seams wouldn't hold.

The molded pipe could be extruded, Fred Krehbiel found. But the fittings could not be molded. It was only when fiberglass was developed immediately after the war that they found a reinforcing agent that would provide the necessary flexibility and integrity of structure.

What they had back there at the beginning was a very low-cost material that had good moisture resistance and was a very good electrical insulator. And they could see a market at Commonwealth Edison for that product also.

The Molex plastic was perfect for those entrance bushings that J. H. Krehbiel Co. had been making—a very smooth insulating material that was resistant to moisture and could be molded very cheaply to any size. And they did that. They molded them in every conceivable size for just about everybody in the Chicago area.

In quick order, they also were able to find a natural market in molding those little black radiator handles.

The basic material used for molding at that time was bakelite (which is usually described as "the old phenolic material"), although polystyrene, a brand new thermoplastic with excellent insulating properties had already made its appearance.

In short orders however, all these materials were appropriated for war work, which meant that they were placed on a restricted list and made available for commercial use only on a government priority system.

Molex, as a wholly new and unproved product, was not on any restricted list. Or any government list. Since none of the established plastics was available for nonessential consumer products, such as toys, that was the field Molex decided to explore in order to survive.

They made flower pots. They made toy submarines. They made toy guns. The submarine looked exactly like what it was, an extruded glob of plastic. The gun, which had been designed by Ed Krehbiel as an exact replica of the Colt .45, scaled to three-fourths size, was so nicely done that it has become a part of Molex lore. There was a news story out of Brooklyn about a bank robber who had been captured when he dropped his gun while he was making good his escape—and the gun had shattered. "That must have been one of ours," John chuckled. "It looked good enough to fool the teller, and it broke as soon as it touched the ground." The more romantic version, which the younger guys in the company prefer to believe, has it that the police had called from all over the country to ask John to please stop making the gun because it looked so much like the real thing that it had started a crime wave.

John Jr. has his own favorite story about the toy gun. If the original Colt .45 was the gun that won the West, the toy Colt .45 may well have been the gun that saved Molex. With a lot of help from the Lone Salesman. At any rate, the company was about to go under when Senior went to a toy show in New York and sold the whole inventory to Kresge and Woolworth. "Got the check, got on the train, came back to Chicago, deposited the check in the bank, and they were able to meet the payroll. That's the kind of competitor he is. All through his life he's been the kind of guy that delivers when the chips are down."

Between the shatterable gun and the unattractive submarine, the company was able to survive long enough to be sought out by manufacturers of the kind of consumer products which had no hope of being awarded a government priority. There was, for example, a clock cover for Hanson Manufacturing of Indiana, the makers of a Swiss clock wherein a Swiss couple came out against the backdrop of a Swiss village to indicate in some way or other, the temperature and weather.

Morton Salt came to Molex when they couldn't get phenolic for a salt dispenser they were anxious to put into stores. You turned the handle and out dropped a tablet of salt. With his instinct for simplicity, John redesigned the dispenser so that it would get the job done with four pieces instead of eight, gave it a rather streamlined design, and lacquered the surface in an attractive tan. Morton was so happy with it that Molex kept that contract for something like thirty years.

(To anybody who wonders why salt tablets had become a hot wartime item, be advised that army tests had determined that infusions of salt were needed to replenish the bodies of their recruits after they had worked up a good sweat. Salt tablets were therefore being dispensed in basic training.

They were in battleships and tanks, they were gulped down by athletes between innings and during halves. Thirty years later, some spoilsport conducted new tests and discovered not only that salt did not reinvigorate the body but that it was actually harmful.)

There was one attempt along the way to do something for the war effort, and the outcome of that gesture had a permanent effect on the direction that Molex would take.

When the American army landed in North Africa in the early days of the war and found itself being battered by General Rommel's tanks, the army put out a call for a nonmetallic land mine that could not be picked up by the enemy's detecting devices. The two basic requirements were that the material could not be metallic, and that it could not be on the War Production Board's restricted list.

Right down Molex's alley. Especially since the introduction of fiberglass into the mixture had given the plastic considerably more strength and flexibility.

Working with a colonel from Ordnance, John designed a land mine that passed the tests so convincingly that the government was talking about building Molex a factory so that it could start to pump them out right away. The next thing John heard was that a ruling had come down that a representative from the WPB had to be at every meeting once the prototype was produced to ensure that no restricted material was being used.

John still shakes his head about what happened next. "The guy from the WPB had been an executive at Onandaga Potteries in Upper New York. He received the designs and testing results and took them to his former employer, and they were given the contract to make these mines out of ceramic-like materials."

Right there, John took a vow that he would never deal with the government again. "Actually, I don't know what we would have done with the plant because by the time the factory had been built, the tide of battle had turned." From what he heard, the government canceled the contract with Onandaga after it had built them a large plant so that they could fulfill the contract they were canceling.

Still, Molex managed to survive without the contract, and when the war finally came to an end, the direct competition with bakelite proved to be no competition at all. Not only was the cost of the raw materials much cheaper, but Molex was so much easier to work with that where it would require eight cavities in the steel mold to turn out molds in bakelite, it took only two cavities to do the job with Molex.

With both the mold and the material costing so much less, Molex was able to turn out a product at one-third the price and still make a good profit.

The direction which the company was going to take came when John decided that the most valuable thing the plastic had going for it was that it was a good electrical insulator. He began to make calls on companies that used electrical insulators.

The first product tooled and marketed was a three-stud terminal block for Hotpoint range (which was GE) and Soreng drier-washer (a Chicago company that would become Controls Corporation of America). The terminal was mounted onto the range or drier, attached to the wiring, and then you put your three lugs on top of it and screwed it down. John designed the product and his brother Ed designed the tools to make the product and also oversaw their construction.

At Hotpoint, they were replacing a porcelain block which was not only expensive in itself but so brittle and fragile that it had to be shipped in barrels packed with straw. Soreng had been using a rubber junction block molded to a wire harness.

The first important bench mark in the expansion of the company came almost immediately when John moved from merely selling the Molex block to Hotpoint to selling the full harness, which consisted of both the molded receptacle and the stamped terminal. Two different technologies entirely.

Hotpoint was profiting from the low cost of Molex, the terminal company wasn't. All they knew was that they were being asked to put their terminal into a cheap product that they knew nothing about. And that meant that John had to make two sales. "We had so much difficulty interesting people on the idea that our part could do the job, we decided, gee, let's make metal parts too, and that way we don't have to go through the business of selling someone else in order to sell Hotpoint."

He took what money they had and used it to turn out a prototype harness: "Then we went to Hotpoint and sold the product and that got us into proprietory products."

In other words, he had a product he could sell, with or without minor modifications, to the market at large.

That was the situation when Dale Miller came aboard in the fall of 1953 as the company's first manufacture's representative. Dale Miller is one of the two manufacturers' reps who would be of particular importance to the growth of Molex. The other was Ed Healy.

Dale Miller had been a project engineer and manager for Bendix home appliances when Bendix was marketing the first automatic washing machines. He had departed, along with many of the other top Bendix people, and started his own rep company after the company was sold to Crosley. He knew everybody in the appliance business. He had total entry. Many of the engineers who had once worked for him had gone on to become vice presidents or division managers at some of the leading appliance manufacturers.

Dale's territory when he signed on with Molex was the whole United States of America. Very shortly, he gave up all his other clients so that he could concentrate his entire efforts on Molex, and with his heavy background in design and engineering, he was very soon spending as much time in the factory as on the road.

They were working during that time, Dale Miller makes clear, on a very restricted budget: "The way the company developed, we'd go out and sell a custom product, where it would be their application and they would pay for the tooling. When we'd hit enough of those to make enough profit, we'd have already designed a proprietory product that we knew we could sell to the market in general. And we'd use that money to tool it. We just kept going that way, using the profits from a custom design to tool our own products until we had a lot of proprietory products in our catalogue."

The best of times came when John was able to nail it at both ends. Solve the problem for a particular company and still hold onto the proprietory rights. A job he did for Whirlpool refrigerator in those early days demonstrates another of the simple, but devilishly clever ways in which John would approach problems. Whirlpool had sent out word that they wanted to simplify their rather sloppy terminal setup. What they had been doing was to rivet two one-quarter inch male spade terminals to a laminated fiberboard. Since that left the rivet head (which was now part of the circuit) exposed on the underside of the fiberboard, they would have to rivet a bakelite board under the fiberboard in order to insulate it. What John did was to design a Molex block in the shape of an "H," bring the two male spade terminals together to form a "U" and nest them in the corner of the crossbar. The rivet was then shot up through a hole from the *underside* of the crossbar to hold the terminal in place. The rivet head was still exposed, to be sure, but the insulation was now being provided by the air between the crossbar and the bottom legs of the "H."

To complete the harness, the female terminal was made in the form of an inverted "U" and clamped atop the male terminal to form a good solid connection.

Cheap, uncluttered, and very effective. Molex has sold a lot of those "H"-type connectors in various applications down through the years.

And then there was the range receptacle he came up with to permit the housewife to remove the heating coils from an electric range so that they could be more easily cleaned.

The heating element on an electric range is a metal tubing which is coiled in such a way that the outer tubing narrows down at the top and becomes an extended neck. Under the old system, the switch that turned the heating unit on was in a housing that sat across the neck. John began the process of disengagement by doing away with the switch and spot-welding a spade terminal where the screw fittings had been. (Actually, he had the manufacturers of the range take care of that part of the process.) From there, he had only to connect a female terminal to each of the spade terminals and enclose them in a housing. That was his receptacle.

The basic ingredients of the plug were a pair of small nail-like rods that he attached to the inside of both sides of the neck. At the end of each of those rods, he attached a simple snap-on terminal. Plug it in, and the rods became the "wires" that conducted the electricity down into the coiling.

In order to unplug the whole heating unit, the housewife had only to lift it up and pull. She could take the unit over to the sink and clean the coils and everything around it. With the heating unit out, she could pull out the drip pan underneath and scrub away whatever assorted gook may have collected. Once the drip pan was out, she could go down inside the top panel of the range itself and clean out any crumbs or spillovers that had fallen through.

Down through the years, John has come up with a hundred such ideas. The company was built on his ability to do just that.

And every once in a while, during those struggling years, they would have a narrow scrape with sudden wealth.

There was a company in Goshen, Indiana, named the Penn Electric Switch Company, which made a product that seemed perfect for Molex. The Penn Switch was on every refrigerator that was made. A lovely device. As soon as the temperature dropped to a certain degree, the switch flipped over and a compressor came on to drive the gas up and cool off the box. As soon as the box became cold enough, the switch flipped back and the compressor went off.

The switch was controlled by a series of contacts that were molded inside a huge phenolic block. A *molded-in insert*, it was called. A very expensive technology. You had to make a stamping, put some pins in the mold, and then mold the plastic around it. Penn Switch was paying its contractor something like $2.50 per unit.

Although nobody at Penn had ever heard of Molex plastic, they were perfectly willing to let John find a way to do it cheaper.

"I took it back to the plant, and my brother and I worked on the thing for a couple of weeks and came up with a way to do it without having to insert the terminal inside. We could just snap these contacts on the surface of the block after the block had been molded. And we could make them for a buck apiece. A tremendous saving."

Penn Switch liked that. Naturally. If, of course, John could really do what he said he could.

Back he went to Brookfield. "Ed and I turned out a couple of handmade samples with these metal parts set in place so that they carried the currents where they were supposed to, and Penn liked it very much. Finally, they said, 'Well, what will it cost us to tool it?' It was going to be a big tool because they were making these things by the millions."

Back to Brookfield he went once again, with visions of wealth dancing in his head. And when he returned to Goshen with the figures, the chief engineer he had been dealing with told him that they had looked up his company and discovered how tiny it was. He said, "I'll tell you what we're going to do, Krehbiel. We are not going to give you the contract, because we just cannot afford to have our business dependent upon a company as small as Molex. What we will do is give you the first call on any project that comes along that you tell me you can make at a competitive price."

The Krehbiels' first reaction, not unexpectedly, was fury. "We were saving them a couple of million dollars a year. That's a lot of money at any time. In those days, it was a huge amount of money."

Once they had calmed down, though, they decided to bite their tongues and swallow their disappointment. The fact was, Penn didn't owe them anything. "There was nothing to show they owed us a dime." In fact, John says, that chief engineer was really a very ethical guy. "We had a little shop with maybe a couple of dozen of people, and they had a big, big business to protect. They had five hundred–six hundred employees in Goshen alone, and that wasn't their only plant. Sure, we were sore as hell at first. But when you're a little guy, you run that kind of hazard."

They had two choices, John decided. "You can yell and scream and go away looking like a horse's ass. Or you can see what you can do to get some money from them. And we did that. They used our design for a lot of years and saved a couple of million a year. But out of that we got some products that were damn good money-makers for us—for fifteen years after that, I'd say. We had a few experiences like that, and they were very interesting and very exciting. But that's what happens when you're small."

Down through the years the competition did not come from other materials. It came from other companies. The Goliath of the industry, the company sitting on top of the mountain, has always been AMP, which went into World War II as Aircraft Marine Products, a little company in Elizabeth, New Jersey, and came out, with the help of all those wartime contracts, as a sizable firm. They grew that quickly because they were good. They were good then, and they get better all the time. "AMP is good for us," Senior says. "They've set the standard for this industry, and it's a very high standard. You're fighting them at every street corner. They're everywhere."

Junior agrees whole-heartedly that AMP has forced Molex to become a better company. "They are very well managed and they are very profitable and they have a strong desire to earn even more profits. And though they're a couple of billion in sales, they're quite light on their feet. They're organized so they can turn around pretty fast. For us to be able to win against them at major accounts means we've had to work to move our company ahead in every area so that we can compete seriously. And we do."

Or, to translate it into the language that Junior uses when he's preparing the troops to do battle with AMP at one of those major accounts, "Let's beat those bastards."

They are so big and so powerful and so good that they get arrogant. And when they do get arrogant they leave openings. And Senior has used those openings to bring Goliath down a peg.

The innovative mind, the innate curiosity, the ability to look at things through his own eyes—that's what took Molex into the connector business and eventually out of its own material.

John's interest in connectors was whetted, really, when the appliance companies using his harnesses asked him whether Molex had anything that could solve some particular connector job.

He knew nothing about the plug-and-receptable type of connection, and so he started with an absolutely fresh mind. And what he saw was something that nobody had seen before.

Consider this: Before John used his eyes, terminals were put in, individually, by hand. And soldered or crimped, individually, by hand. You had somebody inserting a wire and somebody soldering it down. (Or one person performing both operations using crimp-type terminals.) Hands going in, on every operation, and hands pulling out. You now have one machine operated by one worker performing those same functions at the rate of three thousand an hour. And those machines are everywhere, and they are doing it twenty-four hours a day.

And it was all in the way the terminals came off the punch press. John was no stranger to a punch press. He had been working with punch presses all his life. The blank stock is fed into the dies off a reel. Indexing holes are stamped in immediately in order to feed the stock through, much in the manner that film is fed through a camera. The function of the holes is both to feed the stock through and to regulate the time that will be required for the die to do its work as it is passed from station to station.

After the finished product has been fashioned at the final station, it is moved to the final stop, and cut off.

What John's mind did—and nothing more effectively demonstrates his absolute genius of common sense—was to jump the whole process between his punch press and the customer's assembly line and ask himself the question that would change the world of connectors forever. The question was, "Why don't we keep the reel?" We're starting with a reel, we're keeping the reel intact because we need the reel to keep feeding the metal through the die. Why not have the terminals come off the die and onto another reel *so that the customer will have the same natural feeder into his assembling machines that we have into our punch press?*

The implications of that question were enormous. He had bridged the process from his own machine to the application tool he would be designing to receive that reel and feed it into the customer's product. "The razor blade and the razor." Sell them the terminals, and then either sell, rent, or lease them the tool they are going to need in order to insert them.

Application tooling is where Molex shines. Once you have begun to think in terms of feeding the terminals in off a reel, you've eliminated both the lady who inserts the wire and the guy who solders it down.

The application machine will take the terminal off the reel and hold the wire on the crimp barrel until it is attached.

Out of this chain-and-crimp process in its original incarnation came the 1007 flat terminal and, in combination with the terminal, a connector housing. The first time chain form terminals and connector housings had been put together to make a connector series. In its final refinement, some years later, came the .093 connector, the first low cost pin-and-socket. Senior marshaled his tiny sales organization and sold it to Magnavox, to Zenith, to RCA, and virtually put Molex in the color TV business when color television was just starting off.

"They were the first pin-and-sockets made with chain terminals," Senior points out. "That was the secret. There had been pins and sockets before. The navy and army had them for military use. But they were all individual pins and individual sockets. And it was an expensive job to assemble these things together. By having it on a chain and putting it through a crimp machine, a girl just touches a button and it puts a wire in a certain little slot, and she touches the treadle with her foot, and then comes down and takes the next terminal on the chain, and takes that and wraps it around the wire, cuts it off the chain. I watched them in Hong Kong recently. They're going at a rate of almost four thousand an hour. Women can do it, men can't seem to. Women achieve a speed taking these things off a bundle like you're dealing cards."

The .093 (and its smaller version, the .062) is still one of their biggest product lines, twenty-five years later. And, if the rate of growth isn't as high as it once was, that doesn't mean that the sales aren't still going up every year. That's another thing about connectors. Connectors have incredibly long lives.

With the punch presses Molex has today, it is able to stamp out as many as one thousand to 1,200 terminals a minute. Faster than the eye can follow, and almost more than the mind can comprehend. And there are machines at Molex pumping them out, twenty-four hours a day, all over the world.

There are hundreds of application tools in the factories of customers all around the world, inserting the Molex pin-and-socket into the customer's housing.

It's a productivity system. The faster the pins go in the cheaper they are to the customer.

The little company had made a major breakthrough. The question that springs to mind is: Are these things patentable? The answer is yes, no, maybe, and do we really want to? The short answer is that it sure doesn't hurt. Senior has more than two hundred patents in his own right, and the company has them in the thousands. They protect you for either seventeen years, or for as long as they last. Which is until somebody figures a way to put a little curlicue here, or a little button there. And then the question becomes whether you want to go to court about it. And, if you do, whether you'd win.

With the pin-and-socket, the question became academic. Senior had hired a big patent lawyer from a big law firm, and the big lawyer from the big law firm neglected to file for the patent in time.

The chain terminal concept wasn't patentable. There had been other things that had been put on chains and put through crimping machines. Nevertheless, Molex was able to get one patent that was more than useful while it lasted—a patent on the mounting ears that were part of the nylon housing.

Let us retrace some steps. It was with the development of the chain terminal that John had to decide whether Molex was going to be a material company or a connector company. And it was with the final refinement of the .093 pin-and-socket that it closed out of its own material and went into connector housing.

And now we are full circle back to the street fight against AMP.

The first chain terminal, as we have already said, was not the pin-and-socket, it was a flat terminal. The expense of tooling it had been shared equally by GE, Tappan, and Molex. It was successful enough in its own market so that three years later, AMP came out with a version of its own. Not in a chain form, but made competitive by the use of a nylon housing that was not only cheaper but also far more attractive than the Molex version. But it also had a defect. The flat terminal consisted of two spring brass blades that rubbed against each other under pressure. AMP had made the mistake of adding a little locking device, and with the blades already under tension, the engagement forces were so high that it became very difficult to pull them apart. Exactly what you don't want in a connector.

"Senior picked up the information that Whirlpool was having trouble with that AMP connector," Junior says, picking up the story. "And that AMP was not being responsive." Exactly the kind of thing Molex was always looking for to open a door. "The old man got the idea that if he used a round-pin female and round-pin male and butted them together he'd get more contact surface and a better electrical connection. So he scratched one of the things up in the shop and he had one of the engineers build it, and they took it to Whirlpool. It was only a 9-circuit and they needed a 3, 9, 12, and 15. They ran it through their reliability lab. They wanted to use it and funded a good part of the tooling. Senior was smart enough to get them to put up some dough, with the understanding that if we sold it to other people we'd either rebate to them or give them a price deal. But we could still sell the things to other people." Senior put up some money and Whirlpool put up some money; and the round-pin-socket took over the appliance business, and it's still going strong.

That's only half the story. "Senior had the vision to see that if AMP was having trouble with that product in the appliance business, it was probably also having problems in the television industry, where the real growth lay."

It was at that point that Senior went back to the mold shop and came out with the .093 pin-and-socket.

AMP followed, much more quickly this time, with a pin-and-socket of its own. They still weren't using the chain, and yet the nylon housing made their product more than competitive.

There was no longer any question that between the increasing sophistication of the connectors and the emergence of nylon as the industry's molding material of choice, Molex plastic had seen its day. The pin-and-socket housing required a mounting bracket or a pair of spring clips to hold the connectors in place.

But here again, one catches a glimpse of the workings of John Krehbiel's mind. The quality nylon possessed that made it so valuable was its springiness. And so John Krehbiel set to work to find a way to use that springiness beyond anything that was being done by the competition. That was where the mounting ears came in.

Picture a pair of rabbit ears that are sort of shaped like claws. Punch a hole in the nylon, and kind of roll the mounting ears over, down and in, and as soon as they hit the bottom of the hole they lock in place. "You could do that with a springy material like nylon," Senior explains. "You could not do it with Molex or bakelite."

And, as we have said, it was patentable, giving Molex an advantage for seventeen years.

Something like eight years would pass before Molex took on its own nylon-molding operation. And that was going to come—to round the story off nicely again—at almost precisely the same time they were making their next great leap forward. With the pin-and-socket, Molex had staked out an early position as a supplier for the manufacturers of color television. With the KonectKon, they would be jumping, feet first, into the rapidly expanding world of the printed circuit board.

We will save the KonectKon for its own time and place. Suffice to say for now that the first attempts to work with the printed circuit board were more humorous than successful. And that brings us to Ed Healy, and his famous story about the automation machine that was built to feed the transistor socket pins into a PC board for Zenith during the development stages of their mutual programs.

The job of building the automation machine was given over to an outside source. They had to do it that way because AMP, which was competing for the Zenith account, was far ahead of Molex in equipment machines, application tooling, and probably the machines in the plant, too.

They were having it built in a tool and die shop. And tool and die shops think in terms of big hunks of machinery doing big, noisy jobs. And from here on in we are going to turn the podium over to Ed Healy:

"We were working with a guy over at Zenith, fellow by the name of Dar Inman, and the manufacturing guy, John Novacek, who was an industrial engineer and was responsible for this thing.

"We gave the job of building the automation to a guy who was used to working with heavy die equipment. For six months we're building this thing. We show them what we're doing, and they really didn't understand. I don't think any of us did, either. Alex Ewens comes in, looks, and says, 'My God, they've built the USS Missouri.' We were looking at this device and shaking our heads and hoping the guy would put it together so that it would work.

"This little guy, Rocky Manero, worked for Novacek. Rocky had the greatest sense of humor of anybody I ever saw in my life. A little straitlaced but a delicious sense of humor.

"So finally we have it shipped over. This is several months into the program. They never seemed too happy about it, but by this stage of the game they had confidence that Molex would come through.

"Remember, you're talking about terminals less than half-a-thousandth of an inch square. That's not very big. It doesn't take a whole lot of force to put that into a PC board.

"They had this thing set up with the terminals on a reel. Know what a Gatling gun looks like? You see those cylinders going around and around. This thing was something like that, and the machine was maybe 12 or 15 feet long and maybe 6 or 8 feet high. And heavy. And we're only going to put in three of these tiny pins at this time.

"Rocky is standing there, he's looking at this monster of a machine we hauled in, and all of a sudden they turn the thing on, and Rock is standing there, looking.

"They turn the switch on this monster, and Rocky and I are standing there and all of a sudden this reel starts to go around and this terminal comes off this Gatling gun and goes down along the track, which is several feet long, and is heading toward the board. And suddenly it goes SSSSTTTTHHHH, and all the air valves are flapping, and all of a sudden BANG, out comes one of these little terminals, and BOOM, it goes into the board. And we're looking at this in disbelief. To do this one little job, it was like a Charlie Chaplin movie. I mean it was a bad-looking thing.

"So the guy pressed the button again, and now this thing is all warmed up and all of a sudden you hear the bells coming from all over the machine, they're going PSSSHTTT, CCHW-CHAWA, and the air valves are pushing this second little terminal down, and then BANG, it hammers it in.

"This is supposed to be automation. This is supposed to be feeding these terminals in fast, over and over and over.

"Nobody's saying anything. Rocky turns to me and says, 'I want to ask a question. Do you think that thing will do it again?'

"And now we're all roaring. It was such a funny-looking machine and so completely out of character for what it was supposed to do.

"Dar Inman never stopped looking at it. He could see his little printed circuit board—these modulars were maybe 2½ inches wide and 3½ inches long—this little circuit board with these tiny terminals and this great big machine that sounds like quitting time at the gas works, banging away at it. The only thing that was missing was a jackhammer to pound this little thing into the board. Every time this thing would hammer, Dar would get a little excited because he knew his little circuit board didn't have much of a chance to survive in the environment.

"They had a place set aside for it at the Zenith plant over at Claustrom Avenue. They called the manager of the plant, and Dar gets on the phone with him, and says, 'Hey, I want to tell you something. You know the space that's set aside for putting that automation machine into the plant.' He takes a breath. 'To get this machine in, you're going to have to take out part of the wall, you're going to have to reinforce the floor. Because, this is the biggest mother I've ever seen in my life.'

"They were laughing so much that Inman looks at it, and says, 'I may just take it off your hands myself. I got this little row boat for my kid, and I've been meaning to buy him an anchor.' Needless to say, the machine never was set loose on a terminal again. Zenith hauled it away and converted it into a drill press. And that was the start of automation at Molex. Had to be 1967 or 1968."

*   *   *

But that doesn't mean that Molex didn't get the contract. As it happened, Molex had been working on another device. A vibrator. What that meant, in reasonably simple English, is that he was going to shake the little pins into the little holes. And it not only worked, it worked better and faster and cheaper than any of the more conventional automation devices.

The inspiration came from those little paper joggers used to align a stack of paper sheets in assembling a book. Shake them up this way and then turn them around and shake them that way and—what do you know—they've got themselves lined up perfectly.

Fred Gierut, Molex's brilliant die designer, was relatively new on the job when Senior came to him and told him, "Let's try vibrating them into the board."

Says Gierut: "That's when I thought, 'I think the guy's going balmy.' But I got to do it, he's the old man."

Gierut bought a little paper jogger, and then he bought a bigger paper jogger. He and his assistants replaced the paper jogger's wooden board with an aluminum plate to make it lighter and put some springs around the bowl to keep it shaking. A board with matching holes was placed over the circuit board. The matching holes were almost double the size of the PC holes and countersunk to give them a funnel effect.

When the pins were scattered across the board and the rheostat turned on, the pins began to jump up and down in the air. "They went into the holes like a little magnet was drawing them," Gierut says. "Each of those damn pins seemed to head for its own hole like they were keeping an appointment." That's when I said, 'Hey, maybe that guy ain't so stupid after all.' "

Once a pin was in the hole, there was a counterbar built in to hold it. When all the holes were filled, a hinged plate came down to press the pins tight.

There were a couple of sound scientific principles involved. When you change the amplitude of the vibrations, the pin begins to vibrate furiously with its point down, because it is always looking for something to increase its amplitude. That's why it seemed as if the funnel were drawing the pin to it.

The other was the Law of Random Chance. When you have one thousand pins jumping up and down in the air, the chance of one coming down straight enough to fall into the funnel is extraordinarily high. Given the number of holes to be filled, the cycle can be charted on a geometric curve. If you have one hundred holes, they would fill in, say, forty seconds. If you have five hundred holes, it would take fifty-five seconds.

The vibrator was so effective and so cheap to contract that it became something close to state of the art for years. Molex built one system for Burroughs Electronic to fill five thousand holes in the back panel of a computer. The cycle time, from the loading of the board to the unloading, was ten minutes. You could go to the bank on it. The sophisticated and far more expensive Berg machine it was replacing had taken an hour to do the same job.

BROOKFIELD

I looked at this place and I thought I'd stepped fifty years into the past. From the making of the product, everything used to get like Spanish moss on it. The stuff just sort of hung in the air and sort of developed like a draping on the electrical lines and everything else. That's what we used to call it. Spanish moss. It was really the fiberglass that combined with the tar to sort of make a fuzz that hung on everything. And everything was black. Sooty black and your clothes. You'd come home you'd be yellow. Your skin actually absorbed this smoke. Your collar would be yellow, your clothes turned yellow. I used to come in and put my shoes by the door, and two yellow footprints developed by the door of my house. My wife said, "Put them in the garage."

—Don Slavicek—

BY modern standards, the factory
on South-View Avenue was an environmental disaster. By the standards of
the fifties, it wasn't exactly a walk in the sunshine, either. "If OSHA had
been around then," Senior says quite candidly, "we would have been shut
down as soon as their man walked through the door." Or, at least, as soon
as he recovered from his nervous breakdown.

What you were dealing with here, remember, was coal tar pitch that
was melted down in a large vat, in a mixture of asbestos tailings and
fiberglass.

The veterans of Brookfield describe the battle of South-View in such
terms as "purgatory," "Hell's kitchen," and "The LaBrea Tar Pits."

Three more unwholesome components would be hard to find. The first
thing that happens when tar comes to a boil is to give off a green smoke.
The green smoke is pure sulfur dioxide. Liquify it, and you'll have pure
sulfuric acid.

Not to get overly biblical about this, the employees of Molex may not
have exactly "touched pitch," but the sulfur dioxide—so colorfully
described in Dante's *Inferno*—sure did lay its heavy hand upon them.
John Jr. started working at the factory during summer vacations in his
freshman year in high school and did every dirty job his father could find
for him except one. Because he was lucky enough to have skin that was
allergic to fiberglass, Johnny never got to run the mixing machine. "Fred
did, but I didn't. I hauled bags of asbestos. I hauled the fiberglass. I
shoveled the pitch and then I chopped the fiberglass because we got it in
drovings. It was all scrap. We'd haul the fiberglass in and we'd haul the
pitch in and they'd actually do the mixing with a shovel, and then they'd
roll it out, steaming hot, on these trays and run a roller over it and they'd
score them like a pizza. And what I'd do is get these things and take them
with a wheelbarrow into the molding department, and put them into the
molding ovens for the gals to mold. And remove the bars after they had
been cooled. There were three or four guys who did that job and they did
it three shifts a day. They were paid by the batch, so if you were willing to
work you could make a lot of dough. These were guys who were totally
impervious to the fiberglass. It's sooty in there and the more you sweat,

the more the pores open up. The stuff gets in and it's like little glass slivers all over you."

Bob Prosak is Junior's best and oldest friend. They met as Cub Scouts and were fellow jocks together through high school and college. Prosak worked for Molex briefly out of college. "I remember about the second week I worked there, they had a semiload of fiberglass come in, a 40-foot trailer. It was a nice warm day, and they said we had to get this thing unloaded. I had no idea what we were doing. Those bales were 120 to 180 lbs. And we rassled those things, me and another fellow. I tell you, no sooner I got through with that, I went into the locker room and took a shower and that didn't do any good. For three days after that, every time I sat down I felt like I was sitting on a porcupine. That stuff was just murder."

There was only one person in the place who was somehow able to rise above the environment. And that was the founder of the company, Frederick A. Krehbiel. Frederick Krehbiel came in every day wearing a starched shirt, with starched cuffs and a high collar. And, of course, a necktie and vest. "It's 100 degrees in the factory," Junior smiles, "and here's my grandfather back there designing products. Very dignified, he was meticulous. I don't care if it was 120 degrees, always a tie, never an open collar, never the sleeves rolled up. We'd be out there looking like we'd been through a war, and he never seemed to sweat. An amazing guy. A lot of what Dad has learned over his lifetime, a lot of the values he has today he learned through my grandfather. He was a tough guy and a real taskmaster."

Toward the end, he'd leave in the early afternoon, go over to the Cypress Restaurant and have two Old Grandads before he went home. "When he was eighty-six, he walked in and said to my Dad, 'Well, this is my last day.' That was it. He died two years later. That kind of guy you could really look up to."

What greater proof could be found of Senior's personality and salesmanship than that he was able to induce so many capable people to come to work for a very small company, amidst such unappetizing surroundings. Or to hold on to customers who came in to take a look.

Ed Healy's first big sale was not to Zenith, but to Teletype, Inc., another company he had been courting, without success, for years. The conditions for the breakthrough were ideal. Teletype was about to make a small machine that could be set on desks. A new generation machine. Teletype had been using the AMP Mate-N-Lok. Healy came through the door with a 9 circuit pin-and-socket in his hand and a heart filled with confidence. "I knew that Molex had a better product, that it should be easy to sell, and that it would do a real good job for them as well as for Molex. And myself as well."

Except for one thing. Teletype also had a plant near Molex. One of those big, spotlessly clean plants that are essential when you're manufacturing a piece of machinery with hundreds of moving parts. As long as they were right there in the neighborhood anyway, the folks at Teletype could see no reason why they shouldn't go down to take a look at the Molex facilities. And all of a sudden, Ed Healy thought, *"Oh-oh, this could be trouble."*

The visiting contingent consisted to two vice presidents—of manufacturing and of materials—plus two officials from the engineering department. "These guys came in, I forget this Ed's last name, and he's got hold of my arm. He's saying, 'We got to get out of here, I can't see anything.' Like in a panic. 'I can't see what is going on.' "

I thought, *"Oh boy, we're in a LOT of trouble."*

But John had that way about him. "They could see John knew what he was talking about. We're sitting in John's office, and he's explaining what we could do and what we couldn't do. And they gave us, I think, $40,000 for the tooling, which at that time was a lot of money from an outside source. That was the 1292, which was the first one that we tooled on the pin-and-socket stuff where John had a single cavity for the plug and receptacle. He was able to demonstrate that we did have a better product than AMP. It was far better."

It was not the last inspection that would be made. Nor the most famous. There are family stories that develop in the growth of a company, those stories that are repeated again and again, with a warm glow of nostalgia and the heady satisfaction that can only come with having pulled a fast one and gotten away with it. The "Clean Room" is such a story.

In engineering parlance, a clean room refers to an environment that has been made almost antiseptically clean for the manufacturing or testing of a particularly sensitive product. The only way you could have had that kind of clean room at Brookfield was through fire, flood or dynamite. Our Clean Room was a Clean Enough Room.

This is a particularly good story because it involves two men who were not working at Molex at the time, although both are key personnel today. One of them was pretending to be a Molex employee, the other was a leading member of the visiting delegation. It was, in fact, the visiting delegate, Bob Pribish, who eventually labeled it the "Clean Room Caper."

Wearing the Molex colors in this drama are the John Krehbiels, Sr. and Jr., in leading roles, Fred Krehbiel, who makes a brief appearance in a decidedly minor supporting role. There will also be a couple of mystery guests we will get around to. Ray Wieser, the chief of operations, rates top billing for the major part he played and for his ability to appreciate a great movie. Wieser went along with the "Clean Room" appelation until he saw Paul Newman and Robert Redford in *The Sting*. "And from then on, I've always called it *The Chrysler Sting*. Same thing. Newman and Redford couldn't have done it better."

In 1967, Bob Pribish was running the isolectric lab at Chrysler, and the salesman "looking in the door" for Molex was John Krehbiel, Jr.

Molex had been selling terminal blocks to Chrysler for its entire automobile line for many years. By 1967, they had become serious competitors in the connector end of the business as well, and with Chrysler about to change its harness, Senior saw an opportunity for Molex to make its move.

Senior: Essex was a very big provider of a whole wire harness for the Chrysler automobile. That thing was 60–70 feet long, all the connectors were there and all the terminals. Essex had the whole damn thing, and they didn't like to buy from anybody else.

Junior: The way Bob operated appealed to me a lot. He was very demanding to work with as a customer. He was tough. But if you did something to support his project he would try to help you get the business. That's how we really started. He couldn't get Essex Wire who was his big supplier at the time, to respond to an interconnection problem that he had. Without getting overly technical, there were certain terminals he wanted to polarize in a certain way. So we went ahead and had the prototype mold built, had it molded by suppliers.

Pribish tested it in Chrysler labs, found it was what he wanted, and specified it on the Essex harness.

Senior: Prib found that Essex was playing games with their connectors—saying they were having trouble putting the Molex connector on their harnesses. They wanted to put their own connector on there. "We'll do it much faster," and all that stuff. But they did not have the quality and they were losing out.

Pribish: Essex came back with reports from its own lab that sought to make Molex products look bad. Essex was saying that the terminals would back out of the housing, that they were too operator-sensitive. Things like that.

Senior: Essex was rigging its lab tests, and Pribish caught what they were doing. But Essex had been a big provider of Chrysler harnesses for a long time and they had a lot of strength with some of the top people. They were asking him, "Why are you specifying Molex? Essex claims they can do it as well as, and better than, Molex." But Bob is a pretty good fighter, and he fought back.

Pribish: Those were the toughest weeks I ever spent in my life. It took three or four weeks of very, very long days. It was a $600 million corporation versus a $6 million corporation. John never gave up. And he had plenty of opportunity to give up.

At the time, Pribish didn't know how much incentive. Because when John was finally invited to Detroit to make a presentation on his own behalf, he discovered that Chrysler was now specifying that the vendor had to make the entire connector himself. Pribish was under the impression that Molex did its own nylon molding. In truth, the nylon was molded by an outside supplier who was located in Florida.

There was a guy in Crystal Lake, about fifty miles to the north, named Bill Melvin, who had a company which had made some of Molex's molding tools for them.

Bill Melvin: Junior asked me to represent them and go to Detroit and talk as if I were an employee of Molex. I flew out with Junior and somebody else, we met with Chrysler, and they liked everything they saw and heard. And then, just as we were leaving, they said they wanted to come to Molex to see a mold press running.

"Well, sure," John said. "You bet. Love to have you come down and take a look."

Melvin: Then we go to the plane and say, How are we going to do this? "I'll get a molding press in," John said. "But I'll need you over there running it, as an employee."

Ray Wieser: Senior and I and a couple of other people at the plant cleaned up the back room. It had been where we assembled our switches before we moved that operation to Downers Grove. It was being used as a kind of storage room. We had to get the machine in, and in running order, and look like we knew what we were doing. And we had less than forty-eight hours.

Ray had some friends in the business from his old job. "We rented three molding machines, and brought them in and asked if we could borrow some auxiliary equipment that went with it for a couple of days. Overnight, we went from nothing to where we had three machines running in the back room. It was neat."

Since Molex didn't have its own trucks, they had to hire a couple of trucking firms to pick up the auxiliary equipment. There was a certain amount of wiring that had to be done to bring in the power. And the air and the water for the Chillers and Grinders. The Chillers keep the molds cold while you inject the hot nylon into them, and again when it sets up and cools off. The Grinders grind off the raised seam that is left along the pouring line.

Wieser: And we had to have people who knew how to run the machines. There was a fellow from Reed-Prentice Co., which makes molding machines. He was in there with us most of the night because he was the expert on his equipment. Bill Melvin knew the molds. And they showed us what to do and how to do it.

Fred Krehbiel was in during the night, too. Fred had only recently come back to the company to run what was laughingly called the international division. He was tapped, along with Burt Pohlmann, who was assistant sales manager, to wield a paint brush.

Fred: They brought the machines in at the last minute, and we painted the room around them during the night. When we got to the floor, we just painted whatever was not covered. I do remember the rush to get it ready, and wondering if it was going to work. And that we had to have it looking very professional with the proper inspectors and all the rest of it, none of which we had. And to make Pribish feel that we were competent to be a supplier of Chrysler, which we clearly weren't. It was a lot of fun.

Wieser: We got everything running pretty well that night, but it was in the wee hours of the morning. Then we shut everything down and everybody went home and got a couple hours sleep, and came back in the next morning.

Iain MacDonald was there almost by accident. He and Bill Melvin had served their apprenticeships as machinists together in England. They happened to bump into each other in Canada, where Iain was working, and Melvin had offered him a job. "I came in one morning and Bill Melvin told me to hop aboard the truck. I didn't know what was going on. I certainly didn't know anything about the machine I was supposed to be tending, but I remember that Bill Melvin and I both put on white smocks. He was running the machine, and I was told to catch the parts as they came out and pile them in a carton."

They had stacks of cartons packed with finished molds. And they had what amounted to a production line set up.

Wieser: In the morning, we got it all cranked up and running. And when they got there for the visit, everybody was just acting as if it was a routine day. It was a slick operation.

Junior: The purchasing agent was Len Johnson. A straight arrow. We still work with him. I hope he'll be able to laugh about it when he reads about this twenty years later.

In truth, Len Johnson just may have had his doubts. "He came in and Bob came in and another guy, and we took them through the stamping area and to our other molding stuff and then to the back where we were supposedly molding these other parts. Bob took them through real quick, and we showed them the machines and showed them the parts. And Bob says to Len, 'How's that look?' and Len was sort of hemming and hawing."

Wieser: We took them on a tour of the whole facility, into our back molding room. The molding machines were running and we had a couple of our engineering people there too, working as machine operators, standing at the presses. They saw their connectors being molded, and then went back into the front office and met for awhile. I wasn't part of the meeting but John Sr. and John Jr. were in there. The end result of this whole visit was that we did obtain Chrysler approval as a certified vendor.

After they left, we dismantled everything, shipped the molds back to the vendor. Carted some of the auxiliary equipment back to whomever we borrowed it from. I don't know what we did with the machines. We had intended eventually to get into the nylon molding business, but this particular situation forced us to. Quite rapidly. Senior has always been the leader to integrate our manufacturing operations. In other words, what somebody else was doing for us, let's do that ourselves. In fact, I was there when Senior picked up the phone and made an appointment to visit DuPont in Wilmington, Delaware. Senior said, "Let's do it," and we got into the nylon molding business.

Junior: It was funny. We really had our necks out there a mile, but it worked out great and everybody was satisfied. It was strictly a formality because there was no question we could do the business. We were doing a tremendous amount of work with outside suppliers at that time, and that was the project that made us decide to do it ourselves, and really get into the molding business. Now, of course, we have 250 presses that run that stuff. All over the world.

There is both an Afterwards and a Conclusion to the story.

Afterwards:

Through another series of coincidences, Bob Pribish and Iain Mac-Donald came to Molex within a few months of each other two years later. For many years they have worked together.

Iain came in stages. He had left Bill Melvin's operation and taken a job in a factory right around the corner from Molex's Downers Grove plant. There was a restaurant-bar close by, the Keg & Beef, where he'd bump into the guys from Molex after work. Because Bill Melvin had done a lot of tooling for Molex, Iain had already worked with many of them. They began to ask him why he didn't come over to Molex, and since the two guys who were pushing him the hardest were the same two guys who would be conducting the job interview, the outcome was not exactly in doubt.

Bob Pribish had become very friendly with Senior. They played a lot of golf together, both in Naperville and Detroit, and went on hunting trips to Maryland. It was during a hunting trip in the early part of 1971 that they worked out the deal for Pribish to come aboard.

"It's funny, isn't it?" Iain MacDonald says, "that Pribish was at Chrysler and I was at County Molding, and we're the ones who still talk about that day after all these years. And laugh about it. Prib says he knew what was going on, but to this day I don't believe him. In fact, I know he didn't know until we introduced him to Bill Melvin after he came here and told him the whole story. And he was in shock."

Conclusion:

The Brookfield factory ran out of time in 1970. In several ways. For one thing, the lease was going to be up in another year. For another, they were located in a semi-residential neighborhood, and the neighbors weren't all that ecstatic about living with the green smoke floating out of the Molex factory.

The switch operation had just been moved to Mexico as the only practicable way of competing with the cheap labor of the Far East. The offices and most of the manufacturing had long since been moved to new quarters in Downers Grove.

And so Don Slavicek packaged the molding operation and took it to Mexico. "We went way the hell out in the sticks to a place called The Ranch, which was a quarantine-holding station for cattle coming to the United States. The guy who owned The Ranch had this big building he rented to us, and we set up the molding facilities there." They really were a part of The Ranch. "We had cattle pens right next to the building where we were cooking this stuff; you know, making this thermoplastic Molex. The cows would stray into the building, the gauchos would lasso them and drag them out. It was something every day. We used to say if they ate the stuff they'd shit black bricks."

Molex-by-The-Ranch operated until 1977 and then passed into history. It had ended its life pretty much as it had begun, as a good cheap workhorse material for making bulky products, such as terminal blocks.

The importance of Molex, the plastic, in the history of Molex, the company, is that it gave the company both its name and its beginning, and, perhaps even more importantly, it set John Krehbiel, Sr., down on a path that was eventually going to take him into the fastest-growing industry of the postwar years. No, Mrs. Robinson. Not plastics. Electronics.

The exile of Molex, the plastic, had taken place at pretty much the same time that Molex, the company, was going public. By that time, Edwin Krehbiel, the man who had set those forces in motion six years earlier by selling out his share in the company, was long gone.

GOING PUBLIC

Ed was a very quiet kid. He did a lot of reading. He was an excellent artist. And a damn good mechanic. But Ed just did not have the interest in a business that had pressure. He was perfectly content to take a business of a certain size and say, Let's just maintain this. And I could see the fallacy of that. If you say you're not going to sell any more, pretty soon you're out of business.

—JOHN KREHBIEL, SR.—

IT was Ed Krehbiel who forced the company to go public in a bitter conflict which became so bitter that the two brothers never spoke to each other again.

For John Krehbiel, who wanted to keep the company in the family, it may have been the best thing that could have happened. To Ed Krehbiel, who wanted to take the money and run, it may well have been the most galling. By the time Ed died, twenty years later, he could contemplate the fact that the 40 percent of the company which he had sold for $1.2 million had become worth something like $450 million.

Just another example of the Law of Unintended Results.

Even as kids, John and Ed had never been close. The only time they ever spent together was when they were down in the basement machine shop, working with the old man. And even there they were temperamentally at odds. John thrived on the old man's drive and discipline. Ed found them oppressive. "The old man was hard on Ed," a family member says. "He went to California to get away from him."

Ed was an artist. Before going to California, he studied commercial art at the Art Institute and he had worked for several years illustrating men's fashions. While he was in California, he worked at the Disney studios. He also got married. Actually, he was married twice. About the only thing anybody ever learned about his first marriage was that it lasted three years, that his wife became tubercular—a fatal disease in the thirties—and that he had gone to West Virginia with her so she could live out her life on the old family farm.

Ed Krehbiel was such a taciturn man that his second wife, Gay, never knew he had worked for Disney while he was in California. But, then, she knew almost nothing about his sojourn in California. Over the forty years of their married life he never talked about it.

Gay Krehbiel was born in Denmark. She came to Clarendon Hills (alongside Hinsdale), when she was thirteen. Although she and Ed had gone together for two years, she didn't meet her future in-laws until the day of her marriage. And even then the meeting didn't take place at the wedding. As they were leaving the church, Ed told her that his sister-in-law, Peg, was in the hospital giving birth, and suggested that they go visit her.

89

That was how she met Peg. Her wedding anniversary is the same day as Fred's birthday. She didn't meet John until much later. The thing you have to remember about that, Gay says, is that John and Ed were not really working together in the factory. "Ed and his dad were running the factory. John was probably lucky in that respect. He wasn't exposed to the terrible atmosphere."

"John was always on the road," Gay points out, "and Ed was always in there with the machines and the molds and the dirt. In fact, my husband insisted that what really caused his death was the asbestos that he inhaled all those years." Of course, as she immediately adds in all fairness, Ed left the company at the age of sixty-two and lived to be eighty-one-years-old. And if he was constantly complaining about the condition of his lungs, he was also pursuing his not unstrenuous hobby of square dancing until the final six months of his life.

By the same token, it was not until John came into the business on a more permanent basis that Molex stopped being a kind of hobby for the Krehbiel family and became a serious business. But increased proximity did nothing to improve the relationship between the brothers. Both John and Gay agree on that.

Ed had been quite content running a small business. "He was a very good engineer," John affirms, "and an excellent designer." A perfectionist who combined an artistic creativity with an in-depth knowledge of tools. "But," John says, "he didn't have much interest in business. He didn't like the pressure of having to have something done tomorrow in order to make a delivery to the customer."

He never had.

"Why on earth are you going out selling new customers in Indiana and Ohio?" he had asked John back in the early days. "We're so busy now we can hardly take care of the business we've got."

John tried to explain that if he stopped going out to discover what the companies in the appliance industry were looking for in next year's models, they would probably lose the customers they already had and most certainly have no other customers to fall back on. "But Ed was absolutely adamant he was not going to be pressured into designing new molds when we were so damn busy that he couldn't see how we would be able to fill the orders." So John stopped selling . . . and in six months the orders had dried up . . . and John had to go out and start all over again . . . and the lesson he had attempted to impress on his brother, at such a cost to the company, was never learned.

The commitment to growth that was implicit in the hiring of a manufacturer's rep disturbed him so much that when Dale Miller came in with his first good order, Ed wanted to turn it down on the grounds that it was too big. They had a policy, he reminded his father, of not having more than 15 percent of their business with any one company. "By the time we get this order," the old man told him dryly, "Dale and John will have brought in enough business so that it won't be 15 percent."

And then John came in with a bigger order to make gussets for the new Westinghouse refrigerator model out of polyester fiberglass. It was a breakthrough of sorts because it marked the first time gussets were made out of plastic. And once again Ed refused to design the molds. "You're the guy that committed for it," he said, "you design it." So John had to design the molds himself. "We didn't get the thing done on time," John says, "and it was nowhere near as well done as Ed could do, but we got it out well enough so that Westinghouse stayed with the product for a couple of years."

From then on, they tangled constantly.

"It started to get too big," Gay Krehbiel says. "And I know my husband began to believe that it was just a little too much for him to handle. He felt that his one hand didn't know what the other one was doing. It was expanding so fast that I'm sure he wouldn't have lasted as long as he did if he hadn't sold out when he did."

The reality of the situation was that he had started to withdraw. "He'd come to work with an old lunchpail," one veteran toolmaker recalls. "He was as fine a person as I have ever met, but he had absolutely no interest in building a big company."

By the time the move was made to Downers Grove, Ed was sixty years old. He had spent his whole life working in a business that he didn't seem to like very much. And, like his brother, he had sometimes gone for months without drawing any pay. John's son, Johnny, was already the sales manager and clearly, the guy who was going to be taking over the business someday, while his own son, Allan, had just left college to join the Air Force. Allan had not shown any particular interest in coming into the business, and even if he had, it would be four to five years down the road before he had served his hitch and come out of college with his degree.

But look at the irony. As a result of the very growth he had resisted, Ed's stock was suddenly worth a great deal. In 1962, Molex passed the million dollar mark in sales. By 1965, the sales were well over $2 million. He saw the chance to get out with enough money to live out his life in comfort and, since he was convinced that he didn't have long to live, put aside an estate for his wife and son.

John was pushing sixty himself. Ed wanted a million dollars, and John was not going to put himself in that kind of debt at that time of his life.

There was another complication, one that really wasn't. Each of the brothers owned roughly 40 percent of the company. The other 20 percent belonged to Molex's treasurer, Marie Manatte. On the arithmetic of it, therefore, Marie Manatte held the fate of the company in her hand. In reality, there was never any question where her support would go. Marie had come to Chicago from Iowa as a young woman and gone to work almost immediately at Krehbiel Engineering as Fred Krehbiel's secretary. She remained his secretary for the rest of his life. It was because she was so loyal to him that she had insisted, in the face of his better advice, upon being paid in Molex stock in lieu of salary.

And so when Ed began to talk about other people who were ready to buy his stock, John took the elementary precaution of sewing up Marie's support. Not only did Marie pledge her stock to John, but since she was getting up there in years herself, she arranged to turn the stock over, irrevocably, and put much of it in trust for Johnny and Fred and their children.

It was a year later that Ed came back with the solid offer of a million dollars plus from a consortium of businessmen backed by A. G. Becker, a Chicago investment banking firm. A done deal. Except that John still had a right of first refusal. John brought his sons in and between the three of them they bought about $200,000 worth of stock. The remaining shares went to Becker for a million.

Six years later, A. G. Becker took the stock public, as it had a right to under the terms of the agreement. It was not that Becker was unhappy about its investment. Quite the contrary. "We wish we had a hundred more just like it," they told John. In those six years, the sales had risen from $5 million to $17 million. The figure represented such a top heavy percentage of the assets of the company that they wanted to take their profit and use the money for other ventures.

OK, how about it? If Ed Krehbiel had misjudged the potential of the company so badly, what about John himself? "You have to give A. G. Becker a lot of credit," Junior says. "We certainly didn't see it, because we didn't snap up all of Ed's stock. We didn't want to get into hock that deep. Here's this investment banking firm which had more confidence in the potential of the company, I guess, than we did."

But that's Johnny. Johnny is always ready to give himself the worst of it. Senior doesn't see it that way at all. Of course he didn't foresee what the company was going to become, Senior admits. He wasn't even thinking in those terms. "I was still wondering how to make next Friday's payroll." And that's the thing. "We bought what we could afford. We actually went into debt to buy what we did buy." It wasn't as if he was letting control of the company get away from the family. They already had control. The extra stock just padded the margin of safety by another ten percent.

To illustrate his thinking Senior poses a couple of rhetorical questions. "Would we buy another company now for a billion dollars?" he asks. "Obviously we couldn't afford to take a chance on blowing our business. OK, then, how big a company could we acquire? Well, we could absorb one of maybe $50 million, but we wouldn't be comfortable acquiring anything bigger than that or we'd be out of working capital."

Once you go into debt, in other words, the profits that would normally be going back into the business are being drained off to service the debt. "You have certain limits if you use good judgment, and you don't want to go over that or you get yourself in a risk position."

He could have bought Ed's stock by borrowing on the business, and let the business pay it back. That's done every day. But if he had done that, if the future profits had gone to the bank instead of back into the business—with all the multiplier effects that would have involved—where would the company be today, and what would it be worth, and how could anybody know?

John Krehbiel is not a gambler. He is a risk-taker, and the risks he takes—and has taken again and again—are in pushing his pile of chips into the pot to buy the latest machinery. He got all the gamble out of his system when he blew his tuition money in the commodity market. The only gambling he does in business now is when he gambles on himself, and on his own knowledge and experience.

It's one thing to go into debt just enough to guarantee control. That's a worthwhile risk. If he had bought all the stock, what would it have meant other than that Forbes could say he was worth another hundred million.

Having said all that, there is no question but that he did underestimate the value of the stock. We know that because he did his best to talk his friends out of buying it.

In his agreement with A. G. Becker, he would still have first refusal rights for his friends or employees on any stock that was turned back to

Becker by members of the consortium. Not at the price the Krehbiels had paid, but at the higher price A. J. Becker was selling it. As it happened, two thousand shares came back, and John called a select group of friends and key personnel, being careful at all times to express his own opinion that the price they were asking—$48.75 per share—was far too high.

"That's the one thing I will never forgive John for," John Flaherty will tell you. "I'm not a gambler by nature. For me to have bought it, I'd have needed a lot of encouragement."

Flaherty wasn't alone. When the head man tells you they're overrating his company, who are you to argue with him.

Red Thayer and Bill Veeck also passed. And so did Dale Miller. A rep in Kansas City bought a couple of hundred shares. Bert Pohlmann, who had moved into The International Group with Fred, borrowed money to buy whatever he could. And then the next call went to Ed Healy. "How much have you got?" Ed Healy asked, and bet the plantation.

"That's an awful steep price to be paying for it," cautioned John.

"It's all in the eye of the beholder," said Healy. "Is there any chance of getting more?"

He ended up with 1,700 shares at $48.75 and mortgaged his home to the hilt to raise the $85,000 or so that was needed.

When A. G. Becker took the stock public six years later, his $85,000 became something like $750,000. Sixteen years later it's worth something like $15 million.

Talk about getting in on the ground floor, huh?

"I never understood how you got in on ground floors," Healy says. "I didn't sit down and ask myself what the asset value was. I'm not that sophisticated to begin with. It was just knowing the people and knowing the company and knowing in my own mind they had some products that were better than what the others had."

Ed Healy was a salesman, and he knew what he was selling. And every bit as important in his mind, he knew who he was selling for. "I was forty-one years old when I started to represent Molex, so I'd been around a little bit too, and I knew that you had to spend money to make it go."

Senior's very first venture after Ed had signed on to represent him was an illuminated pushbutton switch. "Everything else that was illuminated sold for five, seven, ten dollars apiece. John's switch was going to sell for around 75 cents. It was going to take probably $100,000 minimum tooling and the company was doing under a million in sales. He was willing to take the chance on that tool. He had confidence in what he could

do. That's the 1175 pushbutton switch, and it's still being made today."
Healy was also betting on Johnny, whom he had met even before he was
introduced to Senior. "Here's a young guy who's twenty-three, twenty-
four years old at the time, and you could sense he was a chip off the old
block. He wanted to work. Their work ethic is so strong."

If going public was the best thing that could have happened after Ed's
stock got out of the family, it was not done by design. It was done by
relaxing his vigilance during the negotiating sessions with A. G. Becker,
and doing the one thing he guards against, perhaps more than any other.
Believing what his lawyers tell him.

As part of the original deal with A. G. Becker, he agreed that if they
wanted to take the stock public—"register the stock" is the technical
term—they would assume all the expenses and he wouldn't fight them. "I
remember our lawyers at the time said, 'John, you have absolutely
nothing to worry about. There's no way these guys are going to take a
minority position public.' " So much for lawyers.

"He hated it," Junior says. "He feared what it was going to mean."

Most assuredly, he did not want to let the competition know everything
about his financial condition and earnings. Most definitely, he did not
want to have to deal with "the goddam SEC" and all the rest of that
bureaucratic crap.

"He didn't want to go through with it," Junior says. "But being a man
of his word he said, OK, go ahead and do it. But he was not happy."

Good things began to happen immediately. To begin with, the SEC had
just changed its rules to make it illegal for any party with an appreciable
interest in the stock to become the underwriter. That eliminated A. G.
Becker. "Becker asked me if I knew any underwriters, and I told them I
wouldn't know one if I tripped over him." So Becker arranged to send in a
representation of underwriters for him to interview. Including a representative from Salomon Brothers. A slick article, a fast talker. Along the way,
he just happened to drop the information that Salomon Brothers had just
lent $5 billion to the Post Office. If he thought that was going to impress
the little company from Downers Grove, he could not have been more
wrong. "A lot of interest they're going to have in us," Senior said, as soon
as the guy was out the door.

Not unexpectedly, he chose William Blair & Co., a Regional (Chicago)
investment banker "with a good Midwestern work ethic."

"They had a real great guy by the name of Bill Hodgson," Senior says.
Hodgson impressed him immediately by laying it right on the line. "This

is not fun and games," Hodgson told him. "It's going to require some work on your part."

The lawyers and accountants were going to have to sit across the table and bang heads over endless details. But, he added, there were also good by-products to becoming a public company.

- The employees who were getting stock options would be able to open the paper every morning and see what their stock was worth. "As of now you could tell them that it's worth a hundred a share or $5 a share and there would be no way for them to know."
- The prestige of being listed would translate into the ability to hire better people.
- It was good discipline for them to have somebody looking over their shoulders.

As far as his obligation to brokers or money managers was concerned, the only things he was legally obliged to do were to hold an annual meeting and put out an annual statement. "But if you want your stock to be well recognized in the market," Hodgson told him, "you do have to talk to people. You have to let them know what your company is and what you're doing and what you expect to do."

"Bill's suggestions were absolutely on the mark," Senior says. Senior took over the job of talking to the brokers and analysts. Typically, he took a course at the Dale Carnegie Institute to polish up his speaking.

Molex has a 3 cent dividend, which means nothing. It's in there only to satisfy the needs of fund managers whose articles of incorporation limit them to dividend-paying stocks. The Molex policy has always been to reinvest the profits in the company's future.

Junior is a charter member of the best-thing-that-could-have-happened-to-us school:

- It has allowed Molex to recruit better people.
- It has made the company worth a great deal more.
- The employees have a stake in the company through stock option plans or their own investments.

As for Senior, he doesn't exactly throw his hat in the air, shout Hallelujah, and bless the day, "I don't know how we would have grown. But I don't think that the fact that we went public enhanced our profits except as it helped us to attract good people, and good people are what make good profit."

But if, in the end, it turned out that Ed Krehbiel had helped to make him rich, that was an unintended result, not an intention. After Ed had sold his stock the brothers never spoke again. But the wives remained very friendly. Fred, who has a very strong sense of family and an even stronger instinct for personal relations, remained very friendly with the whole family.

Edwin Krehbiel walked away with his $1.2 million and lived out his life in comfort doing what he loved best: landscaping, square dancing, working around his house, and following the stock market. In fact, he became an expert on the stock market. "Like all the Krehbiels," Gay Krehbiel says, "Ed always threw himself completely into anything he did." He invested in only the most conservative of stocks, and did so well that toward his later years he published a little booklet for his friends on how to make money by investing conservatively. He followed the Molex stock. He never bought a share. When he died, he had a stock portfolio that left his widow very well off.

As far as John was concerned, his brother had ceased to exist. During the preparation for the Fiftieth Wedding Anniversary party that was being planned for Peg and John, Fred suggested to his mother that they take the opportunity to mend past wounds by inviting Ed and Gay. "Don't even suggest it to your father," Peg replied.

JUNIOR

Don't miss Johnny. He's the kid behind all the finances. He's the penny-pincher. He's the one that runs it with an iron hand. He's my pet. I've loved him since he was a baby.

—MARTHA FLAHERTY—

FRED'S a natural," Junior says. "I have to work hard at everything." That's Johnny. He'll give himself nothing. In this case, however, it happens to be true. "He's the most intense person I have ever known," says Bob Pribish. "If it can be done with perseverence and intensity, John will do it. Johnny's not a natural in anything. He is not a natural skier, but he's outstanding. He's not a natural tennis player, but he's outstanding. Nothing flows but everything comes out perfectly. It's concentration. That's the way he's driven the company from the word go. He gets the momentum going. Detail upon detail. John knows what is in everybody's wastepaper basket, he knows what time the lights go off in every office."

He is also, paradoxically, the most ego-less person you will ever find sitting behind the president's desk of a successful corporation. "I always assumed I'd be working for the old man," he says. "Each summer I worked at a different job. The molding department, the shipping department, the tool room. I did more to set back our tooling programs. Those guys just said: Get that guy out, he has no skill whatsoever."

The first year he was in the factory, he was no more than fourteen, and he came home with bed bugs. "He was a grease monkey," Martha Flaherty recalls, not without fondness. "He swept up the floor. He did everything."

Instead of taking a shower and changing his clothes as he was supposed to do, he had come home in his overalls, bringing a lot of little crawling things with him. "Peg and I had to fumigate the room. I remember we took the mattress off the bed and threw it out the window because it was just infested."

"Did I like working in that place during the summer?" Junior asks. "Man, it was awful. But that was paying your dues. The thing that was really beneficial was that I got to know the people really well and I got to know the things that were important to them."

After graduating from Lake Forest College in 1959, he worked as an inspector for awhile (they weren't so presumptuous as to call it Quality Control), and as the company achieved a plateau where the buying became appreciable, he asked for a shot at organizing a Purchasing

101

Department. The department being him. "He saved us so much money with smart purchasing," Senior says, "that when he wanted something more challenging I suggested that he start looking into sales." Which, as it happened, was exactly what Junior had in mind. The year was 1963, the company was beginning to move, and Johnny Krehbiel was just the kid to jump into the saddle and make the run for the Roses.

By freeing Senior from any pressing need to go out and sell, he was also doing something else. He was permitting Senior to turn his full energies to the administration of the company.

Rule of Life: Wherever you find a highly successful organization of any kind, you will find a highly accomplished administrator with a clear purpose and a steady vision.

In 1975, when Senior relinquished the job and title of president to his oldest son, Junior had already been the executive vice president/general manager for eight years. "He had done a great job of controlling budgets, making employees responsible for their jobs, demanding accountability, and exercising good business judgment," Senior explains. "He is the hardest working employee we have."

Don Slavicek, who was able to observe the relationship from up close, describes it in terms that are crisp and to the point. "Senior is the power behind the scenes. Johnny is the driving force."

"My sons and I are perfectionists," Senior has said, "and we sometimes have trouble determining the limitations of people. How far can you push the people." One of Johnny's favorite sayings is, "You take it, you turn the screws down, you keep going, you press for more until people start to get their back up . . . then you back off . . . then you go back and turn it some more. And you do it to yourself as well."

Brookfield was history, the Downers Grove plant had completed its three expansions, and the basic management corps was not only in place but was, by then, well seasoned and fully engaged. And if all but a very few of them had been deprived of the thrill of scratching the fiberglass out of their hides in Brookfield there is not a one that doesn't have his war stories about the weekly budgetary sessions with Junior at Downers Grove.

"Total accountability," was indeed the name of the game. Junior would sit there with his "bean counters"—the accountants—on his end of the table, and the managers and foremen would have to account for every cent. The people who spent the money on one side of the table, the people who controlled the spending on the other, and the battle raged over how much money it would take to produce each product in time to meet the scheduled delivery date.

Iain MacDonald: We would go into a situation and we'd have the foreman in and we would take the late list which was probably fifty–sixty pages, and we'd go over it all, part by part. *Why is this late? What are you doing to fix it?*

"We can't fix it, we don't have the capacity. Our capacity is ten and the customers want thirteen."

"Don't give me that bullshit, fix it."

"But John, that's all we can get."

"That's not acceptable," Junior would say. "I want a plan from you tomorrow morning. Next item."

Absolutely serious. "For him it was, I don't care that you can only build ten, I want thirteen. You figure out how to get it. No eye blinking, no smiling. And this would be done not on one item, but on thirty or forty items where Junior would not release the money to buy the additional capacity."

Bob Pribish: We'd get it from the suppliers. He'd say, "Are they working Saturdays and Sundays?" We were unmerciful with our suppliers. Probably they wanted to do it, but how do you get the capacity? "Tell 'em to work three shifts, Saturdays and Sundays." Is Molex going to pay extra? No. But we expected those parts on our doorstep Monday morning.

One of the classic exchanges involved Art Johnson, who had come to work at Molex in 1960 as a tool engineer at a time when Junior was still the inspector. Art had missed a delivery date, and Junior wanted to know why.

Art said, "John, we don't have the capacity. It is an impossible situation."

"Why isn't the capacity there?"

"You wouldn't sign off on the tooling four months ago."

Junior said, "That's your fault."

How could it be his fault? Art Johnson wanted to know. "I made you a plan and you wouldn't sign it off. You threw it in the wastebasket."

And Junior looked him straight in the eye and said, "It's your fault. You didn't convince me!"

Go argue with that.

"Because of that accusation he made to Art," Iain says, "I never gave up after the first time. He used to throw us out of the office. *Get the bleep out of my office*, and I'd go back to him a third time and a fourth time."

Because that's what Junior had been saying to Art Johnson, wasn't it? *If you really thought you needed it that bad, why didn't you come back and fight me for it.*

You can do that. You can come back, and you can argue. But you have to do it one-on-one. Four guys in his office, and he'll throw them all out. He feels they're ganging up on him. Two of them and he'll say, "What are you, a couple of bookends, trying to squeeze me?" And throw one of them out.

Sure, he was unreasonable. He was unmerciful. He beat up on everybody. But that was part of the excitement.

Jim Geiser: Johnny is one of those type of guys you just got to love. He used to have what you call an all-day production meeting and he would get everybody in the conference room in the old Downers plant. You come in the morning, it was dark, and when you'd leave it was dark. He'd send the secretary to bring lunch in, and you'd never know what the weather was like outside. And one time he was just beating the hell out of me. Every question he asked me I couldn't answer, and the more I didn't know the more he jumped on me. I had one of those old-fashioned pens and I was squeezing it tighter and tighter until it finally cracked on me.

Now, even under the best of circumstances, splattering ink all over your clean white shirt is going to enrage you. And this was definitely not the best of circumstances for Jim Geiser. "I jumped up and told him he couldn't pay me enough. I said, 'The hell with you, I quit,' and I started to walk out. He got up in front of everybody and says, 'You'll quit when I tell you to quit. And not a minute before.' That's Johnny. He'll push you and push you and when he sees he's gone too far, he'll say something to relieve the tension." Even Geiser had to laugh.

It takes a certain kind of personality. Not everyone wants to work in that kind of environment.

There was the guy Ray Wieser hired who was going to serve directly under him as an operations manager. Top level job. He was ensconced in the office next to Junior's and he sat there for a couple of days and heard Junior screaming and pounding on the desk. "This man rules by fear," he told Wieser. Walked out and never came back.

And that fellow doesn't even go into the record book as the revolving-door champion. That honor belongs to the engineering manager who didn't make it through meeting #1. "Dammit," he said, as they were breaking for lunch, "this guy is a madman." Walked off and was never seen again.

On the flip side of that record, we have a guy whom Junior would not allow to quit. A production inventory control manager. "I've got a better opportunity," he told Junior. "You're not going anywhere," Junior said. "I want that report done." He would certainly try to complete it, the guy said, but he had promised to report to his new job the next week. "Dammit," said Junior, "you're staying right here until we get this thing resolved." Kept him there for five weeks.

When the other guys reminded him he was a free American citizen and asked him why he didn't just get up and leave, he said, "Junior won't let me."

"Control of spending," Ray Wieser says, "that's where Junior is at his demanding best."

Late summer and fall are traditionally the most profitable months. That's when the consumer electronic customers are buying all the components for the TVs, VCRs, and stereos that they will be turning out for the Christmas season. After October the orders begin to shut down. "November and December are the slow months. Each year, Junior would get us together and we'd look at the projection for sales and we'd look at what our spending had been. And that's why, he'd say, we are going to have to cut spending in the next two months by 50 percent or some ridiculous number.

"He'd pick some number out of the air that was just impossible and he'd beat on us. We'd have a meeting and we'd be there at six o'clock in the morning and we'd be there until all hours of the night going through every detail in the entire organization where we spend money. We'd have ten people in this conference room and we'd get down to a small dollar account late at night where we'd be talking about $250 items. But that's what it took, and he would just demand on us to drive our spending down. And we would do a good job of it. We would very rarely get to the target but we got a heck of a lot more than we thought we'd have if he hadn't kicked our asses around. We certainly wouldn't have had the good month that we ended up having."

"The end of the year, it was a wringing out," Don Slavicek agrees. "You want to talk about total accountability. You'd fight over $35. 'Last month you said you were going to spend $500, you spent $535. What the hell are you doing?' "

"Or you'd gone over on the account and you needed another $200. If he said, You'll get it out of your own paycheck, you can forget it, you know you're not going to get it. Just like the old man."

The thing to remember in this regard is that Johnny is not an engineer.

"I'm not smart enough," he'll say. What really happened was that both Krehbiel boys came out of high school with a deficiency in math, just like their father. In the early grades, they had attended a progressive private school which did not bother with algebra. In college, Johnny was a jock. A business management major. Business management curriculums are not noted for heavy courses in math, electronics, or mechanics.

Unlike his father, Johnny did not feel any necessity to make up his deficiency by going to night school. ("I don't have my dad's patience. I guess I don't have his curiosity, either.") What he didn't have was his dad's interest in how things work. Senior still loves to fix things around the house. When he has nothing else to tinker around with, he will buy a Heath Kit and build himself a TV set or a computer. Junior couldn't fix a faucet. He has been a hunter since he was a kid roaming the fields around Downers Grove, but he cannot take a shotgun apart. When a shotgun jams on him in a duck blind, he'll just throw it aside and ask for a new one.

Increasingly, as the company has moved into the area of servicing high-tech industries, he feels the lack of an engineering background. So much so that he has been steering his own children in that direction. "Jake feels that every day at work he could do 20 percent better if he had an engineering degree," Posey says.

Don Slavicek discovered how it was going to be right away. Slavicek had been with the company only a couple of months when he called Junior to lay out a problem.

"Who's the bleeping plant manager?" Junior barked.

"Well, I am."

"Then solve the bleeping problem. That's what I pay you for." And slammed the phone down.

"And so," says Slav, "I solved the problem." And got the message.

What you have to understand, say the technical people who work with him, is that because Junior doesn't have a technical background. He wants more information before he makes a technical decision. That was one of the reasons, they believe, for those long, long meetings.

But don't go away. Junior went to night school for courses in business and advanced business, as well as for a goodly representation of the other courses that Molex sponsors for its managers. Despite his disinclination to give himself credit for anything, it is almost superfluous to say that he made himself bright enough to do one hell of a job at the thing that did interest him. Growing the company.

"He's not the wild man a lot of the people in the connector business view him as being," John Klein says. "He's a very logical man. He's a motivator. He says, This is what we want to do, and he may get ten inputs telling him why he can't do that, but he still won't back off his position. Well, is that tough? Yeah. Is that unreasonable? Yeah. Does he think you're going to achieve it 100 percent? He hopes you will. Will he accept 98? Yeah."

But he knows that if he never backs off that top number everybody is going to try that much harder to get it. Ron Schubel is the president of Commercial Products Division. "The guys who advance and thrive at Molex," Schubel adds, "are the guys who set high goals for themselves. And that attitude filters down to their own groups. I know I tell some of the general managers I have at the plants the same thing, knowing full well they probably can't do it all. But if you set the numbers up high enough and don't back off, they will try to find others ways."

That's what it's all about. The Krehbiel philosophy of the alternative course. Of picking yourself up after a failure and finding another way. Senior says, "Have you tried this?" Junior says, "It's not acceptable."

The thing that sets Molex apart, Schubel believes, is the refusal to accept defeat gracefully. "There are always alternatives to anything. And I think this is where John has learned and grown over time. He knows that if he hires this strong group of guys, and he keeps staying after them, they'll continue to come up with alternatives. And you can describe that as tough, and it is tough. Because he never stops driving."

John is tough, and John is competitive. He hires competitive people. Preferably athletes. "You want guys who want the ball, and they want the ball in the fourth quarter, and they want the ball on fourth down and one, and they're not afraid to go for it. That's the kind of guy we have, and we're still looking for those same kind of guys today."

The lingo of sports is never far from Junior's lips. "Goddam," he will say when he's really chewing somebody out, "I could get a fourth-round draft pick and he'd be better than you."

The connection between business and sports is compelling. Athletes know they are going to lose a certain number of times, but they also know that they are going to pick themselves and try to do better tomorrow. And, more important still, athletes know that winning overcomes everything. When you win you feel good no matter what you've had to go through to get there. Losing hurts. The Krehbiels are great talent scouts in that regard. They know that if they give the people they've signed some time they can be very creative and they will come up with numerous alternatives that can either achieve the goal, or better the goal, or come damn close to the goal. As John Klein says, "Junior knows that if he puts another mind thinking about it, and tells you enough times that it's not acceptable, you're going to do something about it."

Nobody knows Johnny Krehbiel, the competitor, any better than his old pal, Bob Prosak. They have been friends since they met in the Cub Scouts. They were jocks together in high school and college. "Johnny banged up his knee in high school. In college, he was average in his freshman and sophomore years. Had an operation on his knee and ended up being captain in his senior."

After they got out of college, they played a lot of handball at the YMCA in LeGrange. "After we got cleaned up we'd watch the other guys play. He'd say, 'I think I can beat that guy.' And he'd practice all week and challenge the guy and beat him. The following week he'd do the same thing. The next week, he'd do the same thing. Find someone who was a little bit better, study him and practice to beat him."

For tenacity, for perseverance, there is Johnny's tennis game. He didn't play tennis much until he was in his thirties. But he had thought a lot about it for a long time. Back in his high school days, he would read the tennis magazines and he'd tell Prosak that he was going to take up the game sometime.

The moment of truth came when he and Posey went off to spend a Thanksgiving weekend together, and Posey beat him. And that was more than John H. Krehbiel, Jr., could stand. "I got pregnant and he got serious," Posey says, in a typical Posey-ism. "It worked out for both of us."

Naturally, he took lessons from a tennis pro for six months before he ventured onto the court. After a reasonable amount of time, he re-injured his knee. Naturally, he kept playing. "The football mentality," Posey says. "It wasn't that he had anything worse than anybody else. He just kept playing until he had no cartilege left. Four years ago he had his last artheroscope, and we all went to the little movie and the doctor told him he couldn't play again."

That's what he thought.

The movie had been made off the artheroscope itself. John has become both grateful for and fascinated by sports medicine. "It was the third operation and the guy had to take out a lot of cartilege. He saw it was getting worn down pretty good. The movie showed that all the cartilege was gone, how it was just rubbing on bone. This was not going to be a good situation." He tried not to play for probably two–three months. "But

I couldn't do it. I just liked the game too much. The worse that happens is pretty soon it hurts enough so that you can't do it, you don't *want* to do it. So long as I want to do it I'm going to do it."

If you wonder where he gets the time, he has a standing date with the pro at the tennis club at 5:00 in the morning. Pays him a premium price.

If you wonder how he is able to get around the court, he wears a big Lenox Hill knee brace. He also wears a neoprene girdle around his waist to protect his back and a neoprene wrap on his leg for his groin pull. Then he wears a neoprene bandage on his wrist. And that's when he's feeling reasonably fit.

Even Bob Prosak shakes his head in wonder. "A couple of years ago, he'd come out with a brace on his leg, and a brace on both arms. His back went out. He'd walk out there like a robot. When I saw the brace . . . I mean it looks like aluminum tubes with a sort of canvas padding."

And then he hurt his wrist. He was playing in a tournament somewhere, and with faultless anticipation raced to the corner of the net, and his opponent wound up and hit the ball as hard as he could right at him, from practically on top of him. The ball hit on the edge of Johnny's racquet, and he felt something go *twang* in his wrist. Naturally, he finished the match. Sure, it was sore. "You always have a sore wrist, tendonitis or something," he explains. It goes with the tennis elbow that you always have. Naturally, he kept playing. To ease the pain, he would fly out to Los Angeles on Friday night to have it treated by Dr. Omar Fareed, who is the doctor for the Davis Cup team. He would take the first plane to L.A. in the morning, rent a car, and drive to Beverly Hills for an injection in his wrist, take an afternoon plane back to Chicago, and be back in his office on Saturday morning. For four months, he did that. For four months, he kept on playing while his wrist grew progressively weaker. Until one day he had no wrist. "Had a guy look at it and he said I'd torn apart the ligaments pretty badly." So he went up to the Mayo clinic where he was presented with two alternatives. He could put the wrist in a cast and wait six months to see what happened, or he could go right in and have it fused. On the latter alternative he wouldn't have any movement in the wrist, but in eight months he'd be able to go back on the court.

"Let's go with the operation." John said. He had three bones fused and five pins inserted into them. In eight months the cast came off and, just as they had promised, he had lost all mobility. ("He can only bend it a little bit," Posey reports. "He can barely shave.")

"A lot of people think you can snap your wrist and that's what gives you the power," Johnny says. "And it isn't. It's your legs and back and your elbow and everything else. You don't lose anything off your service, you just don't have quite the flexibility. You just have to adapt to it."

He also had to adapt to not playing in any tournaments for a year because it took that long for the wrist to become strong enough to allow him to play two matches, back to back.

In 1986, he played in fourteen tournaments. He was ranked seventh in the forty-five and over category in Chicago, and ninth in the over forties. "He's very, very proud of that," Posey says. "Especially that he was able to come back after not playing."

Showing pride in himself is not one of John's most distinctive characteristics. That's the only intimation of ego in him, that he wants to win. Posey has a slight demurrer. She doesn't believe that modesty or immodesty has anything to do with it. "He never seeks praise from anyone. He never tells you anything he does. It's like playing in those tennis tournaments. He seeks situations where he's just another Joe."

Take him away from the business, and he is a very pleasant, smiling, youthful-looking man. You cannot do anything for him. He rejects the spotlight. He will direct any conversation away from himself and towards the activities of whomever he is talking to. During a seminar or a directors meeting, he all but disappears into the background.

For his fiftieth birthday last year, Posey sent out a letter to 150 people asking them to write something about him for an album she was putting together. College friends, and business acquaintances, skiing buddies, tennis players, people he'd put through school. Jake found out about it and told her that she might as well call it off because he was going to be out of town. He hates that kind of thing. He hates being the center of attention. But the replies had already begun to come back, and they were all pretty much the same. "That he's straight and he cares about you."

One of his friends, writing from Australia, was moved to a poetic tribute to Johnny's tennis career. It read in part:

> Alas and alack he was set back
> His knee went first, but soon
> a wrist, a back, went out of whack
> his body became a ruin
> "Bionic Man" he was often called
> as he clanked around the land
> But through it all he stood quite tall
> And quietly said, "I can."

That's Johnny. You drag your leg, you never give up, you win.
And if they throw a party for him, he ain't gonna show up.

Marge Woehler has been Junior's secretary for 13 years. In Marge's opinion, Johnny's tirades were more calculated than was generally supposed. "He was much younger than most of the men he was dealing with below his level, he had to be very aggressive to get their attention."

But that, she makes clear, was in the old days when the company was a-building. "He's mellowed so much in these past few years that he's not the same person. He's much more the gentleman now. I can see him becoming more and more like Senior every day."

The one thing he always had, in that regard, was Senior's integrity. Whether he was coming at you like a blunt instrument, as in the old days, or in the less rambunctuous way of a man who is now, after all, in his fifties, you could always be sure, that what Junior said he would do, you could count upon him doing.

Socially, on the other hand, they are at opposite ends of the pole. Where Senior is so open and easy to know, Junior has always been inordinately shy. Take him away from his desk and his demeanor becomes almost courtly.

He has always been like his father, too, in his overriding concern for the well-being of the Molex employees.

In 1974, Don Slavicek found out that he had a glomular enphritis. His kidney had deteriorated. He found it out after blood vessels had begun to break in his eye. He was able to go to Mayo for a complete diagnosis, and without having to wait the customary three months. "Senior made a phone call, and I was there within 20 hours. And they gave me the whole nine yards. I spent two weeks there, and it cost me nothing."

By watching his diet and taking medication, he managed to stay off the dialysis machine for four years. And never missed a day of work.

Right after he finally did go on the machine, a blizzard hit Chicago. So bad that they were snowed in at the factory overnight, "What about Slav?" Johnny asked his engineering administrator.

"Well, he has to get on the machine to clean out his blood."

"What if he doesn't?"

"Well, if he doesn't get the blood cleaned, I guess he dies."

"Oh no," said Johnny. "Not on my time he doesn't." What kind of crap was that? "I need the sonofabitch to open this place up in the morning."

He put Jim Geiser to work on finding a vehicle that would be powerful enough to cut its way through a blizzard, and Geiser turned up a huge 4-wheel Blazer in Cleveland. Then they found a volunteer from the shipping dock, put him on a plane and the guy drove the Blazer all night through the heavy snow storm and had it as Slav's house in the morning.

"He'd scream his head off for $100 in the budget meeting," Slav says, "and he'd turn around and he'd say, Do that! That's the 'people part' of him. That's the part of him where you say to the guy, 'You can call me anything.' And you'd do anything for him."

FRED—THE
INTERNATIONAL
CONNECTION

The greatest satisfaction? That's easy. My greatest satisfaction is the way the family has developed.

—John H. Krehbiel, Sr.—

SPREAD across the three-panel closet door in Fred's old room in Downers Grove is a map of the world, with each country outlined in crayon and colored in with the hues that were conventionally used in the atlases of the day.

The Krehbiels, father and sons, are endlessly fascinating to the people who work at Molex. And nothing seems to fascinate them so much as the completely opposite personalities of the two sons.

Johnny was ready to leave town rather than submit himself to a 50th birthday party. On Fred's 40th birthday, he threw a lavish party for himself. John has his Porsche washed almost daily, and it is scrupulously maintained. And, still, he will trade them in almost every year. Fred has had his green Corvette for 15 years. He runs it into the ground and then has it rebuilt from the wheels up.

Johnny is happiest playing club tennis in comparative anonymity. When Fred decided to go into sailboat racing at the age of 43, it was Grand Prix racing, against world-class competition. In 1987, his boat, *Insatiable,* won the Newport Regatta and represented the United States in the Admiral's Cup Series.

There are similarities, of course, in their unending appetite for work and in their unabashed admiration for their father. Essentially, however, Johnny is his father's son. Fred is his Uncle Bill's. Bill Veeck.

Johnny spent his weekends roaming the woods around the house in Downers Grove, shooting pheasant or fishing. Fred would hustle over to Hinsdale to spend the weekend at Grandmother Veeck's house and play with his friends in Hinsdale.

They both attended the Avery Coonley School.

Mrs. Avery Coonley was the heiress to the Perry Seed Company fortune. An involved woman. A personage. Upon marrying, she had commissioned Frank Lloyd Wright to design their house. The Coonley house in Riverside has become one of the great man's most famous works. When she built the Avery Coonley School as an experiment in progressive education, the architect was her own son.

The inspiriting philosophy behind progressive education is to promote discipline, not as obedience to an authoritative teacher but out of respect for the rights of one's fellow students. And so, while the student did not exactly control his curriculum, he could establish his own interests and priorities to the extent that if he didn't like what was going on in a class he could get up and take a walk in the woods. The only rule was that you could not walk out of the classroom without taking a reading book with you.

The weakness of such an unstructured education is that you do not come out particularly well-schooled in the basic disciplines. And that's what mathematics is, after all. A discipline. The strength is that there are no walls, and limitless horizons.

The strength of the Avery Coonley School was in the international character of its teachers. Fred still remembers two of them vividly.

"I had a third-grade teacher from England. Daphne Dyke was her name. She was an exchange teacher. And she got us very interested in Europe and its whole fascinating history." In the fifth and sixth grades, his teacher was Mrs. Sun, who was not an exchange teacher. She was a U. S. citizen who had been married to a Chinese bank executive. Mrs. Sun's husband was left to turn the bank over to the Communists. They ordered him to divorce his wife, and once they were finished with him they imprisoned him.

Accompanied by her best friend, Mrs. Sun had taken her son and fled.

She had spellbinding stories to tell the children of Midwestern America about moving from place to place, always in hiding while the fighting was raging around them. There were stories about atrocities committed by both sides amidst the turmoil of war.

"When you're a ten-year-old kid and you hear these stories, it makes quite an impression. And we'd have the maps out to place the localities and trace the route of her escape." Mrs. Sun also had a rather imposing friend who would make an annual visit to her classroom. Pearl Buck, author of *The Good Earth*, Nobel Prize winner in Literature. Every year, Pearl Buck would come in to talk to them about China.

To buttress his interest further, the Regnerys, whose children also went to Avery Coonley, would travel through Europe—and so would other parents—and on their return, be asked to come to the school and talk about their trips.

That early in life, he became aware that there was a great big beckoning world out there.

His father saw his interest and encouraged it. "Let's put a map on your closet door," he said, "and we can find out about each country while we're drawing it."

It turned into a two-year project. "He'd come home after work and on weekends, and we would work on this map. I'd have my map out, and I had to read out to him what it said, and we'd find the country on the map, and he'd draw it, and then I'd help paint it. We did the whole world on this series of doors, and of course I slept right across from it. And I was just fascinated by the shapes, the colors, the size, and the relationships. I lived with this map all the time I was growing up, and it's still there."

Like Johnny, he spent his first summer vacation in high school working at the mixing vat in Brookfield at a minimum salary. Unlike Johnny, he didn't like it one bit.

By the next summer, Bill Veeck was running the White Sox, and Fred went to work for him. He worked the concessions, he took attendance, he ran errands. He also helped to clean the park and worked in the p.r. department.

He continued to spend his summers during college working for the White Sox. A great life for a kid. In the spring, he would work at the park on weekends. Once school was out, he was there full time. One of his more delightful assignments as a sometimes worker in the p.r. department was driving Veeck and his fellow raconteur, Dizzy Trout, around on their speaking engagements. And can you think of a more pleasant or rewarding way to learn about people?

At Lake Forest College, his father paid room, board and tuition. For pocket money, Fred washed dishes. His ambition was to join the diplomatic corps, and toward that end he pursued his graduate studies at Georgetown University in Washington, D.C., and Leicester College, in Leicester, England.

In between, he used Molex to pick up spare money and to support himself. He worked in the sample department and the shipping dock. He wielded a brush on anything that needed painting. It was hourly wages, minimally over the minimum wage, and since he could work for as long as he wanted, he would work fifteen hours a day to make as much money as possible to finance his next jaunt.

"Fine," his father would say when he came back to pick up a few more bucks. "We'll find something."

While he was working in the sample department, his father handed him a folder marked: *International File*. Inside was a collection of letters from people who had been inquiring over the years about the possibility of helping Molex sell its products overseas, or even expressed an interest in buying. Senior had been answering them, sporadically, given the time and inclination, and he suggested that Fred might want to help him out. "Maybe," he said, "you'll find it interesting."

Sounded good to Fred. It was only much later that he began to reflect upon what a perfect way that had been to hook him. "Dad recognized it as a great opportunity, and I think he saw an interest I had and a chance to put those together. I think he wanted to have me join the business, but he was very concerned that I do what I wanted to do. And he saw that here was a marvelous fit.

"Somewhere along the line, I just decided, Hey, this was really what I wanted to do, a way to combine my interest in the diplomatic side, in different people and cultures with business."

He also was realistic enough to recognize that he would have a far better chance to do something in a company that his family owned than in an entrance-level position in the diplomatic service. And bright enough to be able to recognize that he was going to require the help of a consultant. Together, he and his father interviewed several prospects before deciding upon a candidate whose letter of application had been sitting in the *International File* along with a couple of others.

"It was at that point," Fred can say, "that it just started to go."

The consultant was Ed Frume, and if Fred thought that his father was a taskmaster he was about to discover what being tasked and mastered was all about. "A very difficult man," Fred says. And yet a man with a considerable background. Edward Frume had been the export manager for Amphenol before he started his own consulting firm. He came with an engineering background, but his main qualification was that he could speak French, German, and Russian, and could handle Japanese well enough to know what was going on.

Ed Frume was about the same age as Senior. "And," Fred says. "A perfectionist to the extreme." He was also something of a nag. "He reviewed every letter I wrote for three or four years and not one of them satisfied him in the first draft. As often as not, we went to five or six revisions before he was ready to let it go out the door." And it was not only Fred's correspondence that Ed Frume assumed jurisdiction over. "We shared the same desk and he made it a practice to critique every phone call, not excluding the personal ones, so that he could instruct me on what should or could have been said." Same thing for all customer visits or meetings with potential representatives."

Ed was so forgetful that Fred took over the task of packing and unpacking for him. And Ed did not believe in travelling light. We're not

HONOR ROLL
15 Years or More at Molex

AGERTON, RUTH
AKASHI, TAKEO
ALBRECHT, JOANNE
ANTONICIC, JOHN
ARNOLD, ALMA
ASAZUMA, KENJI
BABA, SHINICHIRO
BASSLER, MAXWILL
BAUMANIS, BRUNO
BEATRICI, GINO
BENNETT, JOSEPH
BEREK, DENNIS
BLACK, RICHARD
BLAZEK, JOHN
BOYLES, JAMES
BOYLES, LOU
BRINKER, VERNE
BROWN, COLUMBUS
BROWN, MAE
CANADAY, RONALD
CERNY, MARIE
CHMELA, FRANK
CIEPLY, ALICE
CLAYTON, ISAIAH
CONLEY, ANNA
COX, BARRY
CRAGG, ROB
CREED, JANE
CREED, WILLIAM
DAVIS, BETTY
DAVIS, VIOLA
DICKSON, LAWRENCE
DOUGHERTY, JOE
DUKES, ELIZABETH
EWENS, ALEX
FORD, REBECCA
FUGLSANG, RENETTA
FULTON, WILLIE
FUSE, TOSHIO
GAMAGE, ALDEN
GAUS, RAYMOND
GEISER, JAMES
GESCHKE, CLARA
GIERUT, FRED
GIFFORD, EFFIE
GILIBERTO, JANET
GIRON, EDWARD
GLESGE, LORRAINE
GOLTERMANN, RICHARD
GORSKI, JOHN
GRIGNON, GEORGE
GRUHN, WILLIAM
HABINKA, HENRY
HAMMOND, MICHAEL

HAWKS, LAVERGNE
HOESSLER, JOHN
JANZOW, RICHARD
JETER, ARVATER
JOHNSON, ARTHUR
JOHNSON, IGATTIA
JONES, BONNIE
JONES, JAMES
KATSUMURA, KOICHI
KIM, YOUNG
KIRBY, JOHN
KIRBY, PAT
KLUG, RUSSELL
KOUTEK, ILA
KOWALSKI, BETTY
KRAFTHEFER, KERRY
KRAUSE, HANS
KREHBIEL, EDWIN
KREHBIEL, FRED
KREHBIEL, JR., JOHN
KREHBIEL, SR., JOHN
KRUEGER, JANEY
KUBIK, STEPHEN
KUCHARSKI, ANTOINETTE
KUFNER, KENNETH
LARSON, WAYNE
LOCONTI, MICHAEL
LORENZEN, RITA
LUND, GEORGE
LYNCH, FRANK
MACDONALD, IAIN
MCGRATH, WILLIE
MANATTE, MARIE
MARKHAM, JEREMY
MASKOWSKI, MICHAEL
MASTERS, RAYMOND
MERTZ, CLARA
MEYER, FREDERICK
MILLER, DALE
MILLER, LESLIE
NAKANO, HAJIME
NITO, KOICHI
O'CONNOR, SONDRA
OAKES, WAYNE
OGAHARA, ASAKO
OSBORN, IRIS
OSTRUM, CARL
PALTON, LAURA
PATTERSON, PAT
PELLEGRINO, THOMAS
PETERSON, CHARLES
PETRUCCIANI, PETER
POHLMANN, BERT
PRIBISH, ROBERT

PSALTIS, JOHN
PTACK, JAMES
REESE, MARY
RICHARDSON, ESTELLE
ROCHE, JOHN
RUSSELL, BILLY
RUTA, ANNA
RYAN, MICHAEL
RYAN, TIMMY
SAMYN, DANIEL
SCHALLY, EMIL
SCHNEIDER, THOMAS
SEBASTIAN, ROBERT
SENESE, VICTOR
SHARP, WASH
SHARP, WILLIE
SHINNORS, MATT
SHOUFER, MICHAEL
SIEWERT, JULIUS
SLANSKY, FLORENCE
SMITH, ROBERT
SMITH, WALLY
SNEAD, JOSEPH
SNEED, CECIL
STANHIBEL, DENNIS
STANLEY, LOIS
STRASS, CLAUDE
SUGISAKI, KOWASHI
TAKANASHI, MORIAKI
TAKEUCHI, AKIRA
TAYLOR, CHARLES
TAYLOR, DOROTHY
TOMKIEWICZ, THADDEUS
TORRES, RAUL
TRACZYK, STANLEY
TREMBLAY, JOHN
UPLEGGER, LILA
VARGOS, ALFRED
VIECE, PHILLIP
WARD, ODELL
WARREN, ADA
WEBER, PATRICIA
WEST, BERNARD
WIESER, RAYMOND
WILLIAMS, ARDELIA
WILLIAMS, DENNIS
WOEHLER, MARGARET
WONNELL, LAURAMAE
WRIGHT, STEVE
WYNNE, ANNE
ZAN, JERRY
ZEMAN, THOMAS
ZETTEK, JAMES
ZIDEK, MICHAEL

MOLEX INC. SALES HISTORY

Fiscal Year	Molex U.S. Sales	Molex Int'l Sales	Total Molex Sales
1962	1,063,000	—	1,063,000
1963	1,455,000	—	1,455,000
1964	1,807,000	—	1,807,000
1965	2,391,000	—	2,391,000
1966	3,491,000	—	3,491,000
1967	4,304,000	—	4,304,000
1968	6,263,000	54,000	6,317,000
1969	7,727,000	204,000	7,931,000
1970	8,974,000	776,000	9,750,000
1971	10,253,000	954,000	11,207,000
1972	15,138,000	1,935,000	17,073,000
1973	19,489,000	5,888,000	25,377,000
1974	27,048,000	7,526,000	34,574,000
1975	18,576,000	7,701,000	26,277,000
1976	26,107,000	14,705,000	40,812,000
1977	32,189,000	21,549,000	53,738,000
1978	40,482,000	31,337,000	71,819,000
1979	44,677,000	53,438,000	98,115,000
1980	53,699,000	67,824,000	121,523,000
1981	57,514,000	85,517,000	143,031,000
1982	64,258,000	101,594,000	165,852,000
1983	71,901,000	104,075,000	175,976,000
1984	116,735,000	135,487,000	252,222,000
1985	105,881,000	147,333,000	253,214,000
1986	106,628,000	185,285,000	291,913,000
1987	122,345,000	264,414,000	386,759,000
1988	150,000,000 Est.	350,000,000 Est.	500,000,000 Est.

Lucille Pemberthy Krehbiel
pictured with Edwin and
John in front of their
Hinsdale home in 1911

Lucille Pemberthy Krehbiel

John Hammond Krehbiel Sr.

Frederick August Krehbiel

Margaret Ann (Peg) Veeck and
her brother William Louis (Bill)
Veeck, Jr., 1918

John Krehbiel at home in Downers Grove
the year Molex was founded (1938)

Margaret Ann Veeck at her home in
Hinsdale in 1932

John & Peg's Downe
Grove home

On the beach in 1943 or 1944 in Saugatuck, Michigan. John, Fred and John Jr.

Toy gun made of Molex material designed by Edwin Krehbiel

Molex first Brookfield factory

Three generations of Krehbiels. Frederick and his two sons John and Edwin and their children: Frederick August Krehbiel II; John Hammond Krehbiel Jr. and Alan Pemberthy Krehbiel

Christmas 1954. Peg's mother Grace DeForest Veeck, John Jr., John Sr.'s mother Lucille Pemberthy Krehbiel and Edwin's wife Gay Krehbiel

Christmas 1954 continued. Michael Veeck, Fred II, Fred

Molex second Brookfield plant

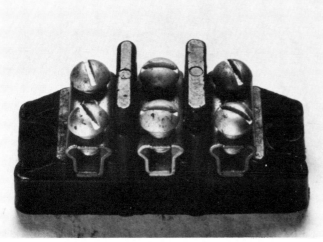

Early Molex Terminal Block designed by John Sr.

Molex first Plug and Receptacle Connector Series designed by John Sr.

Emil and Charlotte Schally.
Emil worked at Molex for 20
years starting in the 1940's.
Charlotte joined Molex in the
60's and retired in the 1970's

Marie Manatte, Molex Treasurer and
major stockholder. Also in the
picture is Pete Petrucciani, Molex
Brookfield Plant Manager

Bob Sebastian and Alex Ewens
celebrating a new order

Isaiah Clayton, John Sr. and John Blazek at John Sr.'s 75th Birthday Party

Molex Dinner for 25-Year and longer-serving employees. Fred, John Jr., Rebecca Ford, Wayne Larson, Art Johnson, Anna Ruts, John Sr. (not pictured is John Blazek)

John Sr. and Dale Miller at
Dale's retirement party

Molex Board of Directors: Louis Platt, Robert Hayes, John Sr., Robert Potter,
Fred, John Jr. (missing from the picture is Edgar Jannotta)

Molex Executive Committee Members: Left to right Tom Lee,
Mitch Primorac, Gorow Tokuyama, John Psaltis

Molex Executive Committee Members: Seated left to right Ron
Schubel, Ray Wieser. Standing left to right Jim Cummings, Ed
Parkinson, Richard Black, Louis Hecht

Molex Executive Committee Members: Standing top row left to right Kerry Krafthefer, Ron Canaday, Tom Schneider. Bottom row left to right Mel Haught, Claude Strass

Molex Executive Committee Members: Front row seat Martin Slark, Werner Fichtner. Back row left to right Hermann Goebharter, Joe King

A gathering of old friends of Peg and John's in Lompoc, California: Left to right Martha & John Flaherty; Nancy & Ed Healy; Peg & John; Ethel & Red Thayer; Mary Frances & Bill Veeck

Summer 1985. Front row: left to right Margaret Ann (Meg) Krehbiel, Peg Krehbiel, Jay Frederick Krehbiel, Kennetha Emig Love. Back row left to right Frederick Love (Pete) Krehbiel, John Hammond (Yaz) Krehbiel III; Kennetha Love Krehbiel; John Jr., John Sr., William Veeck Krehbiel; Kathleen Kirby Krehbiel, Fred

Bob Pribish, J.H.K., Sr., and Ed Healy on the golf course

John Sr. receiving the Electronic Business Executive of Year award (components) for the second consecutive year. Presenting the Award Chat Kelly.

John Sr. and racquet ball
partner Bob Prosek

John Sr. in front of Molex Lisle summer of 1987

John & Peg at home with their dog "Oscar"

talking simply about the usual clothing and toiletries here. "Ed also consulted for three or four other firms, and he always brought along his complete files. In fact, he carried his entire office with him, including a typewriter, office supplies, Dictaphone and at least two cameras.

"In spite of everything," Fred says in pronouncing benediction upon him, "there was much I was able to learn from Ed Frume. He was an incredibly good trainer."

From that other taskmaster, his father, he was being initiated into that same hard school of budgeting that Johnny had graduated from, *summa cum laude*, at Downers Grove.

Fred had not been sent out into the world, like a modern-day Marco Polo, to find his own way. Some basic goals and precepts went with him. Also a budget. Fred would check in with his father for an informal conversation once or twice a week. "He would ask a number of questions on the particular phase of a project that we were engaged in and what course of action I was to take and then make some suggestions."

If it was a question of a choice between two prospective reps, they would go over everything. "We would then list the positives and negatives for each." Often as not, Ed Frume would be asked to pitch in with his views.

"Well," Senior would usually tell him when the drill was over, "you will have to live with these people for many years so you had better make the call."

Not that Fred was under any illusions about what was going on. "He took the time to let me make the decisions but in a way that led me to what he felt was appropriate. It's a style I have tried to adopt, but I don't always have the patience to follow through."

When it came to the budget, the guidance became much firmer. The budget that had been agreed upon for the year had included the consultant's fees and expenses. They were only three months into the fiscal period before it became apparent to Fred how grossly he had underestimated the extent to which he was going to need Frume's advice. "We discussed it in detail, and I received the increase." Six months later, he was back again, and this time Senior clamped down on him. "It was explained to me that a balance had to be maintained between all the needs of the company, and that budgeting was not just an exercise, it was a commitment."

Over the last two months of the fiscal year, he was paying Frume out of his own pocket. And, not unexpectedly, getting back neither tea nor sympathy. Not only would Ed Frume do nothing that he wasn't paid for, he had no compunctions whatsoever about pushing the interpretation of expenses to the limit.

The only thing that can be said for Ed Frume was that he was worth it. He was worth it, in the first instance, because he was able to impart to Fred a vision of the possibilities of the adventure they were embarked upon that went beyond anything Fred himself had conceived of. And he was worth it, even more so, for the restraint he was able to urge upon Fred at the crucial moment of his very first deal.

On December 7, 1967, Mr. Hayashi, president of Matshushita Trading Corp., arrived from Japan with a proposition that sounded straightforward enough. In return for the exclusive rights to sell Molex products in Japan, Matshushita was prepared to give Fred a $50,000 stocking order. Fabulous, thought Fred. Beyond his fondest hope. And right there is where Ed Frume took Fred aside and earned his keep. "You're dying to have this," he said, "because it's your first order. But you're not going to do it, because you're not going to tie yourself up with one company." If he tied himself up exclusively with Matshushita, Frume warned, Sony wouldn't buy from him, Hitachi wouldn't buy from him, Toshiba wouldn't buy from him. His task, therefore, was to negotiate a nonexclusive agreement and still get the order.

It took more than three months to achieve that kind of accommodation, and the order was not for $50,000 but for $25,000. It was his first order, though, and when the fiscal year came to an end, on June 30, 1968, he reported sales of $54,000.

For Molex, the timing could not have been more fortuitous. The conventional route for an American company was to start off in Canada, move on to Europe, and, if everything was working out, take a shot at Japan. There was every reason for Japan to be at the end of the line. Under Japanese law, a foreign company was allowed to operate only by taking on a full Japanese partner. And, anyway, Japan still had the reputation for making cheap, copy-cat products out of the sleaziest kind of plastics.

In actuality, Japan was embarking upon a national policy to move from low quality to high quality products. Within a couple of years, foreigners would be permitted to own their own companies. Before another decade had ended, Japan would be taking over the television, recording, and camera industries, and, shortly thererafter, become the whole enchilada of VCR-land.

And Molex-Japan was going to be right there on the grounds to provide the connectors for those connector-laden products.

Immediately after the contract with Matshushita had been signed, Fred went to Japan accompanied by Senior and Frume to help Matshushita promote its products. By then, they had already laid the groundwork for discussing possible joint agreements with several Japanese firms, including Showa Musen Kogyo (SMK), with whom the first joint venture was eventually consummated.

Three years later, the Japanese government changed its policy, and Molex became one of the first solely owned American companies. Which was perhaps just as well. Strains had developed. Which is usually what happens when you catch your partner adding an extra section to his factory so that he can steal your product. Indignation follows fast apace. Ed Frume, who had a kind of English colonel look and bearing about him anyway, was simply marvelous at indignation. The Japanese partners, having not only stolen but tried to lie about it when they were first approached by Fred, were in such a moral retreat that Fred was eventually able to buy them out for a paltry $250,000. Or, as they used to say in Old Japan somewhere between the *hari* and the *kari,* when you get caught with your face down, kiddo, it's gonna cost you.

Looking back, Fred can see where both the policies that were in place when he arrived and the changes that were made along the way seemed to work to the advantage of Molex.

On a practical level, he didn't have the people to run a factory, much less the budget for maintaining an American enclave in a foreign country.

On a cultural level, the Japanese quite obviously had a better understanding of what was needed to operate within their own country. They understood the intricacies of working with the government; they knew how to appeal to their customers; and, something that has always been of prime importance at Molex, they were able to motivate their employees.

In the beginning, Molex was given a factory and provided office space at the edge of their partner's manufacturing complex. The factory was a Quonset hut in a narrow dirt alley. If you wanted to describe it, rather than categorize it, you'd call it a tin shack.

The office was on the second floor of another tin shack at the end of the alley, and the floor sagged under the weight of the desks and human traffic. Under Japanese law, the company has to provide space for the union's headquarters: The union had the first floor.

To make it worse, the SMK union was a communist-dominated union, and the late sixties was a time of great labor unrest in Japan.

"What happened," Fred says, "was we would be working away, and they'd be down there with their rallies, screaming and yelling. Getting everybody all worked up to go marching off to these rallies and strikes. There were times when it would be impossible to hear what was being said over the phone."

Senior visited them twice before they moved. The first time he came— wouldn't you know—it was on a day when all hell was breaking loose downstairs. For awhile there, it looked as if Senior were going to turn around and go home. But then he saw the humor in having somebody as violently anti-union and anticommunist as himself not only getting involved in a joint venture with a company that had a communist union, but finding himself in a situation where he was actually sharing a building with the union.

The next time Senior came, Fred asked one of the Japanese partners to explain the situation to the union leaders and ask them to stay away while his father was there. So the communist union leader, in the name of Japanese hospitality or something, called off the Revolution for a couple of days.

After they had bought SMK out, Molex moved to a two-story factory that had originally been a warehouse. And which they grew out of so rapidly that it was little more than a holding action. One day they were having lunch across from a bowling alley, which had gone bankrupt. "I think there's our new factory," John Psaltis said.

Everybody sort of looked at each other. Joji Takatsuka, their Japanese G.M., agreed. In fact, Joji could see how the bowling alley could easily be converted into a factory.

They were able, in the end, to buy it for nothing more than the cost of the land, because the owners had expected to have to tear the building down. As it was, Molex had to move in so quickly that the lanes were still there. The employees would set up the pins by hand during lunch time and go bowling. Until finally the iron sheets that were being laid down over the floor to support the molding machines crept down and covered them over.

"Actually," John Psaltis remembers, "Fred had planned to demolish the building and put up a structure more suitable for a factory. But the pace of growth proved to be too rapid, and the old bowling alley was strong enough structurally so that they were able to utilize both floors to accommodate their needs and retain the quite beautiful steel-and-glass exterior."

Richard Black is currently the head of Molex's thriving Automotive Division. For eight years before divisionalization took place, Richard worked for International and Fred Krehbiel. "I don't think I have ever really known anybody with his ability," Black says. In Richard Black's mind, there is little Fred Krehbiel couldn't be if he set his mind to it.

One of the things that Black found particularly impressive in Fred was his ability to deal with people of so many different temperaments.

"To go to Japan and get as big as we are— for our industry—in that country, you have to understand the mentality. The same is true in every country that he goes to." The Italians are very emotional and flamboyant. Fred lets them get it out of their system and seems to know exactly when the time has come to sit them down and lead them in another direction. "When you think of all those different people, with their differing temperaments—the Swiss and the Dutch, and the English and the South Americans—there are so many different ways of growing a business. There are so many different ways of just running a business."

Dealing with people in twenty-five different countries has unquestionably given Fred a chance to exercise the art of diplomacy beyond anything he might have experienced as an undersecretary of state.

That's the good news. The bad news is that gaining a foothold in some of those countries was not so easy as it had been in Japan. Getting started in most countries in Europe, the area he and Senior had originally targeted, was to quote the immortal Bob Pribish—a bitch.

Not withstanding that the first contracts Fred had signed had been in Europe. In the three-month interim between the time of Mr. Hayashi's original offer and the working out of the contract, Fred had signed his first rep contract with Egli, a Swiss firm, and opened up a factory in Shannon, Ireland.

Why Ireland? Because Ireland was close to the European markets, and because Ireland had a Development Program that was making great concessions to attract industry into the country.

But the rep system was only the opening stage.

By following the same conservative philosophy that Senior had followed at home, International was able to hold the risk factor down to a minimum. The formula went like this: Start with sales representatives, build up the sales and warehousing operation, and when sales have reached one million dollars, you lease a small facility of your own and start production.

In Ireland, their original plant was so small that you had to enter through one of those garage-type, pull-up doors. The equipment was whatever Fred had been able to get to them. Pat Kirby can still remember his first day on the job. "We had three Arburg molding machines," he laughs, "and an old obsolete Boy machine." After a couple of weeks, they were told that Lisle was going to send them another Boy. "We said we didn't need it because the first one was such a piece of junk that we couldn't get it to work." Lisle insisted they should have it. "They put it on a train in Chicago and the train crashed. We were all delighted at the news, and we went out and had a few drinks to celebrate."

But Molex Europe was not moving as well as it should.

Fred had gone over with his secretary, Toni Kucharski and John Psaltis in 1975 to bring some order out of the chaos. Toni, who is the sister of Junior's former secretary, LaVergne, had been International's first employee. They began working from a vacated office of a doctor of surgery. "We were seated at counters with our typewriters and telex machines," Toni remembers. "The salesmen worked out of the bathrooms because that's where our files were. The inventory was in the garage."

After awhile, they were able to open an office in Aldershot. In true Molex tradition, it was another converted warehouse. And, also in the Molex tradition, still in the process of being converted. Toni's memories of that do not exactly warm her heart, either. "It was so damp and cold that I had to work with my coat on. And gloves that were cut off at the fingers." It was so cold that they finally decided to get her a heater. "The heater was in the shape of a huge torpedo and it would shoot the hot air right at me. It was the only thing that could keep me warm, that's how cold it was."

Rob Cragg was appointed to take over the UK operation, and new GM's were found for several other of Molex's small struggling European entities. Rob remembers an event during the period which rates right up there with the "Clean Room" caper.

Cragg's caper started when he received a frantic telephone call from one of his salesmen telling him that a major, multinational person was coming into the country to discuss the possibility of using Molex-UK as one of its primary suppliers. "We were not very excited about bringing him to our doctor of surgery office," Cragg recalls, "because we wanted to present a rather more impressive image of our company." So Cragg came up with the wonderful idea of renting a suite of offices in one of the new glass-covered office buildings in downtown London. He fastened the Molex logo on the glass doors, put in the requisite furniture and equipment, and rented a secretary. Then he waited. "On the day he arrived, we brought him to this wonderful multistory building, took him upstairs into this suite of offices, and told him all about this very large, successful company, Molex. He was very impressed."

Rob Cragg was pretty impressed with himself, too. He was still congratulating himself later in the day when he received a phone call from the salesman telling him that their visitor had left his coat in the office and was on his way back to pick it up.

By then, the logo was down, the secretary was gone, and the offices were bare. And sheer panic was setting in.

Fortunately, the salesman had just been having his little joke.

Whatever problems existed in France were solved by the coming of Michel Didier. The French have a certain panache. And Michel Didier is French the way the queen is English.

How French is he? Well, Michel walked into this fancy Paris restaurant with a group of twelve people and was told by the maitre d' that there would be a two-hour wait for a table. "Impossible," says Michel, "I have these people from the United States and England and Germany. These are business people. We have to have a table immediately."

A lot of handwaving goes back and forth, and Michel walks into the restaurant, plucks a tray from a passing waiter, goes over to a table where people are eating, picks up their dishes, and puts them on the tray, and when the tray is sufficiently full, let's it drop on the floor with a crash.

The maitre d' comes running over. "M. Didier, M. Didier, come with me. Come with me." He had, somehow, been able to locate a table for twelve.

That's the French mentality, Richard Black says. "He'd pushed it to the point and he got away with it. If I tried to do it, the gendarme would carry me out."

The quintessential Michel Didier story is rooted in a crucial meeting with Thomson Co., the leading manufacturer of television sets in France. The meeting took place at Thomson headquarters in Paris. Molex already had a small contract with Thomson, but this one was going to be big. Kerry Krafthefer had flown in that morning because Didier had promised to bring in "a specialist" to describe the wonders of Konectkon to the Thomson engineers.

"It was an incredibly important meeting," Fred emphasizes, "because we had just expanded the factory in Ireland, and it was absolutely mandatory that we have this contract."

Ten minutes into Kerry's presentation, the purchasing agent broke in to ask about the price.

"But I'm sorry," Didier said, "we are not a supermarket, we are not selling at discount. If you just want to compare the price of our connector with others, it means nothing." Whereupon Michel jumped up, threw all his papers on the table and told Kerry to pack up because they were leaving.

"What in the world are you doing?" Kerry was asking under his breath. "We've got to have this order."

They started to walk out, and when they got to the door, the purchasing agent, who had come running after them, grabbed Kerry by the arm and pleaded with him to come back. Michel had Kerry by the other arm and was pulling him away. The purchasing agent let go of Kerry's arm and grabbed Michel's. "No, no," he said, "we didn't mean to insult you."

So they went back to the table, and when the Molex contingent left, they had an order that would eventually be worth half-a-million dollars.

When you consider that they walked out of there with a blank contract, they could have filled in almost any price they chose. "Actually," Fred says, "they got a better price than they would have gotten, because the onus was then on us."

Which was exactly what Michel had in mind. He had just wanted to make a point, he explained to Fred. "I felt that I'd get a better price if I sat there and negotiated with them. But I didn't want that. I wanted to create a relationship, not get a price." They'd make it up the next year, he said confidently, and the years that followed. "We have now put the relationship in a way that will be much more advantageous to us than if we had just negotiated nickels and dimes." *Comment c'est vrai;* Thomson has been their best customer ever since.

For the first couple of years, International was looked upon as a kind of backroom operation. As far as anybody could see, the whole division consisted of Fred and a couple of other young people who always seemed to be flying off somewhere. In addition to Fred, there was Toni Kuchanski and John McCabe. In due time, Bert Pohlmann and John Psaltis came aboard, and the group just kept growing and growing.

As for Fred himself, he was heading off into the wide blue yonder so often that the Krehbiels were being referred to as the Father, the Son, and the Holy Ghost.

For the first 14 years, Fred was travelling 60-70 percent of the time. In the process, he was working a fourteen-hour day, six days a week and resting up on Sunday by working less than the regulation 8-hour day.

As the organization continued to grow and prosper, he came to realize that the people on the scene got on quite nicely whether he was there or not. "Actually," Fred says, "things go much better when the decisions are made in the region, close to the customers, rather than in Lisle."

With that in mind, he was able to cut his travel time down to 40-50 percent and his working day to 12 hours. With all that spare time on his hands, he began to take more time for himself over the weekend, allow himself an occasional holiday and take up a few hobbies: Sailing on the *Insatiable*, running in one or two marathons per year and—speaking of a busman's holiday—trekking in Nepal, Kenya and Peru.

In or out of work, no idle time is permitted the Krehbiels.

Gorow Tokuyama, President of Molex Japan, expanded quite considerably on the theme of Fred's management style during an article he wrote in a Harvard Case Study:

"Fred is very talented at managing the multinational operations of Molex. He has given full authority and responsibility to general managers in each country or region. Thanks to this policy we have been able to try to optimize our operations against the unique business environments here in Japan. Fred does not leave the operations alone. We set goals, we follow our progress to these goals. He talks with the managers regularly; he motivates and inspires us but he lets us manage and he has confidence in us. It almost always seems that the general managers want to do what Fred wants to do. I call this control through influencing. However, it is easier said than done. This kind of management style takes a good deal of mutual communications, trust and understanding.

By 1979, the International sales had passed Domestic sales. In 1987, the sales in Japan—Japan alone—exceeded the Domestic sales. And as the Fiftieth Anniversary lifts its golden head, the International Division is accounting for two-thirds of the total business.

Martin Slark and Joe King, who can perhaps best be described as managerial trouble-shooters, attribute a great deal of the success to a strong company culture that is characterized by a pride of accomplishment.

"The success of Molex," says Slark, "has been built on a 'can do' attitude and a family spirit throughout the organization. Despite the worldwide growth of the company, this spirit has continued to strengthen.

There is a total commitment toward improving our results which benefits our customers, the company and ultimately the individual employee."

"For me," King says, "the success has its origins in the early unwavering belief throughout the company that Molex could and would be great, accompanied by the enormous energy which radiates from those who believe in themselves. This belief and energy were contagious and created a will to make things happen.

"In this climate," he adds, "victories were shared and the achievements of each were respected, admired and celebrated by others."

Fred Krehbiel explains it this way: "The International Division has grown because of the work of so many outstanding people. People who believed it was possible for a small company to become a truly global firm. Who shared the vision of people working together successfully around the world.

"People like Joji Takatsukam, who built Molex Japan, and Gorow Tokuyama who is guiding it so wisely today. People like Bert Pohlmann whose drive and energy were so helpful in the early days and who started Molex Singapore, Molex Taiwan and Molex Canada. John Psaltis who gave us outstanding financial controls, something few small companies ever have, and who took on the tough assignments when problems developed in places like Ireland, Japan, the U.K. or Brazil. People like Joe McGrath, who started Molex Ireland, and Pat Kirby who runs it today. Michel Didier, who founded the very successful France Connexion; Vic Senese, who started Molex Italia and went back when problems developed, and who now is wrestling with Zetronic. There is Martin Slark, who started Molex-Nanco and our operations in India and China after very successful assignments in the U.S. and Europe. And J. T. Chung, who founded our fastest growing entity Molex Korea; Denis Rishworth, who built Technor in South Africa; Gunnar Knutsen, who started Molex Sweden and Molex Norway and who is responsible for all of Scandinavia. And then there are the builders: Rob Cragg, who has turned Molex U.K. into our premier sales office; Jim Payne, who built Molex Canada; Klaus Vogt in Germany; Paolo Del Grande in Italy; Frank Tan in Taiwan; Chris Yong in Singapore.

"People like Joe King who after successful assignments in Ireland moved to the U.S. and initiated our worldwide functional coordination in manufacturing, quality, systems and engineering and who is now President of our South East Asian Operations; people like Werner Fichtner who is doing such an outstanding job in turning Europe into a fast-growing, well-focused operation. Hermann Goebharter who after building up Molex Taiwan became Director of S.E. Asia and is now President of the Americas; Mitch Primorac, who is helping us to assure excellence in our worldwide manufacturing and in the coordination of our engineering and quality functions; Tom Lee, who founded our worldwide Human Resource organization. People like Rich Cisek, Richard Black, Ivor Redmonde, Howell Evans, Bane Kesic, and Don Davies who represent a long list of men and women who have worked so successfully in numerous assignments around the world. People like Koichi Katsumara, who has been responsible for so many manufacturing innovations, and Masahiro Enomoto, who has built such an outstanding engineering team in Japan. And, of course, no list could be complete without the name of Toni Kucharski. The list goes on and on. I have only touched the tip of the iceberg. Today in Molex worldwide there are over 5,000 people in 25 countries who share the vision and who are making their own invaluable contributions in helping us to keep moving forward."

THE ROMANCE OF
KONECTKON

*There's no romance in connectors. We're in
the hardware business, kid. If you're looking
for romance try semi-conductors.*

—JOHN H. KREHBIEL, JR.—

KONECTKON is the product that has become Molex's best selling line. By the time its patents—such as they are—run out in 1989 and 1990, it will rank as one of the industry's most successful products.

There is also a dramatically satisfying resolution here that harkens back to the time when the government stole John's design for the antimine detector. He swore at that time that he would never deal with the government again, and he never has. But he did attend a military conference. One time. And that is where the whole romance of KonectKon began.

It happened like this: In his travels around the country making his calls on customers, John was tipped off by friends that the army was gathering a group of connector manufacturers together at Hughes Aircraft in California to talk about a new connector system for printed circuit boards.

And that was where John's instincts told him that he had better be there. Not because he had any interest in a military contract—let alone the money to do the research that military specifications call for—but because the military was such a dominant force in the connector industry that any revolutionary change that came out of such a conference would inevitably be transferred to the commercial sector.

It turned out to be a one-day conference. And just as John expected, the military was asking for a whole new system to replace the Edge connector that was then in use.

The Edge connector system was exactly what it sounded like. The connector was laid over the edge of the PC board where it met the pads coming off the board, to feed the signals in and take the signals out. In other words, the PC board itself constituted one half of the connection. And that was the problem.

The PC board is a plastic made of laminated ephoxi and fiberglass, plus a combination of resins which have been forced into the mix under enormous heat and pressure by a giant press.

As a plastic, you couldn't ask for anything better. As a connector, there were still enough variables in the height and thickness of the boards to make a joke of the military's standards on reliability.

Hence the conference. The army was junking what was essentially a one-part connector that was dependent upon the thickness of the board to complete the connection. What they wanted instead was a traditional metal connector system.

The two engineers who came up with the answer for Molex were Kerry Krafthefer and Bob Sebastian. Although the KonectKon is invariably associated with the name of Kerry Krafthefer these days, the story really starts with Bob Sebastian, one of the remarkable figures in the early history of the little company.

Bob Sebastian came to Molex in 1966 as a trained engineer with all kinds of degrees. He had worked for General Electric back in the pioneer days of television (not too distant in 1966), and had run his own little stamping business.

Physically, he was a big, round, jolly man. He stood perhaps 5'9" and he weighed something in the neighborhood of 280 pounds. He was bald, with a little fringe of hair that made him look like a Friar Tuck assuming that the good Friar always had a big black cigar in his mouth or was chain-smoking cigarettes. The Friar Tuck appellation seems to have been pinned on him by an Alabama distributor who wanted to return some connectors. "Friar Tuck dropped in here last week and sold me this garbage," he told Alex Ewens, "That guy could sell anything to anybody."

Curiously enough, he was a very creative engineer who couldn't sketch worth a damn. (The book on Sebastian was, "For chrissake, keep him away from the boards.") He was an inventor, really. He was a man with a wildly imaginative mind. He could not only understand how things worked from the inside out, he had the ability to shuffle the pieces around in his mind so that they would come out better.

Item: When he was unable to find a camera to take the kind of pictures he envisioned, he went home and made a camera that did.

While he was with Molex he built a prototype television set that incorporated the best feature of each of the major television manufacturers. According to his grandiose scheme, everybody would be putting out the perfect set, and the Molex connectors would, of course, be serving them all.

Would you believe that there were highly paid executives and chief engineers of these companies, good family men all, who were so unappreciative of his efforts as to tell him that they didn't need a connector salesman to design their television sets for them, and that maybe they didn't need one particular connector salesman at all?

His wife called him a genius. Probably he was. He was also, probably, eating himself into the grave. Peg and John would go over to the Sebastians' house a couple of times a year for dinner, and the food would never stop coming. "And then they'd sit by the television and eat potato chips and junk food." John did everything he could think of to try to get him to lose weight, even betting him $1,000 that he couldn't lose thirty pounds in a month. Mrs. Sebastian pretty much told him to butt out. "We eat the kind of food we like," she told him evenly. "Don't you try to tell him how to conduct himself."

They retired to Florida, where, sadly enough, they both died of heart attacks. He went about six months after she did, and since they had no children and, apparently, no relatives, his body wasn't discovered for something like four days.

The part Bob Sebastian played in the growth of Molex, say all three Krehbiels, cannot be overestimated.

"He was the guy I credit with getting us into the electronic business as opposed to the electrical business," Senior says. "With his background in television, he steered us away from the heavy appliance machines, which required a lot of current, and into television, which requires very little." Different technologies entirely.

He had his own plane, and he loved to fly. With his ability to get along with people and his capacity for envisioning what a product should look like, he spent most of his time out with the customers discussing their problems with them. He would then come back to the Molex engineers with the ideas which they were able to work into products.

Sebastian was the original mind behind what became the KK. He had already devised a system, called Inconect, which was the first modular interconnecting system to connect and disconnect the PB board without having to solder the boards together. In the Inconect system, you soldered one part of the connection to one board, and the other part to the other board, and you were able to connect and disconnect them with ease. Up to then, the boards had been soldered together, and to fix anything became such a bother of unsoldering, resoldering, and hoping that you hadn't burnt anything, that it almost wasn't worth the effort.

Kerry Krafthefer was far more typical of the Molex engineer. Young, bright and ambitious, and temperamentally directed toward a small, growing company. His previous jobs had been with the Atomic Energy Commission, the computer department of Argonne National Laboratory; Nuclear Chicago, which was high-tech instrumentation; and Strombecker Tootsie Toys, where he designed stock racing cars. The Tootsie Toy experience was what Senior had pounced upon in the job interview. Cheap electromagnetic gadgets. Little things made of plastic and metal. Mass production, and if you didn't meet the Christmas deadline you were out of business. Just perfect for Molex, he had chortled. "He loved it," Krafthefer says.

A few months before being teamed up with Sebastian, Kerry solved a problem in a way that brought him rather forcefully to Junior's attention as a young man to watch. The 1151 range switch. If you wanted to plug an appliance into the range, there was an outlet to plug it into. A very successful product. Canadian Standards, the Canadian version of UL, had come up with a ruling that in order to be absolutely certain that the plug didn't fall out and land on the burner, the receptacle had to be able to withstand a 1-pound weight pull. Another engineer had unaccountably pulled a complete blank on it, and after six frustrating months, Junior had decided to give this guy Krafthefer a whack at it.

Half an hour later, Kerry came strolling back into Junior's office, handed him a spring, and said, "It works."

He had taken the spring the other engineer had been struggling with, and bent it under one more time with a pair of pliers to form a coil. A very simple way of delivering the requisite amount of force within a narrow range.

Bob Sebastian was working with three different customers when he and Kerry were put together. An organ manufacturer, a TV manufacturer, and an appliance company. Three companies with three distinct problems. The KK, which was the next modular connector generation growing out of Inconect, solved them all.

Kerry took a .025 pin, which is nothing but a square pin that you buy in wire lengths, cut it off in different lengths, and stuck them into a printed circuit board. That was his hard-wired part.

For the female half of the connector, he took a simple spring and added another spring to it on the lower leg. That effectively gave him a double spring, a spring that would spring in two different directions. It was a double spring, double cantilever. The flexibility was enormous.

To make it even more flexible, the springs were set within a nylon housing, designed so there was a little opening, and in that opening he could insert any one of four very thin blades, of minimally varying thicknesses. These blades could be used to direct the pressure and act as a mating device at the same time.

"It was Bob Sebastian," Kerry says, "who saw immediately that it was a system that could be applied to uses other than the three it had been designed for." You could use it as a card reader, you could make the contact a metal post, you could make it a printed circuit board. You could do all those things because the spring was such a good mechanical device. That's always the first test of electrical contact, Kerry states emphatically. "Mechanically, is it good?"

You could use a round wire to plug into it instead of a square wire. Square posts, round posts, four very skinny flat blades, they could all plug into the system. "That's really what the system does," Kerry says. "You plug a lot of things into it and it works."

Because it's called KK, which are Kerry's initials, there is a general belief that it was named after him. "It wasn't really," Kerry says. "But if anybody wants to think so, it's OK with me."

There were several patents given on the system, two of them in Kerry's name. The most important ones protected the configuration of the contact, and how the contact was made to work.

And if that only meant that their competition was going to have to work to find a way to get around them, that would be enough to give the KK a running start.

The design is a perfect example of what Senior had been talking about all his life. "It is a simple, totally functional design," he points out. "The cheapest made pin you can find, just pin stuck into a printed board. And the spring is made out of simple brass. That's what did it. We brought the price down steeply from the way they were making the Edge connectors."

Simplify the design, and maximize the characteristics of the materials you are working with. That's the Molex philosophy. The engineer isn't really doing his job, as far as Senior is concerned, unless he gets the maximum use out of the least expensive material.

Brass springs, nylon housing, and tin-coated brass contacts. You can't travel any cheaper than that.

The cost of the material is only one of the factors that goes into the pricing of the product, though, and hardly the most significant one these days. There is also the cost of the production.

You have the tool-and-die operation.

You have the stamping operation.

You have the molding operation.

You have the assembly operation.

And most important of all, you have the right people in place to run those operations—those graduates of the factories, job shops and night schools, those working men of practical knowledge whom John has always been so fond of.

Although Molex would just as soon keep this to itself, it is now one of the leading stamping companies in the world.

The stamping operation grew with the wonderful Bruderer machine. Senior had read about the high-speed Bruderer stamping machine in a small trade publication, had asked Ray Wieser and his Operations boys to check it out, and when Wieser's figures showed that the Bruderer would increase production by a factor of something like ten, Senior ordered two of them. Given his bank account he really couldn't afford them. Given Wieser's calculations he knew that he couldn't afford to be without them.

The Bruderer was the best stamping machine in the world, and Molex became one of the first companies in the United States to use them.

But at Molex, it always begins and ends with the people. Fred Gierut, the die designer, had gone to work as a junior tool and die designer out of high school. Tool and die making had remained such a passion with him that he would work full time on his regular job and then prowl the city for a chance to moonlight in order to learn something new. He had come to Molex because the company he worked for, Cinch (a division of TRW), had moved out to the suburbs. When the little company offered him more money than the big company had been paying him, he took the job, on what he secretly expected to be a temporary basis, and discovered that he had found the company he had been looking for all his life. "I'm like a mushroom," Gierut likes to say. "Keep me in the dark and throw horseshit in at me and I'll grow you more mushrooms. But don't bother me with all the rest of the stuff."

To Senior, he is nothing less than the smartest die designer he has ever seen.

Fred Gierut was going to get a chance to prove it.

To begin the manufacturing process of the KK, you take a straight wire and put a pyramid tip on it so that you can stick it in the board. Toward that end, Gierut had developed a die—utilizing the conventional system of cams—to hit the top and bottom and trim the side. For the life of him, he couldn't get a decent-looking pyramid out of it. Couldn't get the cuts to match worth a damn.

Unable to get the job done the routine way, he found a better way. He developed a *floating forming pad* that was able to do the whole job with one hit. Hit the top and bottom and trim the side at the same time.

Off that one die, they were able to save 40 percent of the material on the brass strip, and to utilize the speed of the Bruderer to its upper limits. Fred Gierut's 2478 die. It has been in use all over the world now for seventeen years. And it has stamped out pyramid tips by the billions.

As sorely as Senior was tempted to patent the 2478 die, he finally decided not to. In making that decision, he was also establishing as a matter of flat policy that Molex was never going to patent any equipment that would show the competition exactly how they did it.

On the molding part of the operation they found something even better than a patent. It's known in common parlance as a booby-trap.

Engineering had produced the KonectKon. Stamping was sitting there with the Bruderers. The tool and die shop came through with the floating forming pad. But the great acquisition, the "secret weapon" that gave Molex the production capability to handle the KK in all its myraid forms, came out of the molding shop, by way of Switzerland.

From Europe, Molex had received an order to make a series of products which was, in reality, the same product with twenty variations, and Molex International could not afford to tool them all in the traditional way, which would be to make twenty molds. Joel Taylor, the manager of the European division at that time, told Fred about a little Swiss inventor he had come across at a trade show or somewhere who had a concept that would do exactly what was required; that is, turn out multiple parts from one mold. The Expandable Mold, he called it.

The next thing anybody knew they were on a plane to Switzerland. They found Henri Latour in a little studio above a little store on a little street in Geneva. He was a little bald fellow with a little sculptured beard. There was only one drawing board in the studio, and only one drawing on the board.

And yet they found Latour's concept, as he explained it to them, to be positively brilliant. A series of cast-steel cores that could be stacked together in different ways to produce almost every conceivable kind of injection molding.

A concept was all he had to offer, however. Latour had never even tried to build a prototype because he had never been able to find anybody with enough faith to finance him.

Henry Latour had just found one.

Fred Krehbiel was not only going to put up money for the prototype, he also had the line of products that he wanted Latour to turn out. In return, Latour had to promise not to discuss his concept with any other connector manufacturer for a specified period of time.

As it happened, Fred was in the States when he was alerted by one of the Molex engineers who had been sent over to Switzerland that the first test-run was nearing.

In short order, the engineer called again. His first words were, "I've got some bad news . . ."

The bad news was that they had turned the machine on, and everything had gone *Keee-ruuunch*. Not only hadn't the parts been ejected, but the interior workings of the mold were a mess.

It could not be said of John Krehbiel, Sr., that he was terribly surprised. How many times had he seen it happen over the years? Hell, how many times had he come right out and said it. "There goes another one who has a great concept, but doesn't have the practical experience to make it work."

Senior agreed to send a man of practical experience, John Grasso, over there to see what could be done.

There were two things that commended John Grasso to him:

• He had taken his apprenticeship at DeHavilland Aircraft in England and worked in the aerocraft industries around Detroit and Los Angeles. That was the kind of solid shop experience John liked.
• He was the only person in the company who had any molding experience.

Grasso had come to Molex, in a manner of speaking, on the wings of a hurricane.

When the big earthquake of 1971 hit Los Angeles, taking the overpass across from their house with it, Mrs. Grasso put her little daughter in the family car and headed east, after telling her husband to sell the house and pile whatever furniture he wanted to keep into a truck and join them. She landed in Chicago. He had been recommended to Senior, shortly after his arrival, as a good tool and die man who had done some mold designing.

The mold designing was what did it. Grasso was hired to activate the nylon molding operation that had been on the planning board from the time of the Clean Room. He had just begun to design the tools for the implementation of that operation when he was sent to Switzerland to see what he could do with Henri Latour's machine.

He was almost able to get the thing working. Almost, but not quite. Still, the concept itself seemed eminently workable to him, so he asked for permission to crate it up and ship it back to Downers Grove in order to work on it.

The main feature of Latour's machine, aside from the stacked cores, was a positive retraction mechanism, otherwise known as a synchronized positive knockout bar. *Positive* knockout meant that when the machine opened, the bar was activated *positively* to force whatever was in the mold out. The great defect uncovered during all these tests was that it didn't always do so. The Molex parts were small and intricate and sometimes they would tilt or roll and get caught up in the machine, and when that happened all kinds of damage was wrought upon the delicate mechanism by the retracting bar.

Over a period of time, Grasso designed a method of multiple sequential knockouts, which he was able to synchronize to the opening of the machine by tying the bar into the main circuit. Instead of trying to eject the parts in one stroke, the multiple bar was designed to give the mold four whacks and a shake. The machine opened, the knockout system went bang-bang; bang-bang, shake-shake-shake, and any part that hadn't been *positively* knocked out would be *positively* dumped out.

Because Senior had been beefing up his molding department, anyway, there were six workhorse Arborg machines on line when KonectKon hit. From there, the growth was so rapid, that soon there were forty-three molding machines at the new facility in Lisle.

What Molex did not have as yet was any capability whatsoever for building its own molds. They had to have the parts built in the machine shops on the Northside of Chicago, which is not the recommended way to keep a secret.

So what they did was to send out Latour's original drawings, and then recapitulate the whole debugging and synchronization process on each new tool as it came back. Grasso and his little crew knew how to do it, because they had already done it. Nobody else had a clue. "The synchronization was our secret," Slavicek says, "along with the fact that if you didn't synchronize it, you smashed all that delicate tool work to nothing." Who knew better that there was nothing like smashing up a few of those delicate molds—at a cost that could run anywhere from a few thousand to the whole $40,000 investment—to leave you with that awful feeling in the pit of your stomach.

And that's exactly what happened. The feedback from the industry for a remarkable length of time was that the damn tool that Molex was supposed to be using wasn't worth a damn. "You turn it on and it smashes itself up."

Eventually, the competition was going to catch on, of course. Nothing lasts forever. Still, Molex had the field to itself, as far as the Swiss mold was concerned, for a good four to five years.

The KK and the Swiss Mold went together like . . . well, like a pin and a socket. Or a pistol and a bullet. With the KK, Molex was able to offer a product in many circuit sizes, with many variations. Without the Swiss Mold they'd have had to tool each component part individually.

Senior describes what the Swiss Mold did for them this way. "By having a mold that was modular, we were able to shape each mold. Depending on how many steel pieces you put in, you could shape it to several combinations. Because of the Swiss Mold, you didn't have to tool the entire product line. You just had to tool one master mold." Don Slavicek put it this way: "We were able to turn that tool around and make a ten-circuit part with a mounting or without a mounting, with a locking ramp or without a locking ramp. The turnaround was so fast that a customer would call up and a week later he would have the part in his hands. That tool gave us an edge in nylon-molded, inlined connectors, which was what our KonectKon line was."

They worked night and day and still they never caught up. Slavicek was working seventy hours a week and coming back at 3:00 in the morning to check out the third shift. "At one time, we ran forty-seven consecutive days, around the clock, seven days a week. Orders were pouring in that fast."

There were nights when he'd catch people as they were punching out and tell them he needed more time from them. "Nobody ever declined. As hard as we were working, it was fun. We knew we were winning. We knew we were part of it. We knew we would share in it. Don't ask me how they do it, but the Krehbiels have a way of making hard work seem like fun. Even at Brookfield. You'd walk in, Junior and his secretary, LaVergne, would be screaming at each other, and it was like the place was hot-wired."

TALES OUT OF MOLEX

We felt that there was nothing we couldn't do, and the best thing was when you got instant gratification. I mean, RIGHT NOW. Here's a guy that's calling and saying, I'm in trouble, and fifteen minutes later, you rip open the shirt to show the big "S" on your chest and say, "Well, I bailed you out. You can put your people back to work."

—BOB PRIBISH—

L AVERGNE was an outstanding secretary. John expected miracles, and LaVergne would usually pull them off. There was the time, still spoken of in hushed and reverent tones when Johnny wanted her to get ahold of Alex Ewens, the Quality Control man (about whom more will be heard of in a moment.) All he knew was that Alex was in Cleveland with Jim Geiser. He didn't give a blankety-blank how she did it, he wanted Alex on the other end of the phone and he wanted him there quick.

Switch the scene to the Sheraton hotel in downtown Cleveland. Alex Ewens and Jim Geiser are seated at the huge circular bar. There are perhaps 200 people milling around the room. The *maitre d'* comes up to him and asks, "Are you Alex Ewens?" There was a phone call for him.

Johnny Krehbiel was on the line. "How in the hell did you ever find me?" Alex gasped. "I didn't know I was going to be here myself an hour ago."

Easy. LaVergne had dialed the operator in Cleveland and, knowing Ewens, asked her what the action place was in town. She had then told the *maitre d'* that if he looked down the bar, he would see a very skinny man wearing a pair of rimless glasses. Next to him in all probability would be a plumpish, balding guy and the chances were that they would be laughing.

Johnny can be difficult to work for because he is a perfectionist. He didn't like a dress she was wearing one day. "Never wear that again," he ordered. She never did.

In 1975, she got married and moved to Arizona. The day after LaVergne told him she would be leaving, Johnny had to stay home. He was physically ill. She was there, though, long enough to see him through the first wild years of KonectKon.

"The KonectKon hit and everything went crazy," Bob Pribish recalls. "It took an entirely new approach to the problem of interconnection systems between printed circuit boards. There was nothing like it." From the primitive Edge board with wires hanging all over the place, you had this neat multicircuit compact package that could be designed to plug into your product and whip the current in any direction that was wanted.

Bob Pribish and Iain MacDonald, the two interlopers from the Day of the Clean Room, were there to regulate the traffic.

"It was like the invention of pneumatic tires," says Bob Pribish, who is a car nut. "Once the pneumatic tire came out there was never going to be anything else. It was that big."

Pribish had customers sleeping at his house. "They flew in to get parts. Because when this took off, it was a real money saver, and everybody wanted to get it into their product as fast as they could, and we couldn't get to everybody who wanted it."

They couldn't build the tools fast enough, of course. "We had probably two pieces of equipment that built twenty different products. And the changeover time on those two pieces of equipment—the time it took to change from one product to another—was four to eight hours."

Everybody in the world wanted that product. Junior didn't turn down any piece of business. "We'll find a way to make it work," he would say.

"I don't know how we did it, even today," Pribish says, "but we did. I don't know why we didn't get sued."

They set up a War Room upstairs. Nailed pieces of cardboard on the wall with the names of the customers under each of the products. And they'd juggle them. The guy who yelled the loudest had the best chance of being moved to the head of the line.

It didn't help any that two of their very best customers expected to be taken care of on short notice. "I don't care if I gave you no lead time," they'd say. "We're expecting delivery in two weeks." They had the weight. And they were taken care of.

By any normal standard of productivity, piling that amount of down time on an operation that was always trying to catch up is incredibly inefficient. Even with a four-hour changeover time, you'd be losing half a shift. Yet somehow, they made it work.

They made it work by wanting to make it work. And by spending twenty hours a day in the plant.

Expeditors are fellows who are hired to ride herd over a vendor like Molex to make sure the customer gets his parts on time.

A guy named Mike Espary came in one afternoon and introduced himself to Pribish. A little round-faced, rather elderly gentleman. Kind of shy. In a little squeaky voice, he said, "I've got to have my parts."

"Well, Mike," Pribish said, going into the old soft shoe, "Thanks for visiting. And we'll get busy on it right away."

No, Mike said, in his little Elmer Fudd voice. He was just going to sit there in the office. "My boss told me to go to Molex and not leave until I got my parts."

Prib pulled up a chair for him and offered to get him a cup of coffee. "No, I'll just sit here." No, he didn't want a newspaper. No, he didn't want a magazine. Nor a book. Nothing. He just sat there beside the desk, his head bowed a little bit, his hands in his lap. Utterly reasonable, totally resigned, studiously inoffensive.

And little by little, slowly, slowly, he began to seep into Pribish's bones.

"Mike," Prib said after a couple of hours had passed, "I'll get the parts for you. You can go on home. I promise you I'll ship them."

The sad little upturned eyes: "No. I can't come back until I have the parts with me."

Another hour and Prib jumped up and went running out to the factory to ask them to please get the guy his parts. "Because he's camped in my office, and he's not allowed to go home to eastern Illinois until he gets his parts."

It took less than three hours to send him on his way. "We stopped everything. We changed over a unit. We started building his parts." Pribish gave them to him personally.

"Thank you very much for getting my parts," the little man said, in his little squeaky voice. A perfect gentleman to the end.

"He was the single most effective expediter I ever ran across in my life," Bob Pribish reports. "I will never forget Mike Espary."

In many instances, it was more personal relations than Customer Relations.

Pribish or MacDonald or whoever was around would jump into a car at 2:00 in the morning and drive two hours to meet some customer who had driven two hours the other way so he could deliver a part to him. There was the classic case, in the days before Federal Express took all the romance out of customer service, where they charted a Lear jet for $2,000 to deliver a $3 part to a customer whose factory was down.

They had it down to a science, Iain and Pribish agree. Nothing had ever been written down or said, but everybody knew what they were supposed to do to make the thing work. "It was like a crack green beret team operation," Pribish says. "A hundred-pound guy would pull three hundred pounds."

Pribish knew to call Iain at 3:00 in the morning. Iain knew to get an inspector down to the plant. Nellie Welsh, the tough little old lady inspector, would be at Enzo's bar in Brookfield. Pribish would be rousing

Karl Ostrum, Jr., the shipping guy, at his favorite bar in Hinsdale. Or the other shipping foreman, Larry Dickson.

Pribish: Karl knew that his job was to go with it. He would give me a little smoke when I'd call to pull them out of the bar. "Holy hell, you again? It seems like all I got to do is sit down . . ." But these guys knew they were supposed to give me that, and I knew I was supposed to know they were supposed to.

Karl Ostrum, Jr.: My favorite story. He got me on opening day of the Bears season. He got me at the tavern. He said, "Here's my credit card number, here's my phone credit card number. I've got a plane coming from Ireland that's going to land at Kennedy Airport, then I've got to get the shipment down to South Carolina. Do it!" I'm in a bar, dialing all of a Sunday afternoon trying to find this air freight forwarder that could do it for me. That was happening all the time and not always at a bar. Sometimes at home. Got to get these parts to Indiana; Greenville, Tennessee; Minneapolis. Get in the company van and go. I did that a hundred times. I've seen more of the country in the company van than I have on my vacations. It was a lot of fun. I looked forward to those trips. I guess they always said, Call Karl. He'd be happy to.

And then there were the rented trucks during the Nationwide Teamster's strike (Molex does not have a union. Never has. But it was affected by the Nationwide strike). Karl volunteered for that one. Molex was running out of brass, and they had a delivery to make in Michigan the next day. So Junior held one of his "knocking heads" conferences. "I don't care what you do, you get that goddam material up here." They had to have the brass to run those presses, and they had to get the product out to the customer. "Whatever you have to do, whatever the cost." That old familiar cry. He wanted that material there by five o'clock and he wanted the shipment going out that same night.

There'd be no problem, Jerry McElligott pointed out, if they could get the material from outside the jurisdiction of the Chicago Teamsters. And that was when Jim Geiser came up with the idea of renting a truck and driving it to Alton Brass in East Alton, Illinois. It was only with the enthusiastic response that greeted the suggestion that he realized what he was saying. The papers were filled with stories about trucks being shot at from bridges. And bricks being thrown through the windows.

McElligott drove. The other volunteers from the shipping dock were Dick Gotterman and George Musil, who were all big guys, too. And also Jim Geiser. Because it had been his idea, Jim Geiser somehow felt that it was incumbent upon him to go along. He did not feel that it was incumbent upon him to tell his wife about it. She had caught him leaving the house with a suitcase, and he had told her he had an early appointment in California.

"Just don't get killed," John Krehbiel, Sr., advised them, as they were pulling away from the front of the factory. You know what they say about John. You can always count upon him for that good sound, common-sense advice.

Both trips proved to be reasonably uneventful. There was a shipper dispatch driver at their own dock who let them see his .38 magnum and made a lot of threats about what was going to happen to the first guy who boarded the truck. "He was full of baloney," Ostrum says, "and we knew he was full of baloney. But he was pretty loud about it." And it required a police escort to get them through the gate at Alton.

The Molex spirit, the winning atmosphere, was every bit as powerful with the hourly workers, the guys on the floor. Karl Ostrum, Jr., remembers how gleefully the guys down at the loading dock celebrated the first $2 million month.

"Pete Petrucciani had the final audit framed and hung in his office, and we all went to Keg and Beef and had dinner. We had a guy who weighed 349 pounds and they had a hamburger called the Tummybuster, and he had two of these and then was trying to take the french fries and onions off other guys' plates. We used to have such fun. We started trying to make more every month, and every time we went a little higher we'd get all the guys together, the whole shipping crew, and to go the Keg and Beef and have a little feast. We really felt we were in with something."

Ray Goss and Bill Samach ran the maintenance department. Karl bought his son his first bicycle and couldn't put it together. He walked into the pin room, where they were installing some pipe, and asked whether they could help him put the thing together.

Bill Samach was standing on the runway. "Karl," he shouted down, "we're running this pipe here, and you can see how it comes down into the press. Air goes through the pipe and makes the press go up and down and it makes parts so that we can sell them to make money so that we get paid every week." He said, "But to hell with that, let's go put the bicycle together for Karl's kid." Samach jumped down, everybody descended upon the bicycle, and they had it together in a matter of minutes.

"It was like that then," Karl says. "It was all family. We played together. We drank together, we bowled together. And everything got done, and everybody was always looking for more."

They had one guy in the storeroom who was sixty-six years old and dying of cancer. He was climbing up to the top storage boxes to get parts like everybody else. That was what he wanted to do, and nobody was going to stop him.

The Keg and Beef was the official meeting place. John Sr. would very frequently have lunch there, and there would always be five or six of his employees at the table with him.

When he was prepared to leave, John would add up the tab and divide it by the number of people at the table. "That's $4.36," he might say. "Here's my part of it." Tip included.

Everybody would shift around and reach into his pocket. "OK, John, See you back at the plant." Half the time, everybody would plunk down their allotted share. The rest of the time somebody would pocket the money as soon as John was out the door and sign it off on Molex.

Same thing would happen after work. There was something about the night shift that made it easier to get into fights. Especially since Jerry McElligott, the plant manager, was an easy man to get into a fight with. The Quality Control people would shut down one of McElligott's machines, and McElligott would go crazy. McElligott was a 6'4", red-headed, ruddy-faced Irishman who had been a chief petty officer in the Navy and had the foghorn voice to prove it.

"We would have worked all through the night," Iain recalls, "and sometimes we would literally get into fights over Molex." Square off and throw a couple. "Then we'd go over to the Keg and Beef and have a beer and a hamburger." Before they knew it, there would be a dozen people there, and it had got to be 11 o'clock at night, and it was time to go back to work, and there was a hell of a bill to pay. And now the fighting would be over who was going to pick up the tab. "And on a lot of occasions," to quote an unimpeachable source. "Molex picked up the tab."

The day of reckoning came—after a fashion—when Senior went through the accounts during a particularly slow period and discovered that he had a $4000 tab at the Keg and Beef. As soon as they had scraped him off the ceiling, he whipped off a written order, attention every-body, that nobody was to sign a tab at the Keg and Beef from that day forward.

The Keg and Beef didn't exactly suffer a mortal blow. The tool guys would still leave the factory in the middle of the afternoon and say they were going over to the Tool & Die Works for a while. Actually, they'd be going over to Keg and Beef for a hamburger and a beer.

When one of the brothers who owned the place opened up another

restaurant over on Ogden Ave., that's what he called it. The Tool & Die
Works. "I did that," he told the guys from Molex. "So you won't have to
lie any more."

The one thing that is certain, in an uncertain world, is that when
anyone mentions the name of Alex Ewens, he will pause for one reflective
moment and smile.

Alex was a Scotsman and he had a rich Scottish brogue. He was so
skinny (6 ft., 135 lbs.) that it didn't seem possible, and he wore rimless
glasses that accentuated the sharp, bony length of his features.

He would always address Junior as "son" or "young Krehbiel," and
how are you going to yell at somebody who has just called you that?

When Junior went to the hospital for one of those operations on his
knee, Alex sent him a picture of himself sitting in Junior's office with a
cigar in his mouth and his feet up on the desk. Underneath was the
caption: "Rest well, John, things are in good hands."

He was a free spirit. He was an imp. Alex came out of a very specific
era in Molex history. Everybody agrees about that. He replaced a guy
named Erv Nottke, who was so serious and conscientious, and so uneasy
when it came to delegating authority, that he could no longer cope. Alex
didn't take his job too seriously because he didn't take anything seriously.
As a sailor in the Royal Navy during World War II, he'd had two ships shot
out from under him, and after a harrowing week on a raft he promised
himself that if he ever got back on land he would never let anything bother
him again. He kept that promise.

Nobody is quicker than the young Krehbiel to admit that while it would
be impossible for Alex Ewens to survive in Molex's business environment
today, he was the perfect man for the job at that time. "He came out of
another era of American industry."

There is a word in the American vernacular that sums up Alex Ewens'
special talent perfectly. The word is "bullshitter."

When a customer was really upset and asking for his money back, Alex
would get the call. "He would get people to do things you and I wouldn't
have the courage even to ask," Junior says. "He would do it with a totally
straight face. He'd get the job done and ride into the sunset. And the next
time you saw them, they'd say, 'What happened to that guy with the funny
brogue? What's the guy doing, is he still around your place?' "

Before Alex would go out on one of those errands of mercy, Bruno
Baumanis, who was always very conscientious, would try to give him a

full briefing. Halfway through, Alex would cut him off. "That's all I need," he'd say. "I'll go and give them the old soft shoe."

Whatever else Alex Ewens may ever accomplish in this world, he will always be identified with the word NED.

In the early days of KK, before the moisture content of the nylon being used for the housing had been settled upon, the nylon would occasionally become so stiff that it would scrape the plating off the pins as they were being inserted.

The first indication that they had a problem came when Magnavox discovered that it had a whole warehouse full of terminals that were beginning to turn black. Magnavox was demanding a full refund, amounting to $50,000. Off to Knoxville went Alex Ewens and Ed Healy.

Alex took one look, and said, "You've got a case of what they call NED."

"I've got NED?" Clearly, they had never heard of it. Neither had Alex until he heard the word coming out of his mouth.

"Yeah, NED," said Alex, as if he couldn't really believe they didn't know about it. "Normal Environmental Discoloration." And he was off on a long discourse (indistinguishable from a flight of fancy) on the gas fumes that were pouring out from cars and factories, and the rising levels of environmental pollution which had reached figures of such proportions that the statistics became outdated almost before they could be released.

As a result of this pervasive pollution, he informed them, anything that was plated and exposed to the air in a stagnant and unfiltered environment would undergo this slow discoloration.

"I've got THAT?" the Magnavox guy yelped. Geez, was there anything that could be done about it?

Well, didn't he understand what Alex had been telling him? "You have it in the WAREHOUSE." What did he expect? Geez, they had to air condition the place. "Get the blowers blowing up there." He had a whole catalogue of remedial actions that could be taken.

That was Alex Ewens' forte. When he'd walk in, Molex had a problem. When he'd walk out, the other guy had the problem.

"Clickers" came out of the same barn. These were on crimped terminals when his customer reported that he was having intermittencies in his finished product line.

Alex went up and had a big meeting with some unhappy engineers who wanted to know what Molex intended to do about it. They had some samples for him to examine. Alex took one, held it to his ear, and tugged at the attached little wire. "It's clickers," he announced.

"What do you mean, clickers?"

"You have *clickers*," he said. "Here, hold it to your ear."

It would seem natural enough that if you have a solid wire and you don't get a real good crimp, the wire might very well be loose enough so that it would click back and forth. And yet, he would have all these degreed engineers and physicists pulling at the wire, nodding wisely, and repeating, "Clickers . . ."

They weren't doing a very good job in crimping, he would tell them in a tone of mild reproof. That was their problem. The good news was that if they set their machines up properly, they should be able to resolve it, and if they wanted help with the tooling, Molex could certainly be counted on. The old Ewens soft-shoe. When he came in, he was facing people who were demanding a substantial refund. When he left, they were expressing their gratitude.

And, always, there was a margin of logic that allowed him to get away with it.

His fights with Jerry McElligott were epic. Alex was so skinny and McElligott was so big that it was no match. By which we mean that Alex would threaten to perform all manner of atrocities upon essential components of Jerry's body, and what the hell could poor McElligott do about it? Alex would go out to the floor and tell the operator to shut the press down, then he'd hang around until McElligott came charging out, and they'd tear at each other for an hour. Or, contrariwise, he'd shut a machine down and disappear. And Jerry would go crazy trying to find him.

"What Alex would do," McElligott says, "would be to shut a machine down on me and leave town." There was once, though, when the old chief got him. "I was sent to a mill just outside of Boston for some kind of conference, and when I walked in, Alex was sitting there. I jumped all over him, I murdered him. Those people at the mill there didn't know what the hell was going on."

Molex does not operate that way today, Junior emphasizes. Alex's secret was that he never allowed facts to confuse the issue. He would react strictly on the basis of gut feeling. "The whole business of quality has evolved in quantum leaps since then," Junior explains. "Quality Control has become a very precise science conducted by highly professional technical people." The method used today is Statistical Process Control

(SPC), in which the operator has the responsibility of keeping score by placing a dot on a chart after each operation.

In Alex's day, Quality Control and customer service went hand in hand. Alex's other great talent—and a very useful one at a time when selling was done on a considerably more personal level—was the ability to hold his liquor.

Those were the days which Iain and Pribish recall with mixed feelings. "We used to go down to Knoxville, Tennessee, where Magnavox was located, and book a couple of rooms in the Holiday Inn at Greensville, and bring the booze in from Johnson City and just have an open house party for two days." (Or to Louisville for three days to entertain the people from General Electric.) A constant stream of people coming and going. Iain couldn't do it. "A couple of drinks and I fall asleep. Alex could go forever. Alex was a good drinker."

There was nothing too good for a Molex customer, Alex was told. First class all the way. The best in liquor, the best in food. "Give them anything they want." Johnny told him. "But no women. That was Johnny's rule. And he was right. That was the first rule Johnny gave me. And it was a good rule."

And then there was Nellie. Nellie Welsh was a little wizened woman. Probably didn't weigh ninety pounds, full up, and she was of a height for which the expression "Yay high" was invented.

She looked so much like the dirty old lady in the Playboy cartoon who is always trying to do disgusting things with Boy Scouts that somebody would always tear the cartoon out and hang it on the door of the Inspector's office. Nellie loved that. She loved the attention.

By the time the KK came out, Nellie was in her late sixties, and she looked even older. "I was born looking old," she would say, and by way of compensation she would make herself younger every time she had to fill out a company questionnaire.

She had a low gravelly voice, and there was always a cigarette dangling from her lips and a long ash drooping from the end of the cigarette. Bourbon and water was her drink. "A two-drink wash." She would down a dozen bourbons in a sitting, and nobody ever saw her drunk.

She would sit at the end of the bar at Enzo's with a telephone in her hand or on the bar in front of her, and the calls would come. "Is it all right if I ship this . . .?" "Can I set this die up?" She'd love it when they'd plead with her. "Go to hell!" she'd say.

Same thing in the plant. She would always have a large stack of red cards with her as she toured the plant, and she had no hesitancy whatsoever in showing how much she enjoyed using them.

There were times when Senior himself would be called out to the floor to try to reason with her. "You want to talk about bull-headed?" he says. "I used to go out and argue with her. She'd give me a helluva time."

Nellie would say, "No, John, that won't go." And usually that was it. But sometimes he would threaten to pile the stuff in his car and drive it out to the airport himself.

"You do, and I'll get you for that," she'd say. "I'll get you for that, John."

When Nellie retired, John presented her with a replica of the bar stool she always sat on, with a telephone chained to it. She loved it.

The inspector on the night shift was Dolly, a big buxom gun-toting hillbilly. Dolly came from Oklahoma, and she toted a gun because she lived in a very tough neighborhood.

Dolly walked around with her red tags too, and there was nothing she liked more than to drawl, "I ain't gonna buy it."

They were both absolutely dedicated. And they were both tough as nails. They believed they were the guardians of the Molex product, and the Molex reputation. And they were. During the years of the first explosive growth, it was Nellie and Dolly, as much as anybody else, who kept the company honest.

In those days, remember, the operator had almost no responsibility for turning out a good product. The responsibility fell on Quality Control for letting it through.

"With Nellie and Dolly," Bob Pribish says, "they took that responsibility very personally."

Quality Control was Alex Ewens, Iain MacDonald and Bob Pribish, and they are all quite willing to admit these days that they did not necessarily feel called upon to keep a scrupulous record of all the complaints. Considering how hectic everything was, they might even have excised an entry here and there. Recorded or not, Nellie and Dolly would remember every complaint. Because they felt it reflected on them.

Johnny has this to say about her. "She was always very concerned about the company and was concerned about the quality of products that we produced and how our customers thought about us. She was great."

THE CHAIRMAN
OF THE BOARD

———————

Accidents don't just happen. Any time a plane goes down, you can be sure that somebody made an error in judgment or somebody didn't do his job.

—JOHN H. KREHBIEL, SR.—

THE people at Molex somehow believe that John didn't begin to fly until he was in his sixties. That's not exactly true, but it does tell a lot about how they feel about him. John didn't really start to take lessons in order to be a pilot; he took lessons to make himself a better passenger.

Back in the early fifties, when John was out on the road as Molex's sole salesman, there were five major customers—Hotpoint, General Electric, Whirlpool, Frigidaire, and Westinghouse. Of these, only Hotpoint was in Chicago. Whirlpool had its refrigerator plant in Evansville, Indiana, and its other two plants in Jasper, Indiana, and Clyde, Ohio. Frigidaire was in Dayton, Ohio; Westinghouse was in Mansfield, Ohio; and General Electric operated out of Louisville, Kentucky.

In order to get to any of those places, you pretty much had to drive or take a train.

Trains were chancy. "The Pennsylvania Railroad went through Mansfield, Ohio. You'd have to get off at four o'clock in the morning, which I did many times, and you'd get out at the depot and there's a little stove there that somebody had fired up the previous night and nothing's left in the morning. So you would sit inside the cold depot and wait until the plant opened. If you wanted to go on to another town, you'd have to rent a car."

As far as air service to those cities was concerned, there wasn't any. "The airlines went into Cleveland, Columbus and Cincinnati and that was it for Ohio. They didn't fly into Indiana at all. It was almost impossible to get into Louisville, Kentucky, and completely impossible to get into Benton Harbor or St. Joe, Michigan."

He was driving fifty thousand miles a year, and not really complaining that much over the inadequacies of the commercial air service.

"I was scared to death of flying. Every time I'd take a plane, I'd arrive with sweat under my arms, and I'd still be sweating when I met the customer."

There was one particularly harrowing experience while he was flying back from Louisville on an Eastern Convair 240. They hit a thunderstorm and were kept on a holding pattern over Midway for hours. It wasn't only

159

the driving rain against the windows, or the thunder and lightning off in a distance. "This St. Elmo's fire—it's a static electricity—started dancing on our wings. You look out and you think the whole wing is catching fire. It scared us all to death."

As it was, they were on the last plane allowed to land before the airport was closed down. The transformers had been knocked out, and the Convair had made its final descent without being able to communicate with the tower.

When they got on the tarmac, there was four to five inches of water. "The stewardess gave us all an umbrella—I still have the umbrella—and told us to take our shoes and socks off and roll up our pants because we'd ruin them on the tar, that's how black and greasy it was."

And then he drove around for hours trying to get home. The rains were so heavy that half the roads were blocked. Many of them were flooded. He almost went into the drink himself at the main vaiduct at 63rd St., but was able to hit the brakes just in time. "They found cars submerged under the viaduct in the morning. Luckily, I saw the cars piled up there in time."

While he was over Midway, he swore that if he got down alive he would never fly again. By the next day, he was thinking better of it. "Finally, I decided that the only way I was going to get over this fear was to learn what made an airplane stay up in the air." *To know how things work. That's what will do it for you every time.*

He started by taking lessons in one of those little Piper Cubs. "I can tell you that I had no enjoyment in the thing for about five or six hours, until I realized that the wings weren't going to fall off."

And then he began to relax. And then he began to enjoy it. And then he began to enjoy it very much. "I went on to think I might as well get a private license so I could fly around to our customers and cover a hell of a lot bigger territory."

One thing does have a way of leading to another. Once he had his license, he wanted a faster plane. So he bought a used Cessna which was faster and more dependable than the ones he had been renting. Dependable meaning that he would no longer be at the mercy of people like the fool of a maintenance man who had been ready to send him up without any oil in the engine. After a while, the Cessna seemed pretty slow, too. "At least the one I had. So I bought a Beech Bonanza, which was quite a bit faster."

There wasn't much sense in having such a great piece of equipment if you were going to be grounded every time the weather turned inclement.

He decided he should get an instrument license. "Finally, I ended up flying a twin-engine Beech; so if an engine did fail, I had another way of getting to my destination." John loved that plane. And he got a lot of use out of it. "In that twin, I could leave at 5:00 in the morning and be in Dayton by 7:30–8:00, and then fly to Finley or Mansfield, and call on four or five customers, and be home after dark and be back at the office in the morning. No way you can do that with any other kind of transportation."

He logged almost 2,000 hours, and 750–800 of it was instrument time. And then, in 1980, at the age of seventy-four, he turned his license in. Partly, it was because his responsibilities at the plant had changed so much that he wasn't really going "out in the territory" much any more. But mostly, John says, it was age. "As much as I love to fly, I'm just getting too old and forgetful. And this is something where you don't want to forget anything."

It served its purpose, he can say, looking back. "That's one of the real bright spots in my life, learning to fly. The other or primarily good thing about it was I got over my fear of flying."

He has also managed to leave his friends with a treasure trove of stories. Ed Healy's flat-out favorite goes back to the first time he ever flew with him. Ed was going up to Beaver Dam in Wisconsin to make a call on a company called Monarch Range, to whom he was selling terminal blocks, and then going on to Montello Products, in Montello, that did the harness work for Speed Queen Washers and Driers, another customer of Molex.

John had just completed his one hundred hours flying time and was eligible to take a passenger up with him. Ed had just gotten a two-socket terminal specified by Speed Queen.

So John made an offer that Ed may well have found quite possible to refuse if it had been made by anybody but the boss.

Take it away, Ed Healy:

John says, "How about flying up there? I need some practice."

I never was too excited about flying in small airplanes, but he picks me up at the airport at Crystal Lake, and we're over Beaver Dam. It's the fall of the year, the wind sock is down. It just happens to be a bluebird day, a perfect day.

He says, "Do you see any smoke stack?"

There's no smoke stack anymore to let you see which way the wind is blowing.

John says, "I think it's going this way."

I say, "John, I have no idea." I'm not too happy with these smaller planes anyway. All of a sudden, he starts landing. We're landing downwind. I realize all of a sudden that I had seen that airport before, and right at the end of the airport there's about a 3-foot drop into Beaver Lake.

John is coming down. I'm pressing down on the floor as hard as I can trying to get this plane down. I'm pushing it down. When you go down in a small plane . . . this was a Cessna 172, and it's wobbling in the wind.

John, being the guy he is, he does get the thing down, and I've already got the door open, because we're going to end up in the lake for sure.

The plane stops. He says, "I want to ask you something."

"Yeah?"

"Would you mind getting out and pulling us back from the edge of this drop so I can pull the plane around."

We're at the edge of the lake. There isn't a yard to spare. Maybe 2 feet. The prop was over the edge. So I go out and pull the plane back.

We drove over to the airport building. There's one guy working in there. We got a cab to go over to Monarch Range to make our call. When we get back we're talking to this guy, this mechanic there.

John's got the map out. He says there's an indication in Montello, there's a little airstrip there. The guy says, "Geez, that thing's been closed, but I know where the airstrip's at. It's right next to a swimming pool."

Well, in Montello, Wisconsin, population under five hundred, there aren't going to be many swimming pools.

We got into the airplane. By this time we know which way the wind is blowing. Fifteen, twenty minutes, we're looking around Montello, can see where the airstrip is. It's even smaller than I'd imagined, and you can see it has been carved out of the woods. We land there, tie the airplane down, and hitchhike into Montello, which is a small town. There's a guy by the name of Henry Oriente, who is the general manager. First time John met him. We finish our business, and I say, "Henry, can you call us a cab?"

He says, "A cab? How the hell did you get into town?"

John says, "We flew into the airstrip."

Oriente says, "Don't worry about anything. I'm going to ride you out there." He says, "I'm going to see what's going to happen." He says, "The last time anybody took off from there, they didn't get over the tree tops and all four people were killed."

I'm not very excited about this whole adventure. We landed downwind, almost landed in Beaver Lake, and now this guy wants to come out and see if we're going to make it over the trees.

We get out. I'm double-checking everything. I'm watching John. John is double-checking the fuel, the water, draining it out.

I'm pulling the blocks away from the wheels, loading up, getting our briefcases. We climb into the plane.

John pulls the airplane down, and there's Henry sitting on the hood of the car, just waving at us.

I'm thinking, Oh, Jesus, I don't know what's going to happen. John gets his engine warmed up. We're sitting there, and all of a sudden he pushes the throttle all the way in, this little airplane is hopping up and down like mad. It wants to fly. He's got full throttle on. Finally, he takes the foot off the brake, and I'll tell you, we don't go 25 feet and we're up in the air. We missed those trees by 1,500 feet if we missed them at all. And Henry is waving at us, and he's shaking his head. Laughing.

That was my first flight with John. We land on one field and use every bit of available airstrip, and we take off from another field and don't use enough strip to build a cabin on.

Another time, Healy was flying up to Rockport, Missouri, with Senior and Johnny to get in some goose hunting:

We were hunting snows. We go over to Joliet Airport, we get this plane out of the hangar, we get all his gear and everything. I'm sitting next to Senior, and Johnny's in the bed. We don't get 200 feet up and all of a sudden, there's the worst bang I ever heard in my life.

We weren't 200 feet up in the air, that's a critical stage when you're taking off in an airplane. John just kept that thing going around, made an 180 degree turn, came in and landed, like there was no problem.

I'll say this, Johnny's knuckles were as white as mine. John said, "I've got a friend who's got a plane here. Maybe I ought to call him and borrow his airplane."

Johnny and I looked at each other. We say, "Listen, I don't know about you, but we're going over to get a commercial flight in Lincoln, and then we're going to drive down to Missouri and do our hunting there." Which we did. The hunting was really good, by the way.

John Flaherty goes a long way back with John Krehbiel. Flaherty was in the navy, assigned to the A-bomb project, and after the war, the Atomic Energy Commission took him over and transferred him to Chicago to oversee the construction of the Argonne National Laboratory, which was being built in Lemont, practically down the road from the Krehbiel property.

John and Martha Flaherty had two sons, Bob and John, whom they enrolled in the Avery Coonley School. Parents who send their kids to a progressive school are, almost by definition, parents who are going to become very much involved in their kids' education. The Krehbiels and the Flahertys hit it off immediately. Both Johns are tinkerers. Both Johns are laughers. And they both flew their own planes.

Although it was Flaherty who discovered Lompoc, at a time when he was president of Atomics International, it was John Krehbiel who saw the advantages of building a house there for Peg, and it was the Flahertys who promptly followed them.

At any rate, the two Johns did a lot of flying together, and in flying back to Lompoc, they would always pass right over Las Vegas. And while Flaherty would like to have dropped down to visit a casino or two, he was never able to talk John into it.

Here's John Flaherty:

We'd be sitting there, tootling along in the airplane. I would say, "Let's go down because I want to show you around the town a little bit."

John had one answer. "Nothing doing."

One time, we went way down a southern route for some reason, and as we were flying up to Las Vegas, I told John we'd better get fuel. Of course, he was very conservative about airplanes. He's conservative about everything. We didn't really need fuel, but I thought I'd found an opening. So I told him the weather forecast looked like we were going to get some pretty strong head winds, and we'd better go down and get some fuel.

So I finally got him to go to Las Vegas on probably my fiftieth attempt. We taxied up to the executive terminal, got refueled, went in, and they had slot machines right there in the terminal. So John put a quarter in one of those slot machines, pulled down, nothing happened. He said, "OK, you satisfied? I've been to Las Vegas."

The fascination that Las Vegas holds for so many otherwise sensible people, his own salespeople included, eludes John completely. "They think a convention in Vegas is the greatest thing in the world," he says. "I think it's a real pain in the ass."

John's second tussle with the avaricious slot machine came a few years later while the Krehbiels and the Flahertys were flying to Nassau in the Grand Bahamas. "There's a town called Freeport, which is another gambling place. We put down in Freeport to gas up, I put a quarter in a slot machine there and shot that, too."

And, finally, there was the time he invaded the inner sanctum of a Monte Carlo gambling palace, and left with both himself and the casino virtually unscathed: "We had an international sales meeting in Monte Carlo, and I remember because we were in the hotel associated with the casino we were allowed to go into the inner sanctum, where they were really cutting the big chips. And to me it was just drab as all hell seeing some guys . . . idiots . . . putting ten thousand franc chips on a number like twenty-seven because he was enamored with twenty-seven, and losing left and right. Ten thousand francs, and I remember thinking, Christ, how could a guy make that kind of money and blow it at this rate.

"So on the way out I bet one franc on the slot machines and lost. Now I can say I've gambled in Las Vegas, the Grand Bahamas, and Monte Carlo, and every time I've been a loser. And that's the reason I have no regard for gamblers."

If the fear of flying seems to have been wholly at odds with John's normal approach to life, the pleasure he was able to derive from flying a plane once he had licked that fear seems predictable.

John has always been game for anything. Throughout the early part of his life, his achievements as an action-oriented competitor easily outstripped his achievements as a businessman.

At the age of twenty-four or twenty-five, he was part of the doubles team that won the citywide squash championships in Chicago. Well, they did and they didn't. John was one of the better squash players at the Hinsdale Club. One of the players he competed against most often was a fellow by the name of Jimmy Thompson. "Thompson was only about 5'6", and about as big around as he was tall. But he was a very good player. He was probably the best player there." It was at Thompson's suggestion that they teamed together to enter the Chicago city championships. The other entries represented the various YMCA's of the area, the Harvard, Yale, and Princeton Club, the University of Chicago and almost every club, one might say, that could boast of a squash court. For reasons which have become vague in John's memory, the team of Thompson and Krehbiel competed under the colors of the John Marshall Law School.

They won the city championship, and then had it taken away from them when somebody came up with the information that Jimmy Thompson had been an assistant pro at the Racquet Club of Chicago a dozen years earlier.

At roughly the same time, John became deeply involved in sailboat racing. This time, his appetite was whetted by some people he had come across who had suggested that he would enjoy the competition of the sailboat racing at the Chicago Yacht Club. Same thing again. John doesn't "take an interest" in things. He is the world's lousiest dilettante. If he's going to do it, he's going to find out everything he can about it, and the best way to do that, he has always found, is go to the people who know how to do it. Watch: "I met a sailor by the name of Bill Giaver who had been very successful in racing and I said I would buy a half interest in his boat if he would teach me to sail. Those were the Depression days, and he was so hard up for money that he didn't have any other way to get his boat out of drydock and into the water."

Although John wasn't exactly loaded himself, he had the J. H. Krehbiel Company functioning well enough by then that he also sprung for a set of sails that would enable them to compete in the R Boat class. "These were racing sloops, with something like a 40-foot deck, and it took four people to race them. It was a good competitive class. Owing to the construction of our boat we were particularly good in light air, and we had several competitors who were very strong in heavy weather. So it became a matter of what kind of wind came up."

He enjoyed the whole sailing scene tremendously and threw himself into it totally. The crews would get together at the Yacht Club every evening to take their boats out and mingle with their fellow sailors around the dock. "If one of our regular crew members wasn't going to be able to be there the next weekend, we'd have to know as soon as possible so we could pick up a good replacement. All the other crews would be doing the same thing. We took those races very seriously."

John's forte was to work the light canvas on the foredeck, and he earned himself a good enough reputation to enable him to catch crews for four Mackinac Island races. The Mackinac was a 330-mile race.

His first Mackinac race as a crew member on a Q boat taught him the difference between having his own boat and catching on with somebody else. When he and Giaver came back after an evening of sailing on the *Joanie* they would stay on into the early morning hours, tending to its every need. "You'd take all your sails down so they wouldn't rot. They were all cotton then, remember, we didn't have synthetics. They had a sail loft in the locker rooms of the Chicago Yacht Club where you could hang these tremendously big sails up to be sure they didn't rot or get mildewed. Because if they mildewed, they would start to weaken immediately."

During that first Mackinac race, the sails on the Q boat began to tear in the high winds. "I was sewing torn sails all the way to Mackinac. We didn't do very well in the race, but we did have a helluva good time just trying to see if we could finish before the sails collapsed on us completely."

The next year, he sailed on a large Ketch from out of Milwaukee which did much better. "It was named the *Dorelle*, and we won a 100-pound round of cheese for being the first boat to cross the finish line. She wasn't able to make up her time allowance, though, and consequently we didn't win the race."

He still looks back on his two years of sailing as one of the high points of his single life. By the next spring, he had started to build the home in Downers Grove, and while that was another labor of love, it was a labor that was going to be consuming every hour of his spare time for a full year. And then he was married, and then he was raising children, and then he was running a business, and then he was 46 years old and telling himself that he'd be damned if he was going to go through life breaking out into a sweat every time he had to go up in an airplane.

He is, it should be clear, strong-minded and determined. What he makes up his mind to do is going to get done. But first, he is going to learn everything that he possibly can about it.

He had learned early in life that there was a great world of night schools and institutional seminars out there. As time went by, he discovered that there was almost nothing worth knowing that somebody wasn't teaching somewhere.

In the early 1930s, as his business career was getting underway, he piggy-backed onto a correspondence course in General Business that his father was taking from the Alexander Hamilton Institute. The course included accounting, cost accounting, management in manufacturing, industrial engineering, selling, advertising, finance and anything else that seemed applicable.

In addition to those early courses he took while he was working at the machine shop and foundry, a partial list would include:

Mathematics and Mechanical Drawing at Armour Institute
Plastics at Durez Evening School by Durez Plastics
Die Design at Armour Institute
Industrial Engineering (Time and Motion Study) Univ. of Wisconsin
Thermoplastics at Univ. of Wisconsin
Thermosetting plastics at Univ. of Wisconsin
Injection Mold Design at Univ. of Wisconsin
Work sampling at Industrial Education Institute
Industrial Psychology—LaGrange Junior College
Photography at LaGrange Junior College
Flying at Federal Aviation Dept.
Instrument Flying at Federal Aviation Dept.
Meterology and Study of Aviation Weather—Central Weather Service
Increasing Productivity—joint seminars by I.I.T. and U.C.L.A.
Public speaking—Dale Carnegie
Value Analysis—Univ. of Wisconsin
Managing a Smaller Company in a Big Business Environment—American Management Association
Electronic—DeVry correspondence school
Controlling and Reducing Indirect Costs

Then dozens of seminars on:

Product Evaluation and Planning—Schrello Associates—Long Beach, Ca.
Strategic Management of Research & Development—Pugh & Roberts Assoc.
Board of Directors of the Smaller Co.—Assoc. of Board of Directors

You want to find out something about hiring outside Directors for a company as small as his? Well, there is a seminar that is given by the Association of the Board of Directors in Choosing Directors for a Smaller Company.

"The seminar lasted for a couple of days," Senior says, "and I loved it. The fellow who taught the course said there were things you should never do. Don't have relatives on your Board. That was the first thing. He said, 'I know this sounds crazy but don't have friends on the Board either.' Here I had two sons and myself on the Board. Pretty close relatives. He also said not to have lawyers on your Board. I was delighted with that. He didn't even recommend having bankers."

He had come to the right man with that advice. "Lawyers are little better than leeches," Senior says. In fact, he says it often. "They contribute nothing, they generate no business, no money. Nothing. All they are is an encumberance on every transaction you make."

Like when Molex went public in 1972. "We had four sets of lawyers there. You could see all they were doing was stalling, so they could put another few hours in at $150 an hour. All these guys with exactly the same intention, you could see it on their faces. Finally, they were saying things to me like 'Krehbiel, would you be agreeable to saying so and so?' It would take them half an hour to get around the bush. I said, 'Wait a minute, boys. I'll tell you what I'll do. I'll come back when you guys have got this thing to where you have a good draft of it, and I'll take it home and read it over at night. But I've got to get the hell out of here.' I walked away from the table. The lawyer from Blair said, Jesus Christ, you can't do that, we've got this meeting going on here. And it nearly upset the thing with Blair of going ahead with the underwriting. I could see the whole thing was deliberate. Like a goofing-off session. I said, Listen you guys, get back to your work or we're going to fire you, that's all. They were going to have lunch next and have a session in the afternoon. It's just with the idea, How can I take away some money from the guy."

The same thing happened more recently with the law firm that was taking care of his estate. That they were considered the best law firm in Chicago meant not a thing to him. "A very nice gentleman is handling our estates and writing our wills and trust funds and so forth." If he weren't a lawyer, Senior seems to feel, he'd probably be a fine fellow. Knowing how lawyers operated, Senior had told him that he wanted a bill every month.

When the new tax law was passed to take effect in 1987, the distinguished law firm confirmed, not at all to his surprise, that they were no different than their less distinguished brethren. One of the provisions of the new law had eliminated the deduction for legal fees in setting up an estate. "I knew what was going to happen," he says. And he wasn't disappointed. On December 13, Senior found himself in receipt of a tidy little bill for $36,000, covering the period of time between November, 1985, and December, 1986.

"You could almost see these guys saying, Hey, man, we've got to get this all in, but let's make it real late in the year so the guy won't have time to complain."

Man, did they have a wrong number. The bill came bouncing right back to them, along with a demand for an hour-by-hour accounting. And when the distinguished attorney protested that they couldn't possibly reconstruct a whole year's work in two weeks he wasn't telling John anything that John didn't know. "I think it's a goofed-up bill," John told him. "I don't think you put that kind of time in." As for the deadline that they would be operating under, that was their problem, not his. Any tax deduction that was lost because of their failure to send him an acceptable bill in time was going to come right off their fee.

"This guy had to hustle like hell to get a new bill out," John says not without satisfaction. "First time I ever saw him hustle." And it wasn't for any $36,000 either.

Bankers? "Bankers are guys who will loan you all the money you want as long as you don't need it, and won't loan you anything when you do." The distaste for banks has had a considerable influence upon the financial structure of Molex, and, hence, on its success. John will borrow money for only one purpose. To build new plants. Bricks and mortar can be depreciated. John depreciates the buildings and the equipment as quickly as the law allows and treats every dollar that is saved thereby as profit to be ploughed back into the business.

He was taught that hard lesson by Prudential. He had borrowed money from Prudential to build the first unit at Downers Grove, and borrowed again for the first two expansions. "The first addition, the interest rate was increased. The second addition, it went up again." The final addition, which was in 1969, came in the midst of a period of high inflation, and the official he had always dealt with at Prudential called him down to talk about it. "They said the inflation had gone quite high, and they were going to have to adjust the rate quite a bit upward." Well, that was to be expected. But he didn't think they had called him there just to tell him he was going to have to pay the going rate.

They said, "That isn't all. We want some stock in the company, too."

Sorry, John told them. There wasn't any stock for sale.

No, no. He didn't have the idea at all. "We're not talking about buying it," they told him. They wanted a piece of the company, gratis, as a sweetener for approving the loan.

"You can go to hell," John told them, and walked out.

"That is not the kind of thing that endears you to them," John says. But that was OK. Because it was not the kind of thing that endeared them to him, either.

He determined right then that he would never allow himself to be in a position where the bank could get him on the hip and take his business away, as he had seen the banks do to so many of Hinsdale's "700 millionaires" during the Depression.

"I decided we did not want to depend on banks to finance our growth or operations. Or for working capital. One of the reasons we have been profitable is that we will not compromise profit if it is at all possible, and we expect a darn good profit, added to our heavy depreciation, to generate the funds needed to grow the business." As long as he has anything to do with the business, he says, that philosophy will not change. "Most every building we've built and every plant we have constructed was built only when we could afford to go out and buy it or build it ourselves."

John H. Krehbiel Sr. can always be counted upon to speak his mind. When he was first listed in Forbes Magazine as one of the wealthiest men in the United States, he sent a sharp letter to Malcolm Forbes himself to let him know what he thought of his magazine's reportorial skills and ethical standards.

All Forbes had done as far as John could see was to lift the stock holdings of the country's corporate leaders out of their annual reports, run the numbers through a computer and let them settle out.

In John's case, they had managed to double his actual worth by crediting him with the entire holdings of the Krehbiel family, including even the stock that was in trust for the grandchildren.

"They were dishonest," he says. They were also unforgiveably sloppy, in his opinion, for a publication which had, in a very real sense, granted itself jurisdiction over the integrity and work ethic of the entire industrial complex.

"Nobody volunteers information about their wealth," he points out. To do the job right would take prodigies of investigatory reporting. Common sense tells you that there are people around the country of fantastic wealth whom neither Forbes nor you nor I have ever heard of.

But if it was a gimmick for Forbes, it was a pain in the ass to John. As soon as he had been officially identified as the possessor of a $345 million fortune, he began to get letters from a wide assortment of nuts. The letters bore a striking similarity. "They've got the greatest idea in the world, and they need a million dollars so the world could be saved."

Supplicants of more modest ambition tended to work by telephone. Which was exactly what Peg, with her bad heart, didn't need. "It was terrible," Jane Ostrum recalls. "People were calling up and telling her that if she didn't put their kid through college, she'd be sorry. Or they'd say that all their son needed to get to his job in California was a new car. And they'd always say that with all the money she had, she'd never miss it."

For the first time in his life John had to get an unlisted phone number.

When the police reported that his name had been found on a list that had been taken from a burglar, he put in an alarm system and hired security guards to patrol the grounds. Inevitably, there were scenes where the alarm system was tripped and the security guards would come running in. And, just to be safe, sit there through the night with the light burning.

No, John was not happy about the Forbes listing at all.

Neither was the kid who delivered the morning paper. The boy had the misfortune to have the tire on his bicycle go flat in front of the Krehbiel house, and while he was trying to fix it he heard a *click*. There, standing in the early morning dusk was a man and a dog. The man had a double-barrel shotgun. It was, of course, John.

We will move now to Black Monday, October 19, 1987, the day of the great Wall Street Crash. On Black Monday, the Molex stock went down $7\frac{1}{2}$ points, which amounted to a paper loss for John of something like $45 million.

The gloom and doom that had settled upon the corporate board rooms of the nation by the following morning can only be imagined. At Molex, the Chairman of the Board came in, all smiles. "I am," he announced happily, "off that goddam Forbes list."

VOICES FROM
THE FLOOR

So many times you see families where the old man started the business and the sons just bleed off it. It's just the opposite with this company. The old man is the foundation, he's the rock; the two kids just want to go, go, go. If I had this much money I would have sold the business and I'd be playing golf in Arizona. As far as they're concerned—Johnny especially—they want to be in the Fortune 500, and they want to be the best company in the world. I recently heard an interview with Fred where he said, "We're not going to be the second best connector company in the world, we're going to be Number One." This company is going to be there.

—JIM GEISER—

JOHN BLAZEK

I came in 1951 when Molex was very, very small. The old plant in Brookfield. I was about thirty then. John Sr. must have been forty-five. We were making terminal blocks, the different parts that went to automobile manufacturers and parts that went in all your electrical appliances. They were very happy if they made half a million when I started here. But now, what a business.

I saw it grow from one plant to about thirty-seven in the United States and all around the world.

They had the right idea, making the move to go into plastic and nylon.

A fabulous place to work. Anybody that works for Molex and wants to leave and go for a better job, he's got to be crazy. Never in my life have I worked in a place like this, where it's nonunion, all the benefits that we get are terrific. We get everything, profit sharing, terrific hospitalization. You get glasses. If you have trouble with your feet they take care of that.

But hey, I don't want to leave this place. I love this place, it's like my second home, the Krehbiels they treat their employees like they're the family.

The old man told me when I reached sixty-five, John, you take it easy. You want to set your own time. You want to take a day off, go right ahead. Do it your way. Senior and Junior always ask me when they come around, John, you're not retiring on us, are you?

That man looks terrific, doesn't he? He comes over to you. "Hi, Johnny, how are you? How's your health?" Real hard handshake. "Got any problems John? You take care of yourself now, you know." He'll say, "I still got ten years on you, Johnny. Let's see which of us is gonna last the longer."

Junior started working on the real old Molex plant in Brookfield, the one that was next to Montgomery Ward. He was in high school. Who comes walking down one day but Senior. "Good morning, Johnny, good to see you. I'm going to send my oldest boy over here this summer to work. The kid, all he thinks of is borrowing money. He thinks it grows on trees. I want to teach the kid what it is to earn a buck." I said, "John, I give you credit, 100 percent."

175

I call him my young protégé. He gets a kick out of that. "Don't be telling everybody I'm your protégé." I say, "Well, John, you were. I'm not lying. You came up the hard way. I give you credit."

When Bill Veeck had the White Sox, Freddie was in it too. He surprised me. Gave me a season pass. Wasn't that nice of him? I had that season's pass until they got rid of the White Sox.

WAYNE LARSON

Wayne Larson is a veteran of Brookfield. He was hired in 1955 when he was nineteen years old. He had served his apprenticeship as a diemaker at Phillips Control in Joliet, and had worked very briefly for Simpson Optical and for Model Builders of America.

I applied for the job as diemaker. John said they didn't have diemakers there, they had moldmakers. I said, Well, I'll apply for moldmaker then, and Senior's first comment was, We'll give you thirty days and see if you can make it. I figured he was saying, the kid says he can do it, let's give him thirty days to see if he can. I've lasted thirty-three years. Enjoyably. So I go back a little bit with John and Ed and their father, Fred.

I worked originally with Fred making a glass chopper for the fiberglass. It was supposed to be for stripping corn off a husk, and Fred, through his designs, made it so that it chopped the fiberglass into the lengths that we wanted. From there, I worked on spray booths, where we were spraying handwheels for the hot-water registers made out of Molex plastic. I think we had six different variations.

Then we worked for the sump pump floats. You say "float" and you think it would be light. These were heavy. It was water displacement.

I was hired as a moldmaker, but I don't think I was much of a moldmaker. I was doing more of machinery rebuilding, and building and maintenance, anything that was needed from swamping the pitch out of the mold room to actually changing molds over and doing some repair work.

"Swamping pitch out" means all the slag and oil from the molding presses used to run down into a pit that ran in back of the molding machines. Once a month or so we would pull a plate on the side and get in there with a pitchfork and clean it all up.

Working for Molex back then, to any of the employees, meant that you did whatever had to be done. And didn't question that it wasn't your job, you just did it.

The old man, Fred, was very motivated, highly mechanical. When he made a decision, you could be sure it was going to work because it always did. He was a very reserved man, but at the same time he was outgoing in the sense that he was very concerned with people. Like John. I worked for him for about five years, on and off, in different projects, and then he began to sort of taper off.

When Junior came in, his dad said, "Give him the dirtiest job in the house." It was cleaning the pits right alongside of me. He did some mold changeover, some welding, some plant maintenance. He started from the bottom. He was a fun-loving young fellow. It was a summer job, he knew he'd be going back to school in the fall, and he didn't care what the job was. He just pitched right in and did it.

They had just moved over from a small plant on the other end of town, down on Harding Avenue, and as small as the plant was, it was basically empty. I can remember the first year I was there, we had a Christmas party there at the plant. Just knocked off work, there was food to eat, and we opened some packages, and that was the Christmas party.

Before we moved to Downers Grove, the walls were bulging and we had to expand. We had a terminal die that was being run on the outside, and it was brought into the facility, and they had a small punch press, and that was the first stamping ever done by Molex. I'd guess about 1958.

Some of those products from Brookfield are still run on occasion. That's how long the product can hang around. Before the equipment was moved out of Brookfield, we were up into the 1500 and 1600 series, and in 1980 we went back and pulled out one of our designs that had never been used and manufactured the tool. It was 1457. It's in the press running right now.

We would hand-form some of those prototypes, and make about 1500 samples, until Hillside built the new die for us to make the new part, then we were up to three hundred per minute. Since then that product has probably changed twenty times. The Bruderer made a difference. The second product that came in, just before we moved over here, was 1560 and 1561, which was the minimum round terminal. We worked very hard on both of those to get them running.

International started about 1968 or 1969. In 1970, we had a joint venture, and that's when I went to Japan. That was with Fred to set this up and get production running. Then in 1972, I went to Ireland, and I was in Singapore and Taiwan, I think in 1976 and 1978.

In Japan, basically, it was to set up the production and get them so they would be a profit-running company. I don't remember Molex ever running in the red in Japan. But I think from Day One, they had the technology, and the planning was great.

I was there first to set up the building, to get the electric and the machines, to pretrain the people, and show them how to repair the tools. We had an engineer who came over here for three weeks—he was with me most of that time—and he went back to Japan and started ordering the tools he needed, putting everything in supply, getting the building located. When I went over, we finalized getting the presses lined up, the material lined up, setting the tools in the press, getting the safety systems hooked up.

I lived with a Japanese engineer in an apartment for almost four weeks before my wife came over. His name was Kasohiro Doi. He was SMK's top engineer. We were living in his culture, but I loved it. I could sleep on the floor, sleep on the *tatami*. The food was a little difficult because I wasn't used to all the vegetables. More often than not we would go to a restaurant and he would order the Japanese dinner and I would order the American steak. We both liked beer. Japanese have good *tyran* beer. Japanese like sports, so we'd go to the ballgame together.

Ireland was on the difficult side, because this was when the seven or eight people were killed in Londonderry, and they thought it was the British that caused it, and there was an uprising, and they came through the whole district at the time and took everyone out of the facility and marched, and I wondered, What is this going to be? I was excited. In fact, I picked up my camera, I wanted to take some pictures, but the plant manager said it would be best to leave it there.

We marched down the street, eight abreast, and then all of a sudden, we went into a factory building there and a service for the people who were killed and everyone dispersed and went home. A peaceful demonstration. But I didn't know what was going to happen. That was in December of 1972.

The building was relatively small, probably 50 by 75, with one small port. As it grew larger and larger, they get a larger bay, might be ten bays long, and you can have any one of them or all of them, and they might all be 50 by 75 in size, and they just knock out the wall and you go into the next one. The bays were what you might call fire-bricked, with a kind of tin roof on them.

That was all on the airport property. The Shannon Airport. Every plane that came in, came right over the building. There was a lot of activity. Lots of planes coming in and out, and lots of jackrabbits on the airfield. People would go out there and shoot the jackrabbits so the planes could land. And that's what Molex was in, in the first facility. Shortly after that, like a year after that, we moved into another facility.

Taiwan was very different. I stayed in Tapei, which was across the river, so to say. The difference is basically two different cultures. I found it unusual to see armed guards standing at the corner. That was a very good learning experience in Taiwan.

I think that if I were to think of a descriptive phrase for Senior, I would first of all say, "very considerate person." Very considerate. "Great motivator." You could have made the biggest mistake in your life, and he can talk to you and before you know it, you're saying, I know I made a mistake, John, and I'm sorry. Let's go forward. "That's what I want to hear," he'll say. He's considerate of people's feelings. He understands people, and he's a good judge of character, I feel. I think he has that capability of seeing what can be done. Projecting.

Back in 1966, we had a moldmaker, Mike, who built a mold completely in reverse. Ed redesigned it, and the moldmaker reversed it again, which made it a positive instead of a negative. I remember John coming over and looking at it, and the only thing I can hear him saying is, "How do these things happen?"

He wasn't upset so that you could see it, although he must have been seething inside. The first thing Mike said was, We can save it by putting an insert here and regrouping the whole thing, and I think John's attitude was, he knows he made a mistake, he doesn't try to make excuses and he's already thinking of how he can correct it.

John impressed me at the time, because it was a costly error.

I never heard of anyone who said he couldn't communicate with John. No matter how big the problem, or how small.

Design capability, if you're having a design problem with it, go and talk to him. Let him know your problem, and he'll try to help you solve it. And if he can't do it, he'll find someone who can.

That's what Molex is, it's helping one another. It's not a question of whose job it is, it's just, get it done.

I'm the tooling supervisor. Something comes in through products engineering: a thought, a concept, an idea. If it seems like a good idea for a new product, hey, let's talk about it, which is the way it should be, and we'll probably get a new product and design from the engineers. We're always looking into new products, new designs, new procedures. I know these things are in the works. Like fiber optics, not many people thought we'd ever get into that, and we are. But as new products are in the offing . . . Just now, I was talking to an engineer, he says I got this problem with this, can you help me with this, what's your idea here, what's your idea there. It's just talking to different people for different ideas, and then he's going to weigh it, see what he's going to do, and maybe two years down the line, all of a sudden it becomes real. It's a process of talking to people, getting an opinion and looking up design procedures and what your capabilities are. And constantly: Have you got somebody to back you up in the shop while you're doing it?

I don't think Molex has ever overlooked any good idea to put into product. They will never say, "I don't know what you're talking about;" they'll say, "Let's look into it." That's why we have so many products on line, and are constantly putting in new ones.

ART JOHNSON

Art Johnson signed on in July 1959. He had been a tool and die maker for a dozen years, and had been designing dies for another three or four years. He started at Molex as a tool engineer, in charge of the small die shop. He is now crimp and field manager.

I had been interviewed by John Sr. a year before I was hired. At that time, he had already hired a tool engineer. A year later, I get a call on Sunday while we were having dinner, and he says, "This is John Krehbiel Sr. I'm with Molex. I don't know if you remember me."

I drove out to the Brookfield plant, talked to him, and decided to take the job.

At the time, we only had two chain-formed terminals to sell. We were developing a round head terminal—the .093; it's a 3/32 terminal is what it is. What I gathered at the time, John was very new at terminals, so the development of the terminal and the development of a crimping die were probably new to him. It was very interesting the way he came up with that .093. John came up with it, really, and developed it as he sold the parts to customers. We were developing it and also debugging it, so to speak.

Being small as they were, he had to sell the product, he couldn't spend years developing it like AT&T. So he ran into a lot of problems and did a lot of production rework. We ran that production on a development die. It wasn't until, I bet, three years later that John said, "Well, we've got enough money to buy a regular die."

Working with John in that respect was very, very interesting. He was very sharp when it comes to that type of work, and he was a very good person to work for. At the time, we had three toolmakers, we had two project engineers, Ory Klein, and Don Mink, and myself. And, of course, Ed Krehbiel, who did the mold design.

Grandpa Krehbiel worked in that little room. He was designing the air conditioning for an added room that they were building for the product engineers. I got a kick out of him. He'd drive in first thing every morning in his old Plymouth. He'd work until he got tired in the afternoon, and then he'd take off. He was there almost two years while I was there.

We had only three old presses, and they were very slow and very worn out. We finally ended up getting ourselves some high-speed, 22-ton presses and started working our production.

The round pin terminal was just a good terminal. I think it certainly demonstrates his ability. It's successful to this day. When I think: it started in 1959, and here it is 1988, so that terminal has to be something that's needed out in the field. It was a good job in development.

In the development of any product, you really have to push it out fast. And, of course, you've got to know where to put your money, what tooling to use. Which terminal do you think is going to be the one that is going to build Molex? It's very difficult to know which product is going to take off that great, and when it does take off you'd better have some tooling for it.

Johnny was working on purchasing when I came. You could hear him from one end to the other when he was on the phone with the suppliers. He was really volatile, calling vendors on deliveries. Pounding the table. Johnny was always very aggressive when it came to anything he worked on.

Senior is demanding in a quieter way. He's a great one for scribbling notes. Lots of follow-up on anything that he had to do with, whatever his pet program was. He would always drop a note on how's the machine or crimping die? How are the presses going? Should we be looking at buying some new equipment? He's always a step ahead. Should we be looking at something here? Should we be improving something in this area?

I've got to say this. In all the time I worked at Molex, I never saw time fly so fast. I started in the morning at 8:00, and sometimes I was there until 10:00 at night. But I mean five o'clock came around, I'd see someone picking up and going out. I'd say, my God, what time is it. That's how interesting it really was.

And you're thinking about it even when you're at home, and in the morning you're anxious to get back to try something else. That's got to be very unusual. There has got to be something in the company that makes you want to do it. They're a caring company. You're not just a number. All through the years, he's always going around. John talks to all the employees, goes down on the line, talks to the girls there, How's the husband and the kids? Something that isn't done in a lot of businesses.

The people in the crimping area are also service people. We always went out of the way to help customers in trouble, I think, for a company of our size. I'm on the service end where we know a customer's in trouble on the production line. I'll get somebody out the next day if I have to. We set a schedule of various calls from different places. I'll sometimes plan it around a customer who is in trouble. While we're out there we'll hit them, just on a courtesy call. How you doing? Any problems? Any questions? Which I think they appreciate.

BRUNO BAUMANIS

Bruno Baumanis came to the United States at the age of twenty-seven to play professional volley ball, in, of all places, Portland, Oregon. Obviously there is a story that goes with it. Bruno was born in Latvia. He had lived for a year under Russian rule, and then four years under German occupation. When the Soviets returned, he and his family fled to Germany. While he was in Czechoslovakia playing for the champion-ship volley ball team of Germany against a touring U.S. all-star team, he became so friendly with some of the American players that he accepted their invita-tion to join them in Portland. He was playing for the team that won the Northwest regional championship in 1949, when he came to the rude awakening that you cannot make a living in America that way.

He had studied engineering briefly at the Univer-sity of Riga and at Alexander University in Erlogna, Germany, and continued his studies in America at night school. He ended up in Chicago, and came to work at Molex in February 1963. English, Bruno will tell you, is not his best language.

I wasn't looking for a job. There was an agency, they were bugging me about a small company who looks to have potential. I made arrangements to see Senior after work, and two weeks later I worked for Molex. He was looking for Switch and Connector experience. I had worked for Electro-snap, which was a switch company, for six and a half years, and a year at Amphenol, a connector company.

I came from Advance Product design group in Amphenol. That's a glorified engineering department. Came to Molex, we got two tables. I got one draftsman. No air conditioning, no windows. My first thought was, I must be crazy. The main reason for me was it was a small company where I got more personally involved with the people. In my case, Senior was the guy. I many times thought he was my father, yet he's only fifteen years older than I am.

Molex was the main product still. Outside there was a big pot. A little shack that a couple of times caught fire. The office moved to Downers Grove. I lived in River Forest, and Brookfield was very close to me, about fifteen minutes. I could go home for lunch if I wanted. To get to Downers wasn't too bad either, twenty–twenty-five minutes. Then to Lisle. I told them one more move, and I'm going to quit. Now it takes half an hour.

That summer in 1963, Senior went for two weeks vacation, and he left me a piece of paper. There were ten–twelve items. He was very concerned that I don't run out of work. That was my impression. When he came back, he's looking for all the product drawings. I had only finished the first, and I was starting with the second. From there on, he really saw that we needed help, and gradually we hired more and more people, because the workload was there. I always remember that what John gave me for the two weeks, I could work two years.

To me, that was the fun part. The first ten years when they were small and building.

When I started, Johnny was purchasing agent, then he took the sales over. One big job we got from Voice of Music. They made record changers in Benton Harbor. Johnny was the guy who really went after it. They're hard-working people, you have to admit that. When we got the switch project from Voice of Music, we came in Christmas Eve and worked all day on Christmas. We needed twenty-five samples to submit to Voice of Music, and Senior was working all the time making those switches.

Senior's policy was very strong, no alcoholic beverages in the plant. There were Johnny, Senior, and two or three other guys. It was now 2:00 P.M. on Christmas Day, and Senior brought in three or four six-packs. I designed the on-off switch, which was a big item from Molex. Probably built eight million of those for them before they got out of the business.

In the speed we were working, we got the job, we were smaller company, we got parts tooled in six weeks. Junior sent me down to Security Plastics, we cut the parts, delivered them. So wait a minute, what happened if I am wrong? What happened with the tools if the parts were not per print? You go down, accept the part, inspect the part. We were on the go. That was my responsibility. I accepted it. I made the mold myself. I would find out the part that didn't fit. Lots of people are not that diversified. Bigger companies can no longer operate like that. I can't be designer, inspector, quality control. They narrow down on your areas. That's why when the company was smaller, it was more pressure. It was more exciting.

In those days, I couldn't wait for the next day to go to work. I liked my job. I was product manager and got five-six people, and that's as far as I wanted to go. Director of Engineering, that's a lot of paper work now.

Dealing with people. I was more working with the products where I got very much involved with Senior. He was as good an engineer as he was a person, because he got more common sense. Because in engineering, 75 percent is common sense. He would give you an idea, he would not quite push you. You had to be responsible. He gave you an idea, he talked it over. This looks pretty good, that's the way we are going to go. Go back to the board and start playing, what we're talking about doesn't look good on the paper. Where we previously had agreed, now it looks different. Even if it was his idea, he was willing to compromise.

We are all big engineers but when the time comes that had big projects that didn't work out, Senior was very upset. But in engineering when things are really advancing so far and you don't have a product, it's very tough to correct. Certain things are tooled and basically they are wrong. A certain product will have contact problems. Senior will say, "My dog can put these parts together." That was always his expression. Maybe his dog, but it was too late for an engineer.

A couple of times right after the golf game, in the Molex league, six or eight guys a table, everybody has a beer. Time to go home, maybe John has two beers, he picks up the bill, twenty bucks, four bucks apiece. To me, it certainly wasn't the money, that is not the point. That is something like John's style of living. I could be wrong, maybe he feels that somebody shouldn't take an advantage, but it also could be, we're all in this together, I'm not the boss here. Other than that, I have always had the feeling that if I really was in need, I could go to John for a big favor. I'm not considering myself at work the easiest guy to get along with. I've got my own demands. Not because Senior was also my boss, I think there was more to it, that he knew how to handle me, which means a lot for the company.

You never know what John thinks in regard to the customer. He plays it close to the vest that way. But somebody was pulling something once, and he said, "I don't believe in getting rich quick." I had never heard that expression. Who wouldn't mind getting rich, and why not quick? It was explained to me what was meant by that, and it came back to me when it was printed how rich he now was. He didn't get rich quick. Molex wasn't always a gold mine. In 1963, it was no gold mine. These people are hard workers, you have to admit that.

Twenty-five years ago, John started stock options and profit sharing. I was with the company a year and-a-half when it started. They gave us a couple-page booklet. I remember I told Bob Sebastian, "I'm not planning to retire or die, who the hell knows what's going to happen after twenty-five years?" John says to me, "What are you saying about profit sharing?" I had heard things that if they fired you before ten years they didn't have to give it all to you. Ironically, profit sharing is the best thing that ever happened to me. That's what I'm living on. That and the stock options I can make as much as I want as a consultant. I get even today calls from Molex. I have a desk. And drafting board. I'm checking projects. Usually, there are more important projects that you have to pay attention to. They are ready for tooling. You like somebody to check that, a guy who's experienced. Take a little closer look so won't get involved in problems.

RON ADAMS

I came to Molex in January 1965 as a tool and die maker. When I started, there were only a few of us working at our plant in Downers. Seemed like there were about thirty people in the building, if that. Senior used to come out to the plant and work with us.

He used to send us over to Brookfield one day a week to work over there. Everything was black and dirty. I can remember when they came in and vacuumed all the pipes and ceilings and stuff like that. I didn't know they were doing it for the "Clean Roon" sting. I don't know how they ever got away with that one.

He's such a down-to-earth guy, John. We had the golf league when it started, only a few of us then. We'd go and golf and have a few drinks afterwards. He could have a temper. This one time we were golfing, a guy in the foursome behind us hit the ball right near us, close enough so that we could see it land. John went over and stamped it into the ground. The guy came up and wanted to know if anybody had seen his ball. John said, "Your ball's down there."

Junior has a temper too. I've heard him chewing people out. He gets red in the face, and he doesn't let them get a word in. For that matter, so does Fred. When I was there with him in Japan, he got mad at something, and he let four or five of the big shots go there. I don't know, they were keeping secrets from him or something.

It's been a good place to work, no doubt about that. I got sick last year. I'm diabetic. I get these pains in my back. I was talking to Pribish one night, we were at a wedding, as a matter of fact. He said, why don't you go the Mayo? I couldn't see taking time off work, and you got to stay there in Minnesota. He said, "Just go. We'll pick up the tab for everything." Plane fare, hotel, food, everything. Didn't cost a penny. I thought that was really good of them.

The progression dies we make are the backbone of the company, I think. Lots of times I found myself working all weekend if we had a breakdown. Bob Pribish and I, we'd come in, I'd get the die going, and we'd run the parts off, drive them to the airport, put them on the plane. Another thing, speaking of getting satisfaction on the job, after the terminals are made over in another plant, we make these little dies that crimp them onto a wire around to a PC board. We build them and then we travel around the country, fixing them, servicing them. A lot of times people will call: The die's broken, production is down. Sometimes, we can talk them through over the phone, tell them how to fix the die, and if we can't, we'll just go, and Molex pays for all service calls to the customer. They don't pay a penny.

I still remember when we made the vibrator machine out of the little paper jogger. They had a wooden board where you'd lay the paper, and I still got it home as a bread board. Then we got the second jogger, and Frank Miller did the same thing.

Fred Gierut is a brilliant designer. He's brilliant. I used to work with him, then I was in charge of the shop for debugging new dies. I worked with Fred. He'd come out, and we'd go over the prints. Stuff like that. One time we bought a new kind of punch press. It's called the Bruderer. Our punch presses used to run something like two hundred strokes per minute. We got this new type of press, we'd run it one thousand strokes a minute. John Sr. and John Jr. both came over that day to look at it. "Ron," Senior said, "there's nothing like it," and we tripled the speed of the press, and we've never looked back.

They've been fair as far as wages go. In our tool and diemaking trade, a little bit ahead of what union scale would make. We also got profit sharing, we get it every quarter, three or four times a year we get a profit-sharing check. When we were at Downers, the union tried to get in there. They got a bunch of us tool makers and they said they were going to have a meeting. It was across the street there at the VFW hall. So we went over, heard what they had to say. Actually, the union couldn't do a thing for us. They couldn't guarantee us more money, and we knew right away that if we got a union, our profit sharing would go. We decided to kick the union. Because I know John Sr., he's dead against unions.

The stock is good too. Now we're getting it where we can get it taken out of our check, so much a week. I've made a lot of money on the Molex stock. When it first came out, it was $25 a share, and it's split several times. I bought a lot of stock when it went down to $12 one time. I used to get paid in savings bonds, so I cashed them all in and bought the stock. So I've got a lot of Molex stock. Almost 2,500 shares. It's become a nice little nest egg.

When the company does well, the profit sharing goes up and the stock goes up. So you're profiting in a lot of ways.

Johnny has a feeling for the guys in the shop. When I was over at Downers, he called us and asked what we thought of the raise we'd just got, and we said, well, any raise is good but there were some who thought it could have been a little bit more. So Junior came and talked to us, and he gave us more money.

Fred is good to work for. He's good to his International group. A few years back, he took them all to Monte Carlo. He's always doing things like that. We used to send tool makers to Japan a lot. Every night they'd have something for us to do. In fact, we used to go bowling at the bowling alley that is now the main plant. What I'd like best was I'd go home with families and see how they live. They sit on the floor when they eat. The man and me would eat, and after we finished the wife would eat. I guess that's their custom. The younger Japanese, now, they live almost like we do. In modern apartment houses. The old ones, the man would come home at night, he'd take off his business suit, and he'd put on a kimona. I'd think, Ron, you're a long way from Downers Grove. Where else would I have ever got a chance to find out about things like that?

RAY WIESER

Ray had been with Motorola in Franklin Park for two-and-a-half years. He had previously worked for a custom molding company in Chicago.

Six months before I started, they opened the initial part of the Downers Grove plant. They opened that in 1964. Brookfield was still the much larger facility, and that's where they did all the molding. I learned very quick, the hard way. I started in May, which was coming into the summer, and you'd go into that molding room with those ovens, and it was about 240 degrees. It would get so hot we'd sometimes send people home at eleven or twelve o'clock.

I lucked out. The guy sitting at the desk next to me at Motorola had been there for fifteen years, doing the same thing that I had been doing, and one day I sat back and realized I didn't like working for that big a company. So I looked in the Help Wanted section of the *Sunday Tribune* and saw a little ad there and I answered it and was hired. I had a wife and two children. Making a job change from Motorola that everybody knew to a Molex that nobody knew was somewhat of a gamble, certainly. But I really liked a small company atmosphere. I had interviewed with John Sr. and Ralph Kalmar, and there was something about it that I just felt good about.

I had a lot of involvement with Senior in those first six or seven years in projects where we were invloved with building, the manufacturing operations, and the expansion of manufacturing operations—some of the innovations in manufacting when we went to the high speed stamping and into the nylon molding. He was always encouraging us in the manufacturing organization to try something new.

He would get people to start thinking about it, like our high speed carbide die stamping program. That started with a discussion with some of us on what we could do to run the dies faster. He did an awful lot of reading and he might say, I read somewhere about this stamping press that's made in Switzerland. You guys look into that and find out what that's all about.

We'd take off and look into it, before you know it, we've got these Bruderer stamping presses that are the finest stamping presses in the world, and running dies at 1,500 strokes a minute now. Back in those days we were running them at 250 strokes a minute.

Like the land out in Lisle. He went and bought that five years before we ever broke ground on it. That has always been one of his strong points, seeing into the future. He'd sit down and he'd start writing out his numbers of what our sales are, how many square feet we need to support, how many square feet we have now to support our sales, and how many machines, and then he'd start projecting out five years and start running the numbers and say, "You know, in five years we're going to need 100,000 more square feet than we have today." And then he'd do something about it. I'm sure that's what prompted him to go out and buy this land. He wanted to stay in the area, and he was smart enough to do that.

When you look back at the history of the company, the early Seventies is when all hell broke loose. If you look at the years 1970, '71, and '72, those three years, the business grew so rapidly, plus that's when Fred was really getting going with Europe. We started with the Ireland operation in 1971, and we broke ground and started building the Lisle operation in 1972, and we bought the Addison Tool Shop in 1971 or 1972. So you could look back at our sales history for those years from 1969 to 1974 and you'll see that we went from like 9 million to 17 million. We had a multitude of projects going on to handle this growth. Not only the projects with the facilities, worldwide, that we were starting up. It was really a fast-paced time.

I look back on those years and I wonder how the hell we did it. There were so many projects that we had going. If you sat down and made a five-year plan and said you were going to do all those things and gave it to someone at GM or GE, they'd say you guys are crazy. But it happened. A lot of hard work from a lot of people. The Krehbiels really kept everybody motivated and led by example, coming in early and staying late. There was never any doubt where they were coming from as far as wanting to get the job done. That, I think, was always important.

When I would interview people as prospective employees, especially when you started talking to management people, when they heard it was a family-owned company, people who have had some bad experiences would say, oh-oh, tell me about it; and I would say, I don't know what your experiences have been before, but I guarantee you that you have never experienced a family-run company like this company. If they all didn't have the same last name, you'd never know it was a family.

There isn't anyone in this family that's along for a free ride. They're the ones that are driving the company.

The rewards are both financial and psychological. Certainly the employees who perform and get the job done consistently are compensated very well, and given opportunities to increase their own responsibilities and, consequently, their own personal goals. I always like to say that we look for aggressive people who have personal goals and objectives, because they're coming into a company that's extremely aggressive, and if they're not aggressive, they're going to have a tough time operating in our environment.

And Senior. I just know that I have more respect for him than for any individual I have ever met. He's so honest. You never have to guess where he's coming from or what he means. He's just that type of person. I've never known anyone like him and I probably never will. He's an honorable, honest individual. Smart. A nice person to be with on or off the job. He was involved in a sting on me. He and my son got me on the golf course. He invited me to leave early and play golf, and they were conniving with my wife on a surprise birthday. He kept me out on the golf course so everyone could get there. I walked in the door, and it was all surprises, and then he walked in the door. My wife didn't hesitate to recruit him to sting me. That's the kind of person he is.

ED HEALY

I went into the rep business in 1960, and I represented a company named Tri-Metal products that makes metal stampings. That was one of the companies I was representing. It was selling two parts to Molex for their switches—the 1175 push button switch and another switch that was used on electric ranges.

Johnny Jr. was just out of college. We were having trouble getting the parts to him, and if we did they were wrong or there were problems with the plastics, and I just concentrated on working with Johnny on this thing. We got along very well, so he asked me one day if I'd be interested in representing Molex. He said he'd like me to meet his father. That was how I met Senior. Through Junior. That was in the fall of 1961.

Molex at that time had a need for someone who had my background in selling and marketing. You don't have to have an engineering background to be a Rep, but you have to have some engineering knowledge. I had fourteen years of Illinois Tool, ITW. I had a great education from them. A fine company. Engineering-type sales. That's what I was interested in, even though I had a Liberal Arts background.

If you got a little knack for it and the guys at the company you represent are engineers, they can understand what you're talking about.

I could sit there and describe the problem to Senior. He'd take a pad out and he'd start scratching. Was that what I was saying? No. . . . I can't draw a straight line but I know what they want.

John is excellent, and that goes back to his Uncle Al. Albert Krehbiel, the artist. His Uncle Al taught him how to do it. Selling is like everything else. If you're good, it's recognized, and if you're not, it's recognized. A rep is sitting with his own business; he's a contract sales person. I represented several different companies. None of them as successful as Molex became.

They present a challenge to people. That comes from John Sr. We were out in California on one of our trips. One day it was raining and we couldn't play golf. John says, let's go in and play racquetball. I had never played racquetball, I had played handball. But this was fifteen years ago. John was sixty-five years old, I was 50, and he ran me right into the floor. It didn't take long.

I made up my mind I was going to learn to play racquetball after that. He's a competitive guy. I'm like that myself.

John invited me over for a golf tournament at Naperville, and after we were finished we went in to have a drink. We're sitting there drinking, the pro comes in and says, Geez, you two guys had better be careful, I think you're going to be in a playoff. We say, What do you mean? We had no idea where we were, never bothered either of us.

Sure enough, we're in a playoff. John is behind me on my drive, the other guys were ahead of us. They're better golfers, it's a handicap tournament. One of them was the club champion. His handicap is two. The rest of us carry a ten. So John hits his ball nice. I hit a ball and it's OK. John hits his second shot, and he's only about 10, maybe 20 feet off the green, which is pretty good under the circumstances. I get lucky and hit a ball about 2 feet from the hole. These other guys, all of a sudden, one guy is out of bounds and the club champ is over the green.

We won $700 and a TV set each. John had never gambled. He didn't know what he was going to do. I said, I've got no problem. I'm going to take mine. So he gave the money and the TV set to Pete and Yaz. A year later, we went over there in the same tournament and this time we won watches. Pete and Yaz are home and they said, "Would you get us another television this time, Gramps?" They expected him to win again. That's the way they feel about their grandfather too, I guess. They expect him to win. And he will win. He does.

John makes things work. It's got to be will power. It's got to be strength. It's got to be something. How many people have you met who are like that?

Iris Osborne

December 14, 1964

I came in as a secretary to the purchasing agent, who was Pete Matts. I had come from Continental Insurance, which I found so boring that I finally told my husband I just couldn't stand it anymore. He said, Well, he didn't know why I wanted to look for something else, because I wasn't looking for a serious career. I was just looking to help out.

After I started working at Molex, I did become more serious about what I was doing because I felt what I was doing did have more impact. There were four other women at the office at that time. Marie Manatte, of course, and LaVergne. Florence Slansky was the switchboard operator and payroll clerk. She died about ten years ago. Edith Lindgren was the bookkeeping department. She had an antiquated bookkeeping machine of some kind, I don't know what it was called. She would sit at this big, monstrous machine, I didn't even understand how it works. It wasn't something that you sat on your desk, it was a big machine that she had to have a chair and sit in front of.

And Ila Koutek, who retired. Ila used to write up the orders. They had this old duplicating machine that made those purple copies. Remember? Like they had in school when I was a kid. That was what they used to send the copy of an order out to shipping.

Pete Petrucciani was in the warehouse in Brookfield. Oh, I was afraid of him. He'd call from Brookfield yelling at me because I didn't get something in that he needed. He had such a rough, hoarse voice. I was really not too happy when he called. Then I met him. He finally came over to the Downers Grove plant. He walked up to my desk and said, "I'm Pete Petrucciani," with that real rough voice, and I started laughing. I said, "You're just a little guy. I've been afraid of you all this time. I thought you were a great big monster because of that voice." He said, "I fool a lot of people that way." He was a very likeable person. A sweetheart. And a very hard worker.

I remember when Pete came in, all excited, to announce that we had just had our first $1 million month. The next day, Peg and Posey took all the female employees out to lunch to celebrate. There were other times when we'd had some record-breaking occasion and John Jr. took us all to the Drake over in Oakbrook for lunch.

Fred was in the sample department when I started. He was the only person who made samples and sent them out. He didn't have any interest in the business at that time. He said he wasn't going to stay. He had just come back from England and he was very interested in castles. He had visited a lot of castles and he had put together a little book about castles, and I still have mine.

When he started with International, nobody thought it was going to amount to anything. He hired a secretary and he hired a consultant and that was all. And then he started traveling some. Hired a few more people. Opened sales offices. That's all we thought it was going to be. Sales offices. He handled everything very quietly. Then he was traveling all the time. He was flying to Europe twice a month and to Japan once a month, and everybody was saying, "He is never going to be able to keep that up."

KERRY KRAFTHEFER

Kerry Krafthefer was hired in 1968. He had been working in a company in Des Plaines and wanted to work closer to his home in Downers Grove. He was twenty-eight years old.

I was told that there was this company that was owned by the Krehbiel family, and the old man was president and chief engineer. They had four engineers and were looking for a fifth. He had two sons in the company who were not engineers. And this guy was sixty-two at that time, and he had taken the company with $6 million sales. Hmmm. Two sons who are not engineers. He's sixty-two, probably ready to retire.

I had gone to IIT. I had worked in the computer department at the Argonne National Laboratory at the University of Chicago which was the Atomic Energy Commission. From there to a company called Nuclear Chicago, which was high-tech instrumentation. And then Strombecker Tootsie Toys, where I designed those stock racing cars and also did the instruction sheets for putting them together that people woke up to on Christmas morning. Yeah, I was that guy. What interested Senior when I interviewed with him was the toy experience. Cheap electromagnetic toys. I agree. It was mass production, and you had to be fast, because every year the push was on to make the Christmas market.

It's not the little place it was when I joined. We were two hundred people and we knew everyone by their first names. I succeeded because I spent all kinds of hours here. My in-laws, I think, are still upset with me for being at a meeting on a Sunday night when my wife was over at their house in Lombard in labor. I was at a Molex sales meeting the night my son was born. I had to go pick up my wife, and they were yelling, "Why aren't you with your wife, our daughter?" I took her to the hospital and she gave birth the next day. At the sales meeting I was passing out cigars. That was my youngest son, Kevin, and he's seventeen years old now, so I've been working at Molex longer than I've had two of my sons.

It's not everyone's cup of tea. My son would sit here and draw on the drawing board while I was working on Saturdays. Now he's an architect.

I've told people, it's not that you're wrong; we're probably wrong. We're nuts. My daughter graduated from high school and I wasn't there. I brought them in here on Saturday. They'd play with the toys and things and have pens and draw. She's a University of Illinois senior in architecture.

My wife will often say when she finds something in my suit pocket, "How can grown men get so excited about something like this?" I'll come and say, Look at this, this is super, and she'll say, "It's a little piece of plastic and metal, what's the big deal?"

Actually, what I liked about it was that the chairman of the board was also the chief engineer. And that meant I'd be reporting directly to him. A few things Senior has told me over the years is how you invite competition if you price the products too high. So we regularly base our selling price on the cost of the product, but only to make our corporate objective profit of 10 percent—we don't try to get 30 percent or 40 percent if that's what the market will bear. We would rather make it as low cost as possible and then put our price on it such that we could make a fair profit.

One of the important things I learned from him is his philosophy—to design and maximize the characteristics of the materials you're working with. That is to say, if you're using a metal, and we think that brass could do the job—it's a low-cost copper alloy—we'll try to get by using brass, and we will press that material to its limits to get it to function. We might have to design the product a little bit differently. But we would really try to get the most out of that material. When it comes to the contact surface itself, a lot of people would use gold in many applications. We tried very hard to understand that mechanism, that contact interface so we wouldn't use gold unless we absolutely had to. We tried to use a low-cost plating such as tin, or solder; we tried to use a low-cost contact material such as brass as opposed to Phospur bronze of copper, and we tried to use nylon instead of phenolic which is a thermal plastic. His philosophy, which I think is very fundamental to our style of engineering and one that I have learned (and I'm concerned whether Molex will be able to keep it), is to maximize application to the least expensive material. I admire him for that, and to me that is the Molex engineering philosophy.

Many people take the conservative route: I've got to be sure it works, overkill it. Very wasteful. He's adamant about that. Not only for Molex engineers but for American engineers, that an engineer isn't doing his job if he is overkilling a design.

It depends on how you approach the challenge. Either you say, this is my design, now I have to find the material to work with it, or you say, given this material, come up with a design. That's more Senior's philosophy. Given this material, come up with a design. He thinks you do a good engineering job when you take inexpensive materials and turn them into outstanding performing products. I think that's, really, even beyond John Sr., the Krehbiel philosophy. His father was very much the same way. Use the inexpensive materials and see what you can do with them. One man's garbage is another man's gold. He doesn't consider it a good engineering job when people just automatically come in and use the most expensive product, gold plate it, put it in. Sure, that's easy, but are you doing a good job for your company? Not only for Molex. Is that engineer doing a good job for our customer?

It was very loose when I came to the company. We lacked a lot of things. We wanted to change a drawing, we just changed it. We wouldn't tell anyone. They didn't know what to make in production. I'm ashamed to say that, but that's exactly how it worked. Loosely structured. See, I like that free-wheeling, being a little bit entrepreneurial. Now it's so many systems.

It's a big company now, and I wasn't hired by a big company. I was hired by a small company.

FRED GIERUT

Came to Molex in July 1967 from Cinch connector (which is now a division of TRW). Cinch had moved to Elk Grove village, 25 miles north of Chicago, and Fred wanted to work closer to home.

After high school, I went to work for about three years as a junior tool and die designer, then went back to college, then back to work as a die designer and went to night school at the same time. I took courses in electronics, air conditioning, radio and TV. I thought I was going to be a TV and air-conditioner repairman. But as I got involved more and more in tool designing, and got better at it, I became more in demand. Because people with a lot of practical experience in that area are hard to find. I worked at a lot of places. Some of them did the same thing as Molex. I also worked at a company which did a lot of big automotive type of things. Real huge stuff. I was doing a lot of moonlighting too. Ninety-nine percent of my education has been practical experience, but I do use the things I learned in my two years in college. I learned a great deal about all this sort of electronic stuff we make. I did a lot of machine design, and I had to know a lot about electronics, and wiring, and air cylinders, and gears, and things like that. In my case, it all went together.

After Cinch moved, a headhunter called me up and said there's a company in Downers Grove looking for a die designer with my experience. I never heard of Molex. I said it doesn't sound so good. A little company like that, it might be shaky, and I had kids already. But it was half the distance, I was only twenty-nine, so I interviewed with John Sr. It looked like a very ambitious company, and the pay was right. I had been assistant chief engineer at Cinch and I came to Molex as just a die engineer, but the little company was actually paying me more money than the big company had. I didn't care about the title. Eventually, I became the manager of die engineering, which I am now.

The good thing about John Sr. is if you have a crazy idea he says go ahead and try it. His approach is a lot like mine, a kind of shotgun approach where you don't have all the answers but you do have a lot of ideas, and he would say, Go ahead, can't learn if you don't try it. He told me that many a time, he still tells me that today. Go ahead, try it. He's not worried about investing money on a good idea. He's thrifty, but when it comes to inventiveness, it seems like money is almost no object. He won't say any stupid idea you come up with, try it, but if it's a logical idea he'll tell you to go ahead. How else are you going to find out?

Because I worked in so many places, and moonlighted in a lot of electrical companies, a lot of shops that make stuff for people who are our competitors nowadays, and a lot of automotive distributors and places like that, I am very familiar with their construction. And on construction we do a lot better. We get longer life out of our tools, and they run faster, and we keep on working on new ideas to make the dies more changeable on the press, and with less maintenance on the toolmakers.

If you're not involved in our industry, it's hard to visualize what we go through. The people here have to be very, very creative; it's almost like creating songs and poems except we do it in technical language.

I always figure a designer is something like a painter. You have to have a talent for it. When you start designing a tool you really don't know exactly how it's going to look. You can't picture the tool before it's done. You start, and you start developing and drawing, and little by little you progress through the tool, and all of a sudden you're finished and you say, OK, that's what my tool looks like.

If you've got the talent, the word gets around. We're looking for a die designer now, comparable to what I was when I came here, and our personnel guy is combing all our competitors trying to find out who is available. There aren't too many young people who get into our type of profession. Or even know about it. And it's tough when you start out, because there's so much to it, so much to learn. And you never learn it all. The more I'm in this business the less I feel I know.

I enjoy the competition. There's always so much more we have to accomplish and learn. The day I don't have a challenge will be the day I don't want to work here anymore. I enjoy the pressure, and the game. The Krehbiels have a way of making it seem like that, like it's a game that I know somehow I'm going to win.

All the guys in my department are tool designers, and we all work the same way. We work hard, put in long hours, and there's no fooling around. We bullshit like everyone else. We have our discussions, talk about fishing and hunting and the usual things. Then we all hit it again. I think you have to have that attitude to take the challenge and run with it, see what you can do to win the game. If you have a guy who just wants to come in and coast, this ain't the company for him. All our guys run with the ball.

Through the years, a lot of people have come and gone. In the crimping department we used to have a bowling league. Bruno Baumanis and

Bruno Rice and me were on a team, and we took first place. I was still young then, and everybody after bowling would make the bars around here. I don't do that anymore. Same with the golf league. After golfing, we would sit around and have a few beers. They still have it, but I don't get in that any more. I live thirty-five miles away. There comes a point with kids growing up, I got four kids, and I just want to spend it with them. I spend so much time here already. And I go home and have different troubles with the kids, the home, the car.

JIM GEISER

Purchasing. Came in 1969, as a result of one of those accidents that wasn't really so much of an accident.
"That was a funny story. Probably the first company which I interviewed with that I didn't really want to come to work for." Geiser was working for Honeywell, in Boston. One of the buyers who worked for him showed him a blind ad in the Wall Street Journal, *told him he'd never get Jim's job unless Jim died or quit. Jim answered it, had lunch with the headhunter who had placed the ad, and was so little impressed that he ducked a couple of interviews and was finally shamed into going to New York, instead of spending his usual Sunday on the beach.*

I was interviewed by Johnny. The most unusual interview I had ever had. He sat there and talked for about two hours about Molex and then we went out to lunch, came back, and he said, "Tell me everything you ever did since you graduated from high school, and don't leave out any details." That was the whole interview. I went back to Boston and I never thought I'd hear from him again. The next day he called and said he wanted me to come to work for him and would I think about it. I said, "Hell no, I don't know anything about Downers Grove."

Johnny said, "Come out Saturday and have dinner and meet my dad," and from then on it was just like a love affair with the company. The

Krehbiel family to me is the most interesting family I've ever met in my life. It's almost like the old saying in the army, there's a right way and a wrong way and the Molex way. Coming from big industry, the Honeywells and that type of thing, and working for a small company—and even as big as we are today—the Krehbiels have a hands-on pulse of the situation. When I first went to work for Junior, I used to tell my wife, if the phone rings at three o'clock in the morning and nobody's died, you can go back to sleep. Johnny would just wake up and dial the phone and say, "Hey, Jim, what about that thing we were talking about yesterday." The Krehbiels demand a hell of a lot of you, they'll bust your balls, there's no doubt about it, but at the same time the rewards have been great and I've been able to grow with the company. I'm in my midfifties now and I could never work for another company. I'll either quit, retire, or start my own business.

Molex to me is not just a job, it's a way of life. You can walk through an airport, LAX or LaGuardia, and you seem always to find a Molex person. They travel at night, they travel at all weird hours of the day. You'll always see someone on the road again. I had lunch with a gentleman today, and he said, "I've never seen a purchasing group that travels like your people do." Most purchasing people don't travel. I have as big a travel budget as our sales and marketing people. Again, the Molex philosophy is that if you're going to do business with a company, it's better to sit across the desk and go eyeball to eyeball. We put our buyers on the road constantly. They're looking at what's going on, what the market is. Every time we talk about budgets when business is going down, John says, "What about your travel budget," and I say don't touch my travel budget, because you can't do business sitting on your ass. Johnny always agrees. Johnny was a football player and he says you've got to hear those knocking heads, one-on-one. The day I leave Molex is the day it's not fun to come to work Monday morning. Because it's fun. I've been here nineteen years, and it's fun to come to work Monday morning. To see this company just boom. We're like the Bears when they won the Super Bowl. We have a lot of controversies, we fight amongst ourselves, but I tell you, it's a lot of fun. If you don't have fun doing business, then get the hell out.

There were times we could drive into walls as we grew. There's always more to do than you can do. I think a lot of their philosophy is to give you a hundred things to do and if you do eighty-five of them you're doing damn good. I've seen people who couldn't go along with this. It seems every time there's a crisis, it happens the day before a holiday. It's either

Christmas Eve or New Years' Eve or the Fourth of July. There are people from larger corporations who are used to working from eight to five and going home. And that's not the fact with Molex.

Johnny is here at six o'clock when he's overslept. There's not a manager at Molex who works less than 60 hours a week. Or a Krebhiel who works less than 70 hours.

As we grew, we hired people who just couldn't keep up with our folks, no matter how good they were in the companies they came from.

Any manager who works here can take all the vacation time he wants. They just say, Hey, you do your job and you get it down, when it comes time to take a trip, if it takes three weeks, go ahead and take it. They demand a certain perfection, and I think most managers here give it to them. I think that's the secret of Molex. It's all the good people in this company.

They treat you like you're one of the family. In 1971, we were negotiating for the Mexican border operation. We had a committee consisting of Ron Canaday, Ray Wieser, and me. When we took Johnny down the first time, we were in the Cavern Cafe and they had one of those guys walking around drawing caricatures. Johnny had him draw a picture of me as a Mexican bandit and he says, "That's how I want my purchasing agent to be. A Mexican bandit." I never knew it, but he had it framed, and on my second anniversary he gave it to me. It says: The Cavern Cafe, 1971. I have it hanging in my office.

During that same time, John comes walking into my office and says, "You're going on a trip, right? Do you have a pair of alligator shoes?" See, John used to have a pair of alligator shoes, and Posey would say she always knew when he was going out of town because she'd look in the closet and his alligator shoes were gone. I said heck no, I can't afford alligator shoes, I buy my shoes at Thom McCann. It wasn't a day later, his secretary walks in and says, Here's a present for you from the boss. It's a pair of alligator shoes. That was back in the Seventies, and he probably paid $150 bucks for those shoes. Johnny comes in and says, "Every time you go out of town, I want to see those damn 'gators on your feet."

They're like that, and yet Senior is so down to earth. People around here read about Senior being one of the four hundred richest men in the U.S. At the same time, it's funny, he's driving a Plymouth K-Car. He says, I need a new car. I said, OK. Since I'm a purchasing agent, I buy all the new cars. I'm thinking BMW, Mercedes. He says, "That K-Car looks nice. Do you think you can get me a sun roof? Peg would like that." He says, "Nothing fancy, one of those kind that Montgomery Ward has for about three hundred bucks."

KEN KUFNER

When Senior hired me early in 1969, he was chief engineer and company president.

It was ironic how I was hired. I was working at Continental Can. I was on the board and I sat next to a guy who was a headhunter. Molex was advertising for an automation engineer. I was interviewed by Senior twice in March and again in April 1969.

As chief engineer, he hired me as the first of the automation engineers. I worked for and reported to John from 1969 to December of 1975. He's a gentleman, honest as they come. If you have heroes in your life, he'd be one of mine. Obviously.

We did a lot of traveling, back in 1973, '74, '75. John had his own plane. Magnavox was a major customer, we flew back and forth to Greenville a lot. We also made lots of trips to Europe, and Senior is always a lot of fun to be around. We had this German kid, Pete Kohler, who presented these seminars. We were in Heidelberg, Germany, seven days during a seminar, and we had a couple of drinks at the hotel restaurant while we were waiting to be served, and it turns out to be one of those affairs where they come and cook the bird at your table. There's this guy, in the big cook hat, and he's making a big production of it, with the arms flapping and the fingers flicking. And he's wheeling the serving truck this way and that, and after what seemed like forever, he pours wine or something on it, does a little pirouette, makes a magic pass and pft— there's a burst of flame. And silence. "What are you going to do now," Senior said, "throw it out the window?"

You had to be there.

Like all the Krehbiels, he goes to bed early in the evening and gets up before dawn. Peter and I would have dinner, put John to bed, then we'd go out on the town and pick him up at 6:30 in the morning. Did it five, six days in a row. Came down to breakfast the last day, and he says, "Gee whiz, you guys look awful. What's the matter?"

"We got the flu," we said. "Lot of that going around Heidelburg."

When I hired Tom Schneider, I had been here about two months. We had him working on a special project, and Tom was working Saturday, Sunday, late every day of the week to get this machine done by a certain time.

Then one morning, after Tom had done this for about a month, John walked in around 8:30, and Tom was sitting down drinking a cup of coffee.

John took me aside. "What's Schneider doing?"

"Tom's working on this machine. The 1500 assembly table."

"No, what's he doing right now?"

"He's having a cup of coffee."

The story is in the timing. The guy has worked something like fifty-five hours straight. He takes fifteen minutes, and John walks in and catches him on his one break.

When Senior was mad, he'd get mad for a long time. He had a tic, where he'd put his finger into his shirt collar, straighten his neck, and straighten his tie, and get all red in the face. And for a couple of days, he might pass you in the hall without acknowledging that you're there. They'll all let you know when they're mad, all three of them. Junior has a library of items on how you embarrassed yourself. Johnny loves to throw the grenade and run behind to be there when it blows up. He likes to wound you, not kill you. But WOUND you. Overspending will do it. We were quoting a machines system for Burroughs in Daley, Pennsylvania. This was years ago. I estimated twelve grand. It went way over that, more like twenty-five grand. That was a lot of money back then. That's the kind of thing he loves to bring up. He'll bury you that minute, but an hour later. . . .

Junior had no engineering background back in those days. We had a machine in back, and we were trying to feed little tiny pins down a plastic tube into a fixture and then finally into a wafer assembly. What happened was, as the pins went down the tube, they would create a static charge and effectively cling to the tube.

We're getting nowhere, and Junior wants to know why, and when I try to explain, he says, "Don't give me that static charge bullshit. Go out there and fix the machines."

I sent Schneider down there. We're trying all kinds of lubricants, Free-on, everything, and two weeks later the machine still isn't running. So Johnny calls Tom in, and Tom starts to tell him about static charges. Johnny almost threw him out the window.

TOM SCHNEIDER

Tom Schneider was twenty-six years old, in 1969. He had worked for two years at Continental Can Research Center.

Senior is still to me the same as he was when I walked through the door and was interviewed by him in 1969. He's never changed. His speech is the same. His memory is excellent. No sign of age. Maybe walks a little slower, maybe does spend an hour or two less a day here. Other than those minor things, he's here.

He interviewed me along with Ken Kufner. He knew I was only out of school for a little bit, knew what I wanted to do as a person and with my engineering career. We were talking about salary. I had just left this company, and he hired me for about what I was making at the other place. Twenty-five dollars a month more. It's what I'd asked for.

I came in as an automation engineer. At that time, Senior had charge of engineering so I was under him. The equipment part of it, kind of went in two different directions. There was inside automation and outside automation. I had one of the groups, with four or five fellows in the beginning. That was in 1969. Now I have fifty in one group and in my other group maybe one hundred engineers.

As far as the automation on application tooling goes, I remember Senior's theme, which is absolutely correct, that the future of Molex was in the automation side of the business. Specifically saying years ago that we have to automatize customer tooling. I think Molex is known in our industry as pretty strong on application tooling. It was his vision that got us there, knowing what we had to do. He stated that many times.

I have been at this company since it was a $6 million company. It certainly has made a difference in my life, in terms of my career. I don't think my career would have been the same if I had been with a different company, because of the growth and the changes. They wanted it to grow, and they wanted it to be successful and the people in it to be successful. What will always stand out in my mind is the striving for excellence. To be a better company. And as far as the Krehbiels go, fairness too. Senior is a down-to-earth gentleman.

When we have bonuses, they go all the way down to every level of the company. Profit sharing the same thing. And stock options. There is always some type of sharing if we're doing well. They have all that stock, but the money goes back into the business to make it grow. That means a lot to a lot of people.

We recognized that lots of people were making robotic systems. IBM makes a robotic system, and Telex Adapt, and Unimation, and several others. We decided not to make robots. We decided to make the systems that would go on robots, so that if the customer said, Hey, we're using an IBM robot, I want your production, OK we have a delivery system that will work with an IBM robot, or anybody else's. So we recognize that. That's our niche in the robotic market. We are making delivery systems for our products to be used in anybody's robot system, in any of their plant operations.

That's a new market for us. We're not trying to sell equipment, we're trying to sell products in that market. We'll deliver the product. Whether it's tubes or boxes or cartons, using our technology will allow the robot to replace it.

Senior used to do the automation equipment. At one time we were repairing an old machine from Brookfield, it was real old. We had it at Downers and we couldn't get this thing working. We had a couple of engineers working on it; Senior came through and asked us what we were doing. This engineer said, "I don't know who designed this thing, we'll never get it working." And John just said, "It worked pretty good years ago when I built it."

My secretary was thirty-nine years old. She worked for us for seven–eight years, and did a very good job, a very aggressive lady. She didn't feel too well, so we got her into Mayo Clinic and we found out she had a brain tumor and she had it operated on and passed away not long after that. I know that John put some things in motion that took care of her two girls and made sure they were OK, and took care of a lot of things that normally another person that owned the company wouldn't even think about.

A lot of times people would be ill, and Junior or Senior would do something special to get that person up to Mayo to make sure he's OK. That happens a lot. It happened I had a fellow working for me, a twenty-year-old employee, factory worker, worked in crimp area, hadn't felt well, had some back problems, and legs were bothering him. We fly him up to Mayo Clinic, pay all expenses. Get him examined. Had a problem. He retired, and that's something they did out of their own instinct.

Molex is a family thing, they look at it as a family business, not in terms of the Krehbiel family. We're all very close. It may not be that way through the entire organization any more, and some of us are not very happy about that.

Pat Weber

Pat Weber came to Molex in 1969 under circumstances we will go into later. She came as production inventory control clerk, which meant she was working on the shipping dock. She went on to become a customers order specialist, then one of four regional field supervisors. And since 1983, she has been in charge of one of the New Business groups.

Every promotion came about because she heard there was an opening and went after it. With every promotion, she was breaking new ground for a woman in the company.

I get up at 5:00 in the morning and I'm here by 6:00. My husband will look at me. "How do you do it?" You're up and at 'em and ready to go the next day. You walk in the door and you're electrified. I recruit for the company. I go out to college campuses and recruit. I'm looking for people who are about to get their engineers degrees and don't want to be engineers. Who want to go into sales or marketing or manufacturing. In five years I've promoted about thirty kids out of here.

I've experienced just about every emotion that a human can on this job, since I've been with this company. All of them except one. I have never been bored.

I have been so angry that I go out and I slam my car door, go home and kick the door. I get so angry because things don't go right, or because we lost a piece of business, or a program didn't work. I'm elated when one of the kids graduates. One of my graduates last week pulled a contract worth a half-million dollars.

I hire them and I train them, and to see them grow and go on to do things like that is just phenomenal.

I was the first woman in a lot of meetings. Having come up through the organization, having worked with a lot of different people, and having had a lot of opportunities since the time on the dock, I have probably heard colorful vocabulary for a woman. Not having just come in on a load of cantaloupes, I understand most of the terms.

I don't ask for any concessions because I'm a woman, but in meetings these men were used to John and his very rich and colorful vocabulary. One guy got involved in an emotional outpouring and he let loose with some very colorful terms. And John just stopped the meetings and turned around and looked at him and said, "Watch your mouth. Pat's here."

To me it didn't make any difference. To John, it did. For years he called me either Lady or Madame. I wondered about Madame, but I decided that it was a term of respect.

Yes, John Krehbiel, Jr., has walked out of his office and asked me to go get him coffee. And a roll. And he even specified what kind of roll. I did it. I grumbled about it to myself, but I went and did it. But that was more than ten years ago. Because I have been training my boss and training all these gentlemen. Until three years ago, John still had me doing a report for him on the billing on the dock that was ready for shipment. Everywhere I went in this organization this little report followed me. I laughed about it. Finally got with people over at the tooling building and we got another way to address the problem. We got John out of the loop.

Senior has been an individual I have a great deal of respect for. Each anniversary they give us an award. From ten to eighteen years, they send you out, for a dinner. On my thirteenth anniversary, I picked up the phone. "Pat?" I didn't recognize the voice. "This is John Sr. I have a little gift here for you for sticking it out thirteen years. Probably don't want anyone to remind you of that, though."

So he came up to my office and gave me the award. He likes to give out the awards. He always says, "We're very thankful for your contribution." That's one of the fun things of the job.

Getting praise from the Krehbiels, it means so much, it really does. Because they don't hand it out. I can remember that my mom was a hard taskmaster. She was a role model. I am what I am today because of my mom. I remember that any praise from my mom, that was everything in the world. It made me so happy. I feel the same way when they praise me. It's a paternal feeling. You look upon Senior with the same type of respect as you would your father.

They had done things for me on a personal basis that . . . actually I guess you could call it an endearment and a debt. They have done those things for me that no employer would ever even think of doing for an employee, and because of that I will be here until they take me out on a stretcher.

It's like you're sitting around and you're worrying about something and all of a sudden someone reaches out and touches you, and you don't have that problem anymore. And you don't know how they know, and you don't ever ask because to thank them would be to embarrass them.

Let's go back to 1969 for the type of thing I'm talking about.

I joined Molex in April of 1969 and in May I found out that I was pregnant. I was pregnant when I came to Molex and I didn't know it. Because I had been trying for years to get pregnant and couldn't.

The doctor had told her that she could not get pregnant while she was at a bill-collecting job because she was under too much stress.

So I left and I was sitting at home and my uncle, Lou Boyles, called me and he said this job won't be stressful. All you have to do is clerk work. At that time I was one of three women in the State of Illinois, one of the seven in the country, that had ever held the position of assistant branch manager for a loan company. I was a bill collector. Back in the sixties, women didn't do things like that. I went into bars after people and knocked on doors. Having achieved success with that career, came the moment I was going to be a clerk, and then I found out I was pregnant. And the next month my husband decided to leave me. I had been on the job three months. He left on Sunday, and on Monday morning I went to my boss and I said, "Mr. Kalmar, I'm pregnant, my husband is gone, and I need this job." He said, "Well, Pat, I can't make any promises."

I said, "OK, I'm not asking for any promises. All I'm asking for is a chance."

"You've got that."

Well, I did everything at Molex outside of cleaning the bathrooms. Nobody else wanted to do this? I'll do it for you. And really, I worked very hard and I would come in very early and stay very late.

They looked on me as someone who really wanted to make a contribution and someone who really needed the job. And so they let me work up until three weeks before I was due, which was absolutely unheard of at that time, because you left the job when you started showing and you didn't come back.

So when I left to have my son, Ralph Kalmar said, "Pat, if you're feeling all right, would you mind doing some work for us at home? We have all these reports that have to be done."

I said, Sure, I'd be happy to. There was no mention of "pay me" or whatever. I was home ten weeks. My son decided to be late two weeks, and when he was five weeks old I came back. And my paychecks never stopped.

My paycheck arrived every Friday, registered mail. And, again, that was unheard of. Absolutely unheard of. It enabled me to pay my hospital bill and bring my son home without any financial burden. At that point, you can't imagine how I felt.

I still don't know who told who, or how it came about. Senior or Junior. Or Fred. I sat right in front of Fred's office.

They are absolutely incredible. When you work for somebody who works as hard as you do. Or harder. And is always there to talk to you, and knows who you are, is going to give you advice if you ask for it. He's going to praise you, but you're really going to deserve that praise. And if you deserve a smack he's certainly going to do that for you.

No, it hasn't always been easy. Everything you heard about John is true. And then more. But, O my God, when you need him. When you need these people they just seem to know.

IAIN MACDONALD

Iain MacDonald arrived in March 1970. His title was assistant quality control manager.

I was about thirty-five. What was exciting about those days was that we were struggling in Molex Domestic to get into major customer bases, and at the same time we went into International. In the old days it was tough because we didn't have a base to build on and we had to get that base. Now we've got a good base to work on, but the competition is absolutely ruthless out there. Fifteen years ago, we went into those other countries, and they're obviously coming back and pitching at our base industries now. The Japanese are one of our biggest competitors in Domestic. And every week we see new things coming in from Korea and everywhere else.

But the Krehbiels' philosophy is, this is fine. The three of them, they've never backed away from competition. Sometimes, in the old days, we used to swear they enjoyed it. In fact, we used to have meetings in Downers Grove, and Junior would be there bringing out what we had to do. We'd do anything, fly anywhere. It wasn't unusual for us to fly around the country, take the red-eye special out, approve something, bring samples back the next morning, and then be with a customer that afternoon. The first trip I ever took for Molex was when I was sent down to the Security Plastics in Florida. We took the evening flight to Miami, went into the molding house, spent all night and all morning there, and I got the twelve o'clock flight back to Chicago, and by late afternoon I was on my way to a customer with samples in my hand. We still do those things. We will do anything we have to do to satisfy our customers and keep their production lines going. People have said to us that's one thing that our competition doesn't do as well as Molex. When we say service a customer, it's not just a slogan, it's something that we work very hard to do.

I remember the time Art Johnson and I went down to a company called Amco in Indiana. That was an all-day deal, and we're coming back late at night, and Junior was waiting for us at the airport. He had committed to this customer that we would be in Huntsville, Alabama, the next morning. We had ticket checks we could fill out, for the 5:00 A.M. flight out of Midway, but between the three of us we couldn't put together $5 to carry in our pockets.

What we do nowadays is that we are much more certain in our procedures. For example, we come out with a new product, then we sit down as a group—design, automation, quality control—and we discuss what we describe as product reviews. If we're going to make a terminal or an assembly, we sit down and review the design, and each representative of the department has comments to make about the designs, myself from a quality standpoint, from a processing standpoint; and from my experience with the customer on similar products. We discuss the areas where we have potential problems. The reliability lab people come up with their testing requirements, we come up with our manufacturing requirements. Automation people may have some comments on what they require.

All these years I've been here I've known people to quit Molex and I will guarantee you that nine out of ten of them, if you bump into them and ask how are things going, they say, you know, I made a wrong move, I should have stayed at Molex. That's because they want that success and they want that old-fashioned pride and they want that feeling of family loyalty that we have here.

You have a whole mix of people but they're all of a certain quality. The enthusiasm, the dedication. And there's also a personality about a lot of people around here. Doesn't matter if you're in top management or the guy on the floor. It starts with the Krehbiels again. There's none of this big boss, little guy, shop floor thing around here. That's the type of excellence you come across as well. It's the people, personalities, work ethics. Get the job done, that's it. When I interview somebody now I tell them I try to be as fair as I can. What I need from you is to get the job done and I don't like to have to say, "Can you come in Saturday?" I expect them to come in Saturday. I expect them to come in Sunday to get the job done. I don't like to have to ask. The people around here, that's what they're going to do. They know they have to get the job done and they'll do whatever they have to do to get it done.

Senior has always been a rough guy when he makes up his mind about something. I always remember when I got a letter from him saying, this is absolutely the last time I'm going to tell you, and he puts that in writing and, whew, that kind of shakes you up. But Junior would never buck Senior, and a lot of times Junior would say, I want that done, and Senior would say, You're absolutely not going to do that. So you think Holy Mackerel, what are you going to do? I felt like that guy in that stage play, *Mr. Roberts,* for a long time. If I stayed out of Senior's way for a couple of years and let him wonder who I was, maybe I'd be smart enough to maneuver between those two directions.

Don Slavicek

Started out as an apprentice with GM, and went through the metallurgy department and tool design-ing. Got his foot into design at GM's electromotive plant where they made the Diesel locomotives and went to school at night to learn design. Then he went to work on Ford aircraft when they were making the first jet engine. Throughout his life he's gone to night school. He was hired by Molex in 1970 to get their nylon molding operation going.

I ran the old plant where they did it all, where they started. When I came there in 1970, I came from a pretty modern stamping facility. When I walked in there and looked at that operation, I felt that I had walked back in time.

Senior's approach to most things was a very practical applied logic. I know we would get involved in quality discussion and methods of manu-facture or design. Usually, his resolution to something was, "Well, what's the practical logical way of doing that?" And then all of a sudden people would get off on their engineering tangents. And it would be very practi-cal. "Well," someone would say, "if it was like this. . . ." And he'd say, "Well, then, why the hell isn't it like that?" And usually when he left that hanging there, you had the solution. We used to get into situations because I was the plant manager. My responsibility was production. You had to get that stuff out the door, because what went out the door paid the bills.

You got results, you got recognition, you got paid well. You expect this. You know, I always felt that I'd be working as hard for anybody else as I'd be working for the Krehbiels, yet the Krehbiels seemed to be more appreciative. I've worked for people who sort of looked down their noses at me and thought well, you know, you're one of the guys that works in the factory where you get your hands dirty and the dumbbells work.

He hasn't changed. One day, the old man was listed as the fifth richest guy in the state, and then it changed from $450 million to $245. "How's it feel to lose $200 million, John?" He says, "I never considered it in the beginning."

He hasn't changed. He and I went to the design show one day. I had a better company car than he had.

We were merging onto the Stevenson Expressway, and there was a big gravel truck bearing down on us. I'm saying, "John, step on it." He said, "I've got it to the floor, dammit. Next time I get a car I'm going to get one of those goddam turbos in there, so I can go when I want to go."

I said, "John, why don't you get the purchasing agent to change it for you now?" It's like he doesn't want to bother anybody on personal things like that.

There aren't many John Srs. left in the world; there should be a tribute to a man like that.

Senior had a good philosophy about banks. He wasn't a big financier. When we went out and bought things, we bought for cash. He had strong debt capabilities with the bank, like $20 million. We were never in a debt situation. I worked for a company where their debt was always hanging over their heads. You could never do anything.

Like when John Grasso and I hit him up for a couple of Arborg machines. He said, OK, but it better do what you guys say it will do or you can walk east until your hat floats. But you don't have to go through a Board of Directors and a bunch of accountants who are going to tell you they walked through the factory last week and it seemed like half the machines there weren't running, why should they buy you two more.

When Senior points a finger at you, that's the time to look out. It was Alex Ewens who first said that. And when he says, "f---" you better get out of there. He's used that word maybe four or five times in his life. It was like this sumarai who swung the sword so fast the guy didn't know his head was off until he saw it on the floor. He'll use hell and damn often, but that's all. When Senior walked in and said, "What the f--- is going on here?" look out. Heads were going to roll off the end of the truck like watermelons.

I had a heart attack because I'm my own worst enemy. I put stress on myself. I can remember hundreds of times I was wrestling with a problem, and I would get up at night and go back and sit at the table and write down all the thoughts I had, or even sit down with a calculator and do the math. Otherwise, I wouldn't have been able to get any sleep at all.

My wife understood. I had two kids eight years apart. One kid I was very close to. The other worked for Molex in his growing years. I was never close to him at all. He was never involved in any of the extra sports activities, or the extra above-work things that I did with my other kids, because I never had time for him. I was married, and Molex became my child.

RON CANADAY

Ron Canaday, vice president–controller. Started in June 1970. A graduate of the University of Illinois, he served seven years with General Motors and four years with Miles Laboratories.

I never actually worked at Brookfield, but the first time I saw Brookfield was kind of funny. I came in on June 15, and physical inventory was June 30. Being the new kid on the block, and not having seen Brookfield, they couldn't wait for me to get over there in my white shirt and tie. I was accountant-controller when I was hired. Some of my staff went along, and I know they expected me to take one look and start reeling. I never batted an eye. Went out and talked to people, rummaged around in the boxes. I was a great disappointment to them. See, I'd heard from some people what it was like over there, and I knew just what to expect.

I was recruited. My last job at General Motors was plant accountant at Guide Lamp, which had three thousand employees at the time, and then I went to Miles Labs, where I eventually became a division controller.

I had spent eleven years in two fairly large companies, and always in Indiana. Coming into a company the size of Molex was interesting to me. But I'm not sure that was the primary factor. My wife and I both grew up near Champagne-Urbana, where the University of Illinois is located, and our families were all there. And then, I interviewed two or three times with John Sr. I thought he was a great man. Still do.

He had certain things he wanted done, and you could just could see in his face how intense he was, and you knew if you came to Molex it would be a challenge, and you would have a clear direction of what you were supposed to do and you would have to figure out how to do it. You could use your own ingenuity and resources and have some autonomy to accomplish the things that were laid down.

Two years after I came here, the company went public. I, being the chief financial representative of the company at that time, and John, being the president at the time, John and I took the brunt of dealing with the attorneys and the accountants for the registrations of stock.

Most of the meetings were held in Chicago at the William Blair offices. The ride to Chicago was about forty-five minutes, so every day for several weeks, we were in the car, chatting.

We were in a roomful of accountants and attorneys, and they get rather nitpicky—that's their job—for the SEC and so forth. It got hairy many times. It was such a long, long process, and we were very small, our sales were about $20 million. You have to start disclosing some of your major customers—where you sell your products; what you compensate your principal officers—just a myriad of things in a registration statement. It was very difficult for John. We had a lot of long hard conversations on what he really wanted to disclose. Now you have to bear in mind that some of that you have to do legally. But John is a good teacher, and I certainly learned very quickly from him that you don't automatically give them what they want.

It's not just black and white. There are different ways you can supply the information, and in certain cases the way it ended up, they didn't get quite as much as they said they had to have. But that was a long siege.

We do talk about the old times, and a lot of the newer people just can't comprehend that period of time. You had the facility at Downers Grove, you came into a little foyer and there were a few offices, and then a very small area for manufacturing. They can't comprehend what it was like to be a $20 million company, with the whole bloody company in one office, including Fred. From our perspective—the people, who have been here fifteen to twenty years—we saw the company go from $20 million to $385 million. It's remarkable.

We have facilities all over the world, and we spend $40 million to $50 million annually on new tooling, new equipment, and brick and mortar. When you look at the track record and the growth, the worst thing you can do is have the business and not have those things already in place.

The philosophy of 25 percent increase in sales and 10 percent in growth is very aggressive, no question about that. But that's why we're in the Fortune second 500, and should be moving well up this year.

I got to tell one story. This is between 1970 and 1972, I can't remember exactly.

Junior assigned Ray Wieser and Jim Geiser and me to find a suitable place to relocate our factory. We needed to have some low cost operations.

At that time, we had some mechanical switches that some of the old molding went into. We looked around and decided Mexico probably was the place that we should look at. As you know now, we have too large facilities in Nogales, Sonora.

This is the funny part. During that period I contracted Bell's Palsy, which is uncommon, but not *that* uncommon. They don't know what causes it. What it is, is paralysis. You can draw a line from the tip of the skull down through the middle of the nose, and the right side of my face was paralyzed, and the left side was completely normal. And so your eye begins to droop on one side, and your mouth. And your speech becomes slurred.

Jim, Ray, and I were the team. We went to Nogales. They had a reception on the United States side for some of the potential businessmen who were there. There must have been fifty or sixty others besides us. One man, who was a wealthy individual in the city, was at the reception. He had some stores and also a freight company, and he really came at us. He was not very pleasant at all; perhaps even hostile. He said he was very concerned about all the business coming into Nogales, Sonora, and also Nogales, Arizona, because it was their Shangra La. A nice community. He said, All you people come down here, and we're going to have to build more schools and our sewage systems will have to be revised, etc.

Here I am with the side of my face all drooped over. The only way I could speak without slurring was if I put my finger at the edge of my lips and stretched my mouth out tight. Then I could speak normally. And I was doing it by then without thinking twice about it. He said, "Where are you from?" and I pulled my mouth over and said, "Chicago," and he just went bananas. CHICAGO! Let's face it, Chicago does have a little bit of a background about Al Capone and all that. And here's these Chicago gangsters, and this crazy guy with his face all drooped over.

Wieser and Geiser are saying, "Naw, we live in the *suburbs* of Chicago. The suburbs!" At any rate, we became one of the first U.S. companies to locate there in the industrial park.

TED TOMKIEWICZ

Ted Tomkiewicz is the vice president of products engineering, commercial products division, the largest engineering department in the organization. Commercial products include the appliance industry, home entertainment (which is primarily television), office panel industry (which is something new) and electronic games. He has thirty engineers under him.

Years back, I worked at a competitor, Methode, a considerably larger company at that time. I had been contacted by an employment agency and asked if I would be interested in talking to a small company that had pretty sound things about it. The one thing that impressed me was that I came over to Lisle to interview and, hell, they're opening up a new building. Nice carpet. We didn't have that at Methode. It kind of struck you. They're expanding into a new facility, maybe there's something happening. In two weeks I got called and I said, hell, I need a change. Two-and-a-half years at Methode and nothing interesting was happening. The thing that convinced me was that one of the important people I was very close to at Methode told me he had heard about those guys. He told me it was a very good company, and they were coming on very fast. I talked to Senior and Clete McDonald, the chief engineer, and the personnel guy, Ralph Kalmar, and they sounded like they were regular guys.

They offered me all kinds of things at Methode to stay, but I had made up my mind and nothing was going to change me.

It was a little bit of a shock because I had been working on nothing but military products, and when I came here it was all commercial stuff. Nylon connectors. Cheap and dirty stuff. Molex had found a niche in providing what they called "affordable technology." Not giving you the best contact materials or top-notch plastic materials but materials that would do the job.

Of course, I still designed with the Molex material, too. Senior would come around and look at the design, and we had a lot more time to have close contact with Senior. He would look at our design and see too much wall there, too thin, and he'd say to core that thing out, get rid of that material.

I tell you this is a tough place to work for, this is a very tough environment as compared to the environment I came from, but at the same time they give you an opportunity to show what you know and show what you're capable of doing. They reward you accordingly.

We have our picnics and we have our fun. I go to Senior and we talk about golf and other things but, boom, it ends and you go on to what you're there for. As far as I'm concerned, I've learned a lot and I respect these people a lot. They don't change their positions from month to month or day to day unless it's a business decision that they have to make. But they have character, all of them. I've known Fred and Junior. Obviously, I've been the closest to Senior, but I've known Johnny quite well also.

I always was fascinated by the way Molex was able to identify business, and when we found it, boy, could we keep it. There was so much attention given to projects. Never a letup. Weekends, Saturdays, Sundays, Mondays. Whatever the hell it took we were always meeting and talking and making sure the thing would happen. We still talk about it, driving here in the morning and seeing those two lights on and then driving out of here at night at seven o'clock and the lights still on, and then you go on a trip and come in here from O'Hare at 8:30 at night with a limo and those lights are on. You didn't have to know a hell of a lot of anything other than what was happening from the top management, and the guys who were successful at Molex follow their example.

I didn't know how good I was or how good I could be and I maybe would never have known if I had worked in companies like Methode. They're still a company and they're making money and keeping a lot of people employed. I'm not knocking them from that standpoint. I don't think they offer the opportunity on a broad scale like this place. When we were growing I had opportunities to go to other areas in management here and I had to refuse them because I wanted to stay in engineering. The challenge is always there to find out how good I can be. And the more you work, and the more you get to do, and the more opportunity you have to keep learning, the more you understand that if you're lucky and work as hard as you possibly can, you never will find out. And I think that's the secret of Senior's philosophy, and that's the success of Molex. The challenge is always out there in front of you.

Affordable technology was a Molex thing for a long time. It was more than just a slogan. You knew that there was some obligation for you to make that thing work with a little bit less than what was possible. Really trying to get total value into the total analysis, beyond the connector itself.

The equipment. How to put it together faster. Build that in at the front end. Optimize the sucker. Don't compromise the integrity. Work on optimizing it from material usage. And that happened everywhere. Connector design, die design, and mold design. And sometimes we cut corners and we got burned, but that's how we learned. I think it was a term that stayed for about five to ten years. It kind of went away with the high-tech.

There was a situation I'll never forget as long as I live. I was given the responsibility of overseeing constructing a connector from Clete McDonald because he was going out of the country. Clete was a hell of an innovator, and it was great for me to get the opportunity to work on the project. I got into it and analyzed it, and I told Kerry Krafthefer, who at that time became chief engineer, that I wasn't going to work on the thing unless I totally redesigned it, because it wasn't going to meet the customer's specifications. Bob Sebastian told Senior that the connector wasn't going to work, and Senior said, "My God, we made some commitments."

The next morning, Senior called me and Kerry in, and I wasn't through the door before he said, "You're giving up on this thing? That's it? That's all you've got to say?" I mean, he really put it to me stiff. "You're just giving up?" I really got scared because the last thing I wanted was to give up. And then I was excused from Senior's office, and I guess Senior went after Kerry pretty good. I think Kerry had a lot of good things to say about me, and we got together with the marketing guys and the application guys and everyone. I presented the details of my problem, and everybody agreed that I was going to have to redesign. I made some modifications, and we did have a great model shop. You had to do everything with a pair of pliers.

A couple of weeks later Senior came over to me in the shop and said, "You did a helluva job on that connector." That really impressed me. Because he didn't have to do that.

I live very close to Senior. One time I was going to pick up some firewood, and he said, why don't you come and get it from my area? I intended to take my son and go over and help him chop. Instead, he called me and told me to come over and pick the stuff up. It was all stacked up for me in front of his garage. He loves to do it. He's got a splitter now, attached to the tractor. The first time I went over there he showed me the mallet he used. That thing was so heavy, I thought it was going to take him over backwards. He was chopping away. Now he goes down to the woods, cuts the wood with his chain saw, splits the logs, and brings it back on this little wagon he pulls behind his tractor.

I would never go and ask him for it. But every year, he says, come and get your firewood. I just loaded up a beautiful pile. I say, I'll come and chop it myself, but he loves to do it and it's already there.

The man is unbelievable to me. I had a recent experience with him and my son. When my son got interested in flying, I went to ask him who was a good instructor, and he called the guy who had been his instructor and had my son come in after school so they could meet each other. Last year, my son graduated from high school and got his pilot's license and he's now studying aeronautics at the university.

I don't often go and sit in Senior's office. Sometimes we don't talk for two months and then he'll come and say something and it's like we were working together and we're neighbors or something. It seems like you're addicted to his way of doing things. You say, damn, that's exactly what my father told me. That's how things happen. He never changes the values of what he is trying to pass on to us.

I conduct myself the way they conducted themselves when we were working from that end. I'm groomed, and, I'm sure, so are all the other guys in the company. We may in certain situations change things, but we go right back on track and work according to the Molex philosophy. When we get real big, things may be less controlled and all that. But I'm sure everyone feels the same thing.

JOHN PSALTIS

John Psaltis, joined Molex as an assistant controller in the summer of 1972. He had been working for Touche Ross, one of the big eight cost accountants.

Molex was a small company then. What drew me to the company was that it was young, aggressive, vibrant, and looked like it had good potential. I started in International, working with Fred when International was only five years old. We had a small subsidiary in Ireland, and we had just bought out the joint venture partner in Japan. And we also had a small office in England. That was it.

The quonset hut in Japan was just about what I expected. Japan was still looked on as a less developed country, industrially. As hard as that is to believe now. We stayed there for a couple of years before we moved to a bigger quonset hut and remained there until about 1975 when we bought our bowling alley.

That was really a great job of negotiation. After Joji told us the price he negotiated, we said, all right, now we have to do one more thing. Now, you go over there and tell them we want the bowling alley torn down because we just wanted the land. So he went back, and when they agreed to tear it down, we said, All right, instead of waiting for you to tear down the building before we sign the documents, you reduce the price by another $50,000 and we'll take care of that part of it ourselves. To this day, we are still using the bowling alley as a factory. We didn't have to do anything. We had to reinforce the floors to handle the greater load that was put on them. We had to gut the whole inside for all the new electrical fixtures and piping and everything else. But as a bonus, they left a whole bunch of bowling shoes, and for years our employees used bowling shoes at work.

We developed very quickly, but not always quickly enough. I remember with our first general manager, Joji Taksuka, the business had just started growing, and there was a scare on the commodity markets. We used a lot of brass material, and business was starting to go up and it looked as if we would not be able to get brass. Joji decided to do a good deal and bought a lot of inventory. We didn't need all that brass, that was close to two years' supply in those days, so needless to say we found ourselves in a cash-flow problem. And Fred said, You guys got yourself into this, you find a way to get out of it.

So I went to Japan, started talking to our bankers about arranging a loan to pay for this material, and the bank says, Sure, we're going to give you the money, but we want a parent-company guarantee.

Fred was not going to ask for the parent company to give International a guarantee. He said, You fellows have to mature and learn that you have to pay your own way. So find a way of making it go.

We finally did manage to get our line of credit established with one bank, and we did get out of the problem, but that was before we could afford to go to that restaurant for lunch. For luncheon, we'd have cucumber sandwiches. Two slices of bread and a slice of cucumber in the middle.

In 1974, we were planning on starting a European headquarters in

England. In the winter of 1974–75, the oil embargo came, and it was very difficult to find fuel. So the government decided to conserve electricity. One day we'd have electricity, and the next day we'd have heat. So we would have these storage units for heat, and we'd plug them in during the days when we had electricity and allow them to trickle slowly the other days, so the place would not be frozen.

I remember Toni using woolen gloves with the fingers cut out on the manual typewriters, and she used to stick a candle on top of the typewriter so that she could see when she typed. That was a sight to see.

We finally decided to move away from the doctor's office and found a new location in Aldershot. But it was brand new construction, and we didn't have any of the utilities hooked up yet. Behind the place was a storage tank for natural gas, and to hook the gas up so we could have heat, it took a long time. It was just behind us, but to draw the line from there and hook us up took three months.

It was a cold winter, and we hired those industrial warehouse heaters that looked like torpedoes, and sounded like jet engines taking off. In the mornings we'd get in and crank them up so the chill would go away. But by the time the people got in, we had two choices: being deafened and suffocated with the kerosene smell, or freezing to death. There was no in-between. When those things were working, it was warm, but you couldn't hear yourself think because of the noise, and the kerosene smell was pretty strong. When you shut it off, the building was not very well insulated, and five minutes later you'd cleared out the smell and every-thing else, but it was cold and damp. Just before we froze, we'd turn it on for a few minutes to get the chill out and shut it down again. We were there for one year.

Brazil was a comedy of errors for a long time. Or, as we prefer to say, a learning experience. We started in Brazil in the late seventies, and we just never could get the thing going. By the time we made the decision, a recession started in Brazil. Inflation started shooting up. We couldn't get the right people who worked with the right mentality, and it just kept on going farther and farther down. It was time for a re-thinking of our approach.

In 1983, Fred asked me to go down there and straighten it out. So we took another look-see, and put a squeeze on expenses, increased selling prices, and immediately our sales ran from $100,000 a month down to $30,000 a month. After a few months of problems, sales started picking up again, and we were able to get bigger margins and build it up. And finally, last year the Brazil plants basically balanced the inflation, at least for ten months, and gave our company time to breathe and show a profit, and prove that it can be successful. But it was many years before the turnaround, and quite a bit of money went down there. It was a learning experience.

The one thing we really need to focus on and continue is not to lose the people orientation and the can-do attitude as we grow larger and larger. I used to know everybody around the world by their first name, from janitor to general manager. I'm having a hard time now remembering just the managers.

I have a favorite story about Fred. It is not Fred's favorite story. Right after we moved to the Epsco building, myself and a couple of other people decided, we'll get new furniture and paint the place, it will be nice. We also decided that Fred's old desk and old chair were going to be totally out of place in the new environment.

He was out. We just picked up his desk and his chair, put them in back of the warehouse, and put in a new desk and a new chair, and waited. Fred walks in, and he hollers at all of us. He says, "I'm going out for five minutes. When I get back, I want my desk and my chair back here or else all of you are fired."

He got his desk and chair back. The desk is still in his house, and he still uses that same chair to this day. Although at least we finally got him to reupholster it.

Fred's strength is in knowing how to be flexible when he is dealing with different nationalities. Flexible not where you forego your beliefs or your principles, but flexible enough to accept the different temperaments and idiosyncracies as long as the structure of what is being done is correct. What color you paint the wall isn't critical—to use a metaphor—as long as it's a good solid wall. And different countries, different nationalities, have different preferences for colors, and will paint it differently. So you have to make sure that the Molex culture remains the same, yet at the same time allow for the flexibility to paint the walls different colors and maintain the differences that make us a truly multinational company. I think it's very important to be able to make that distinction.

JOHN STIPANUK

*General manager, engineering and marketing. He
has a degree in mechanical engineering from the
University of Wisconsin.*

I came here in 1974 from Sunbeam Corp., which is an appliance corporation, and their R&D headquarters are in Oakland. I was working a lot on
product design there.

One of the guys in the Advanced Development group came to this
company about a year before I did. Back then we were in the $20 million
range. The feedback was that this was a growing small company. I like a
small company as opposed to a larger company. I sent in a resumé, and
they turned me down. I guess they didn't have an opening, because they
called me back a year later out of the clear blue and asked me if I would
still like to have the opportunity. So I came out and was interviewed. I
looked at these little parts—little stampings and housings—as opposed to
the household products like a mixer or a blender. I said, How can that be
exciting?

I came in as a product designer here. At that time they didn't really have
an R&D department. We just went to the customer and looked at the
problem, came back and designed a product for them, instead of maybe
looking and designing something that's in the future and takes a lot of
R&D.

I came here on quite a commitment. I was thirty years old and my wife
was pregnant. In fact, we had twins six months after I started here. I had
just bought a brand new house and here I left my secure job and took a
risk with a small company. Sure turned out to be a fine risk.

I hadn't heard it was a pressure cooker or anything like that, which I
later found out was pretty much the reputation.

What I had, though, was the exposure right out of the block. Two
weeks after I started they gave me a credit card and a business card, which
I hadn't known as the tools of the profession, and sent me to RCA to sit in
front of engineers to design a brand new product. I knew nothing about
the connector business before I came here. But they were growing so fast,
and they needed people to do the technical side and develop the products.
That was the kind of start you had. There wasn't a six-month training, or a

year development, or working with somebody. You were on your own and sent out to do the job.

Later, we got to developing our own people. For three or four years in a row there, I would go to campuses and recruit right out of school, so we would have these fresh engineering graduates and place them strategically throughout the company.

I'd look for a roll-up-the-sleeves type of individual. You had to look for somebody who was willing to get into all aspects, not just be one of the cogs in the gear. The engineer covers it from womb to tomb. We covered it from the manufacturing standpoint back to the development of the product, the customer interface. It really was hands-on. If you had to be in here Saturday making some samples with your hands, putting two parts together, you did it. If you had to draw the project, as opposed to giving it to a draftsman, you did it. You did whatever was necessary to get the job done.

Most of my association with Senior is in either of two areas. One is in Advance Development, which he heads up, so we had quite a little bit of interplay there. The other is on the golf course.

Certainly he's a hard-working individual to be in here every day at his age, and plugging away.

He has a philosophy of working very hard to accomplish something, and nobody retires. I'm amazed at how sharp he is for a man his age about what's going on here on the business side of it.

In Advanced Development, he's a kind of catalyst on new ideas. Nothing seems to be impossible. We have a consultant that comes in, he works for Martin Marietta, he comes in with a lot of what I'd call Blue Sky ideas. We're all talking how tough that might be, and how we'll never be able to accomplish it, and the next thing you know John is saying, "Yeah, that's pretty exciting. Let's get it on our action list, let's work on it!" John contributes quite a bit in the A.D. meetings. It's not just being there and putting his weight to the projects. He's thinking about ideas. I've seen him step up to the board and start sketching ideas. "Let's take a look at it this way." He has a lot of credibility.

As to golf, we have a league on Tuesday night in the summer. The league is divided by ranges of scores. 'A' Flight is the best golfers, and there's ten of us in that group. You usually play your opponent, plus you can team up with two other guys out of any Flight for the foursome. So he gets to play with a wide range of people, not just the golfers of his own caliber. But he's very competitive. He enjoys the game and he's a very consistent, very disciplined golfer. Most of us are certainly a lot younger, and we're hitting the ball all over the place, always trying to recover, and he's just right down the middle every time. One of the things he gets a kick out of, he likes to take a buck from you.

What I get a kick out of is when he leaves work and gets into a little Chrysler. He used to have a K car. Here's your multimillionaire, as reported in a publication, and he wanders out in the gravel parking lot and gets in a K car. He sure doesn't seem to live the success story.

BANE KESIC

Bane Kesic is international marketing director.

The first time I went to the plant in Downers Grove, eleven years ago, they had a guy named Jerry McElligott, who was the plant manager. At that time I was in the liaison engineering group, which was just forming. That was the first step in the effort to pull everybody together and work with the customers, with production, and with our QC control people. So I go there and I had to shut down one particular product they were running because it was out of the specs. I was telling the lady who was QC operator that we had to stop the press, repair the die, and get it going again. She went into the office. This man opened the door, Jerry McElligott, he's 6'4", and when he opened the door, the door literally flew wider. He said, "Who are you?"

And I introduced myself. I said I had just started today. He said, "What do you think you're doing there?" I said, "Well, shutting you down, Jerry. Because the parts are not being produced to specifications."

He said, "Bullshit. This is my plant. Get the hell out of here."

I started to ask myself did I come to work for the right company. What the hell's going on?

I said, Hey, you can scream, you can hit me, you can do whatever you want. But this doesn't go as long as I'm employed. If you fire me, fine, that's a different story. Then he starts accusing me that he has to lay the people off, he's going to have to send everyone home. I stuck by my guns. Half-hour later, he flew out, yelling something; just slammed the door and it shook on its hinges the other way.

To get out of the factory at the time, you had to go through his office and I heard the voice, "Hey, kid, come over here," he said. "You know, I give you credit. You stood up over there. Let me buy you some coffee." Since then it's worked out beautifully.

I'm from Yugoslavia, graduated in Yugoslavia as a mechanical engineer. I got all my courses when I came to this country and got a job at Zenith Radio. I took courses at IIT just to see if it was really what I learned over there. Then I took a couple of additional courses later on. And from that point I took a lot of management-type courses. Plus Molex had the U. of Chicago design a special program which was for six weeks. Nobody got the degree or anything like that, but we covered economics, statistics, marketing. We went through all the disciplines that MBA graduates do. Then finally they sent me to Harvard MBA school for two weeks, for an advanced marketing management course.

Bob Sebastian would come in when I was with Zenith and say to me you're wasting your time. If you're happy to work from 8:30 to 5:00 and have your little projects for the next sixty years, you're in the right place. But if you like excitement, if you really like a good company, I've got the place for you. He started telling me more and more, and I said, Bob, it sounds fantastic. We had to clear it with the two guys I reported to because at that time Molex had just started selling to Zenith, and we didn't want to upset anybody. And they said, Hey, if it's a better opportunity, by all means. I took the job for less than I had been getting, but in two, three months they gave me everything. I never regretted it. Never. As long as I live I think that was the smartest move of my life. And the one person who is happier than me is my wife.

I was there two years, when Uncle Bob came downstairs and he said, Bane, with your European background, I think you can contribute much more to Molex if you go to International. I tell you, kid, they are growing. He always called me "kid," because he used to call me that when I was with Zenith. I said, Uncle Bob—I called him Uncle Bob—I said, Uncle Bob, if you think that's the right place to do it, hell, I got to rely on you to show me the way.

He said, "It's all set up. You go upstairs and talk to Fred."

It's always exciting. Can't wait to get back in the morning, because half the stuff is not done yet. Constantly. Everybody gets this feeling where you want to dog it for an afternoon, or you don't feel like doing anything. But I'm telling you, that's the main reason why I quit Zenith, because I found myself working on one project, and if I'm a little bit late, nobody says anything. If I want to doze off all afternoon at the bench, nobody would say anything. I just could not stand it. If I'm not busy, I go goofy. You look always for what's next, what's next.

And the funny part is days go very fast. I think you fulfill your dreams or whatever the case may be. You feel you are doing something. And I'm contributing. Not just for the company. I'm contributing, after all, for myself.

When you go on a trip, believe you me, you're starting like 6:00 in the morning, you make all the customer calls with the local guys or with the customer, you have dinner. During the dinner, believe you me, nobody talks about how nice the weather is in Czechoslovakia. We talk business. Afterwards, we go to the bar for a nightcap, and it's still pure business. You get back to your room at midnight, and it's been business for eighteen hours solid. Day after day after day while you're on a trip. Couple of times I was physically tired and did not want to discuss, but you never find yourself saying, hell, why am I doing this, is there something else in life than just talking? But you just get that excitement. A couple of times I got comments from European guys or Far East guys. Hey, don't you guys in Lisle know how to talk about anything else than just business? And then, OK, if they feel like that and it's late at night you apologize and start talking about something else. But it's business, business, business all the time. That's the total commitment. Total. And what Fred is doing is getting the wives involved in a very nice professional way through seminars, and a little bit here and a little bit there, they're a fantastic support. My wife never, ever questions why're you going, what's happening, she just knows that I enjoy it, she sees the rewards. I mean what else is there?

We had an International meeting in Santa Barbara, and Senior has a house close by, and we had one evening where the entertainment was a Western hay ride. And at dinnertime he and Peg showed up. It was up in the high country, and we were bused to one of their ranches for this Western-type dinner with the square dances and we had a band and we had steaks cooked right there, barbecued. A fantastic set-up. And then we took the wagons with hay on the top to sit on, and that part of the trip was winding roads, downhill. And all of a sudden what happens, Peg and Senior are seated next to me and my wife. Peg just jumped in and sat in this open flat wagon, with hay in the middle, a horse and buggy actually, and Senior sat next to me and they went with the whole group down the mountain. They waited in line for their steaks. I remember for Zenith, the president would be served first and everybody would cater to this guy. He wouldn't know half the people there, and this man—Senior—knew almost everybody, even in International, by the first name. That's what gets you hooked 100 percent. You realize, geez, you're not a number, you're a person.

The funny part is, when we go out for a sandwich, all of a sudden the bill comes. OK, $3.42. Everybody puts in their $3.42, and if he owes you 2 cents, he brings you the 2 cents next time he sees you, or you give it to him.

It's a dedication from the people. It's not fake. It's real dedication. Camaraderie. Unbelievable camaraderie. It makes no difference whether it's International or Domestic, unless two guys really have a conflict with each other. The camaraderie, you can count on somebody to give you a hand, no matter what. Somebody's going to come through and help you with whatever you need.

I'm very proud to go in front of a customer and say, "Molex." We are recognized as a very, very high quality product and company. You go in and you pound on the desk. We're the best. That makes selling much, much easier when you know the product is good. The people are going to back you up. The whole approach to selling is different than if you felt like, my God, we got one weakness. I would say those two are the keys, and the personal touch by the three owners with the rest of the employees, where you are still a name, you are not a number.

Welcome John H. Krehbiel Chairman
of the Board   Molex   Shioya Factory